Peggy Dean's Guide to

NATURE DRAWING & WATERCOLOR

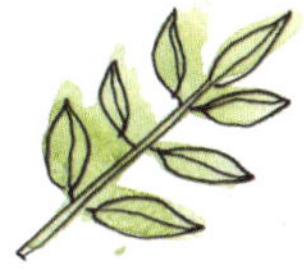

Learn to Sketch, Ink, and Paint Flowers,
Plants, Trees, and Animals

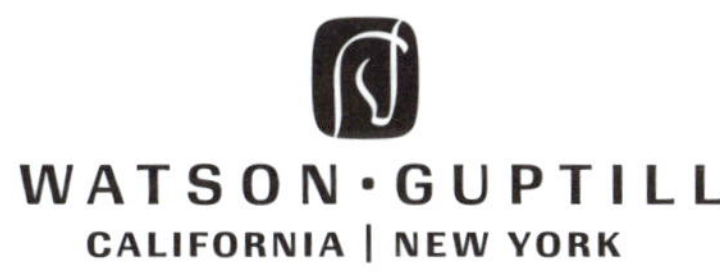

WATSON·GUPTILL
CALIFORNIA | NEW YORK

CONTENTS

I wish to
live a life
that causes
my soul to
dance
inside
my body

— Dele Olanubi

INTRODUCTION

I can't draw—seriously. It's not something you'd expect to read from the author of a book you pick up to learn about drawing, but a couple of years ago, if I'd been asked to sit down, look at a blank piece of paper, and draw, it would have been hard for me to make expressive stick figures. I maybe could have done a flat daisy shooting out of some choppy lines that I'd try to convince you was grass (it was that bad). So if I can't draw and you can't draw, let's "not know how to draw" together.

Here's the thing: Drawing is all about viewing your subject differently by breaking it up into lines and shapes. Step-by-step illustrations create muscle memory and allow our skillsets to expand and, in turn, this muscle memory and skill helps us create our own masterpieces.

If I can draw, trust me . . . you can definitely draw.

I remember an afternoon when I was young. My cousin was visiting our house, and the art supplies were out. We were on our knees, with well-used crayons and streaky markers, using the piano bench as our art table. I don't know why that was the surface we decided was best to draw on—maybe we couldn't wait to dive in, maybe my brother's five million LEGOS were taking up other surfaces, or maybe we wanted to be near my mom while she cleaned. No, I remember why—we were kneeling over the piano bench and drawing because my cousin was trying to get away from me and the bench was her final destination before she gave up. She was older than me and I admired her; I wanted to draw what she was drawing. I remember she formed faces and dresses and shoes differently than I did, and I was desperate to learn a new style. So I hovered over her shoulder and watched with laser focus, memorizing every stroke.

When I was growing up, my mom enrolled me in lots of art programs so I could dabble in different media, and I loved all of them. But the problem with a lot of art programs for children is that they're so guided. Although I was young, I felt stifled

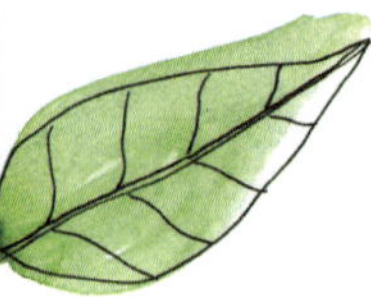

by the over-instruction. I didn't think I had my own creativity or that I could draw anything without copying something else.

In my late teens, I could be found outside at the patio table until the wee hours of the morning after convincing a group of friends to have a paint party. This was one of my favorite activities. The only thing missing was that I never painted anything original. Every single piece I painted used something else as a reference, which wasn't satisfying. I needed more. That's when I decided to take ownership of my own creativity and to embrace learning through the discouraging journey of trial and error. Because I've always been attracted to creating, the journey became a need.

Let's get personal for a second and think about why we create art to begin with. Unfortunately, as we near adulthood we tend to stray from some of the things that used to bring us so much joy in our younger years. In turn, we lose our creative outlets and find other ways to cope with everyday stresses. I found myself scrolling social media and sites such as Pinterest for far too long, or wasting my time watching television, never creating anything. Mindful practices were practically nonexistent in my life. Then one day, I met my biggest trigger: Rejection. Rejection and I don't get along, and Rejection makes me destructive; at least then I feel in control. This one day, though, I decided that instead of internalizing the emotions that stemmed from Rejection—which I knew would result in me putting up walls and stifling my progress in general—I sat down on the couch and picked up some old watercolors and a cheap pad of mixed-media paper. I started to paint without reference, without thoughts. I started to paint what came to mind, and in little time, I felt full—connected to myself, to my emotions, and to my journey. Every night for two more months I painted, without trying to better my skillset or worry about progress. I did it for me. I did it to heal. I fell in love with the child that still lives within, the one I quieted when I became an adult. I had found my outlet again. Once I felt connected to why I was creating, I wanted to learn and absorb as much knowledge as I could to expand what I could create. It was then I realized that I had truly found my version of mindfulness. Now it was time to explore.

I've been heavily inspired by the nature around us. Coexisting on this planet with so many amazing plants and animals and inspiring colors is incredibly grounding, so to speak. Nature is imperfectly perfect, which is something I fully embrace and adopt in my art. Rough edges, asymmetry, texture, exploration . . . these are the features that translate to so much character on paper. Let yourself breathe and release the need for perfection. Let yourself grow.

Self-Taught

I have found that being self-taught is a long, difficult process chock-full of mistakes. You're getting less excited, aren't you? Bear with me. This is good stuff, I promise. When you want to learn something on your own, passion is the most important thing you need. Without passion, you're likely to go through the motions, lose interest, and feel as if the process has become a chore that will eventually fall by the wayside and likely never surface again. But passion sparks a drive inside of us that we don't have control over. It ignites us and we have nowhere to go but up.

During the process of most illustrations, I don't like my work. Ask any designer or artist about this and you'll likely hear that the process is the hardest because we want to see the end result but we're stuck looking at our incomplete "meh" work. While you practice your drawing skills, I challenge you to persevere through this very natural stage of creation. I find that the work I dislike the most during the process is the work I end up loving and reusing over and over again. I also encourage you to take breaks if you feel stuck or that you're "butchering" your drawing. Trust me, you will feel this way at some point—we all do—and it's just as much a part of the process. Stand up, do something else, and come back to it. Returning to your work with fresh eyes will jumpstart your motivation because you'll see that your progress has actually been pretty impressive after all.

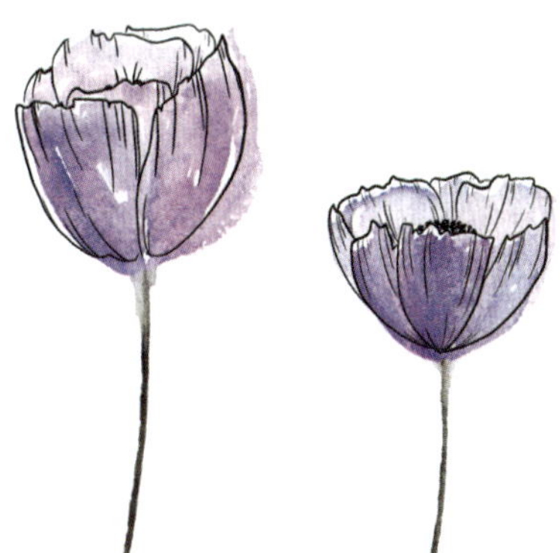

Find Your Style (and Not Just One)

There's an art to art. One of the questions I'm regularly asked is about how to develop one's own style. Oftentimes, it's followed up with another: *How can I form my own style when I'm learning from other artists? Isn't that just copying?* Fret not, for no matter how much you imitate another's style, it will inevitably evolve into your own style with practice. Once you have a solid understanding of a particular way to execute a design, begin experimenting by slowly introducing small tweaks in your artwork. Let's say you start off with wet-on-wet watercolor techniques but you're also interested in trying your hand at some offset black-line sketches. These two styles don't generally complement each other well (so they say), but does that mean you shouldn't try it? No! Art is about the journey. We don't create for instant gratification, we create because we enjoy the process of expanding our minds and watching the way our art reacts when we apply different techniques with our hands. The final product is always a bonus; it's something we can look at and be proud of, and it's personal because we built a relationship with that project while creating it. After you've spent some time learning, experimenting, and learning some more, it's quite possible that you'll have a go-to technique or medium that fits you and your style best; you might decide to hone in on that and continue to develop it more and more, always becoming more "you."

Then there are the artists who can't stop experimenting. They experiment because the learning process feeds them even more than building an image or a brand. Many times I've reflected on my work and have been frustrated because I can't decide which route I want to take. Actually, more than anything else, I just don't want to commit to only one style. Let's look at the pros and cons of each, and why neither is right or wrong.

Unique Style

Once you have a solid understanding of your own creative expression, the number-one benefit is that your work will be recognizable as your own. I envy people whose work is recognizable, because I am not one of them.

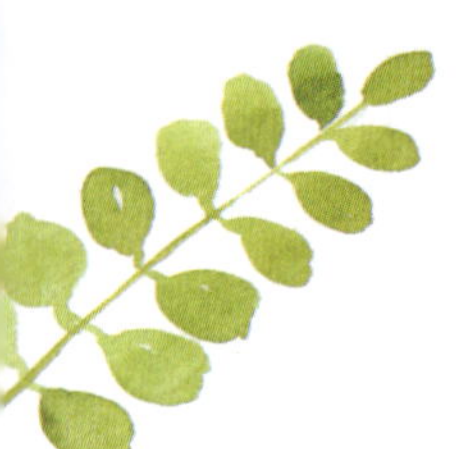

Some of the ways we can identify the work of our favorite artists are by their choices of media, their color palettes, their use of lines and texture, and more.

I admire artists who, for example, focus solely on folk art. It's such a unique art form, bursting with energy, with a simple color palette and layers of solid silhouette forms. It also has a rich history, and the things modern-day artists can do with this style is pure brilliance. Additionally, I enjoy art created with only light watercolor washes and wet-on-wet techniques, using a low-volume color scheme with little detail to achieve a soft and delicate look. I also enjoy works created with bright colors that capture energy. Some sketch artists' illustrations are bold, rough, and imperfect, yet full of character. When you have work that is easily recognizable, you've instantly built a self-branded image. Your illustrations will reach a particular audience that might absolutely fall in love with your style. Your style will develop organically.

Someone might have a similar look to someone else, but they can't possibly do exactly what the other can. There is room for all artists in this world because we all have a unique twist on what we create. There is room for you.

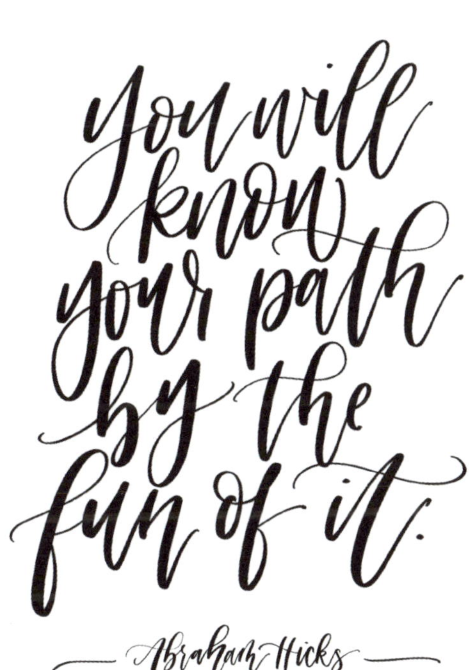

Jack of All Media

Some artists just can't-stop-won't-stop—and you're looking at one of them. The phrase "Jack of all trades, master of none" stands true for me in a major way. We all have our own reasons as to why we want to learn more than one way to execute a project or why we want to create with a bunch of different media. It's like people who have several hobbies. While some people play one sport and get really, really good at it—eating, sleeping, and breathing their sport—other people like to knit, quilt, play backgammon, host dinner parties, enjoy the occasional badminton game, go swimming, play cards, do some computer coding, etc. The point is, some like to dip their toes in a lot of different bodies of water, and I'm talking big bodies of water. And this isn't to say that these two types of people don't have things in common; chances are they absolutely do.

Some of the benefits of working in various styles are:

- You continually expand your mind by challenging yourself to learn new skills.

- You create a skillset that will be helpful during your journey.

- You develop versatility in your craft.

My suggestion is to try, experiment with, and commit to the art media and styles that make you happy. That's what this is all about, anyway—isn't it?

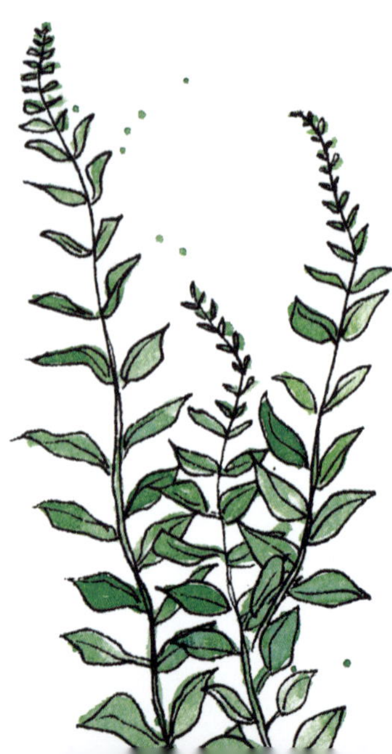

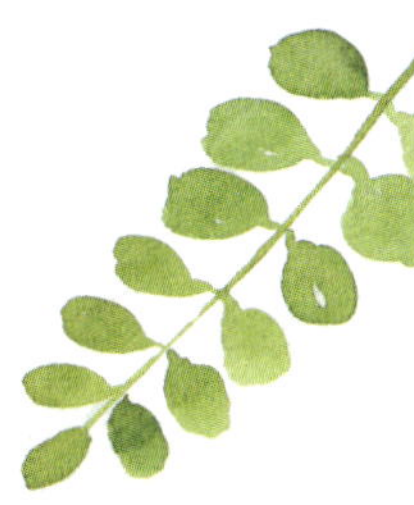

Art Is in the Eye of the Beholder

As you jumpstart your journey through nature illustration, there are a few things to keep in mind.

Practice makes progress. The word *progress* replaces *perfect* in the phrase we're used to hearing—because you shouldn't ever strive for perfection. You should strive for your journey, your own unique style, and for how creating makes you feel. Once you have a fundamental understanding of how to interpret objects to draw on paper, you'll be able to explore styles and find not only what you like most but also a style that organically becomes your own.

I've seen too many cases where someone's admiration for another's work is a subconscious comparison, and they ultimately give up on their own journey because they don't see the results they want. Here's the thing: Learning curves are a natural progression, and our work can get straight-up uglier before it improves. It's not a competition. If you must compete, do so only with the person you were yesterday. This mindset shoves our doubt in our own abilities behind us and allows us to align with amazing creators that we admire because we're all working toward the same goal: bettering ourselves, improving the skill of our craft, extending our reach, and embracing mindfulness and the peace we feel doing what we love. We must remember why we're starting or why we started: because we have a passion for this creative outlet.

The last point I want to make before we jump in is one I can't emphasize enough: If you "mess up," keep going. You might find that you can save the illustration by getting creative with how to fix it. Some of my favorite pieces are ones I thought I had almost ruined, but I kept going and challenged myself to utilize the error to my advantage. Through doing this, I've discovered techniques and styles I may not have tried otherwise. Mistakes can open a new door in the creative process. The more we dive in, the more doors open that we never realized we wanted to walk through.

Ready, Set, GROW!

A History of Art Products

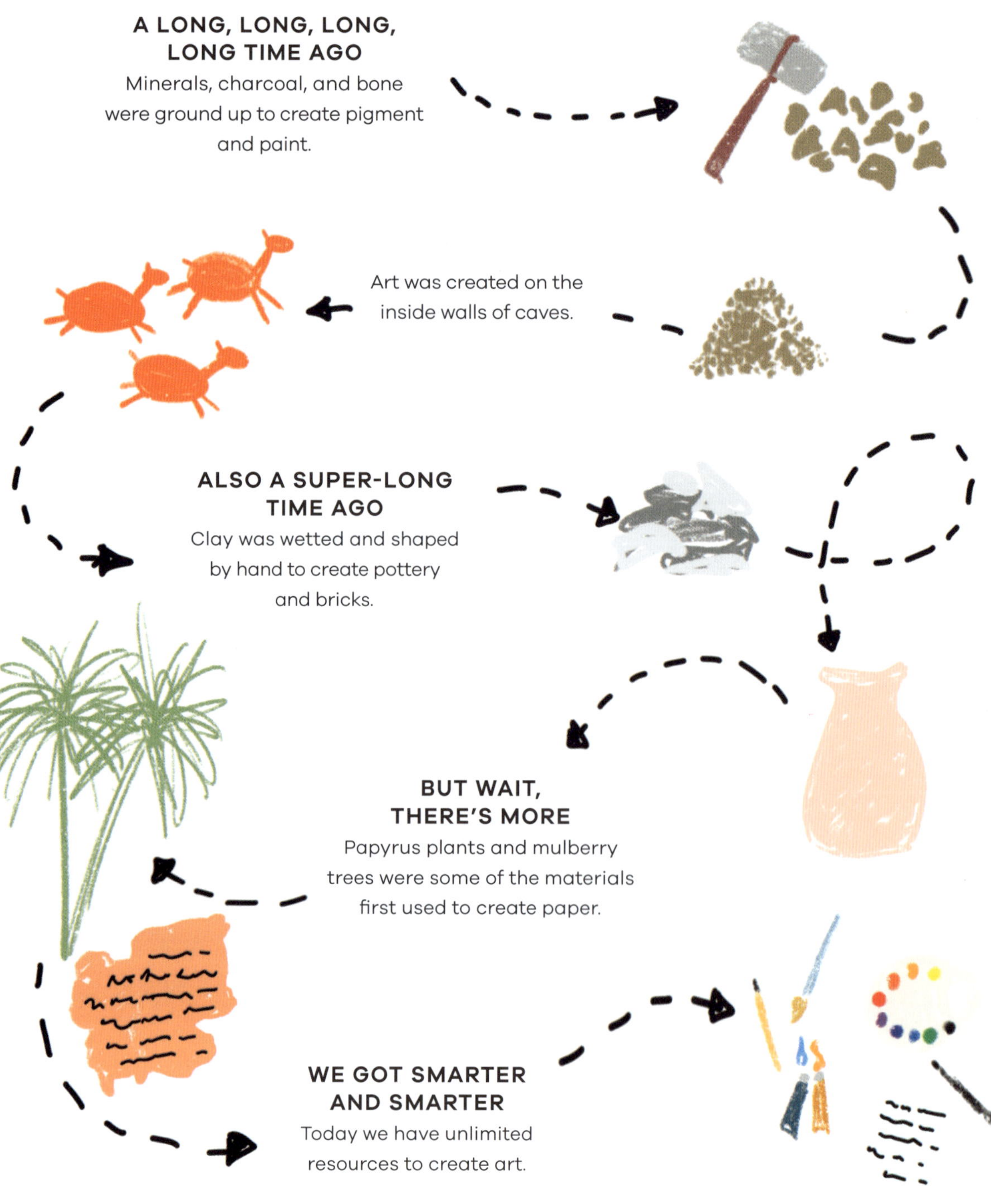

MATERIALS

Being resourceful means seeking out information that will help you learn and grow. If you're asking yourself whether or not you're resourceful, allow me to squash any doubt by telling you that just by reading this, you're nailing it. A couple decades ago, resources were few and far between. Today, we're inundated with options and it's hard to know what to choose. From books and classes to pens, paints, and paper, it's inevitable that you'll be overwhelmed. When you finally do decide, you might experience buyer's remorse because you feel like there was probably a better choice and you didn't make it. Let's face it: having too many options can be a problem.

Historically, art products were created using sources found in nature, such as clay, minerals, charcoal, animal bones, plants, spit—you name it and it was probably experimented with at some point to see how it could possibly be used as a medium. I love thinking about this because, too often, people feel that they need more products to create. They say, "I don't have the right paper," "I need different pens," and "I wish I could, but I don't have . . . ." I hear these comments all the time. Just because our technology has advanced doesn't mean we can't create! Just work with what you have and you might surprise yourself. Some of my favorite art supplies have been random finds, whether at an art store or outdoors. You might find a great twig with a hard-spiral end, perfect for dipping into ink and using for calligraphy. Maybe you'll come across a spongy plant that, when applied to wet paint and used as a stamp, creates a texture that you wouldn't have otherwise been able to develop. Look around! Art is waiting to be created. Remodel your living room, build a fairy house out of twigs, pour a perfect bubble bath, fold a cool origami shape out of a crumpled-up receipt, or paint your nails. Art can be produced in many ways. So open your eyes a little wider and take in your surroundings—be a modern-day caveman.

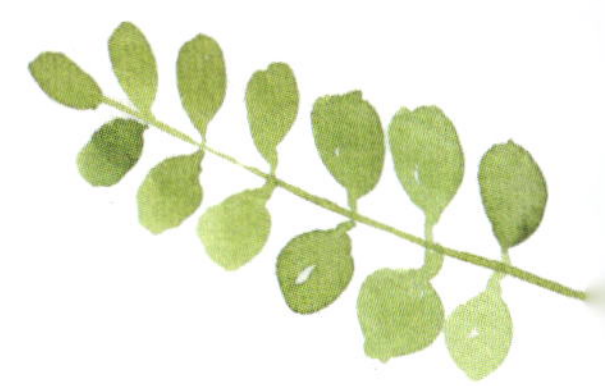

Allow me to help you find materials. First of all, a lot of products out there are great choices! Internet searches will show you "the best" based on paid advertisements. Influencers will show you "the best" based on sponsorships. Artists will show you "the best" based on what they've used and prefer. Is this always true? No. But chances are, you're going to be pulled one way or another. I'm going to introduce you to some of my favorite products and explain why they're my favorites. Just because a product is one I prefer, though, doesn't mean it will be the best for you; nonetheless, through this journey, I will share my personal recommendations. My strongest advice when it comes to product discovery is to grab a few options, play around, and decide what you like best. Once you become comfortable molding your skills with tools that allow you to advance, invest a little more in some new ones you haven't tried. Repeat the experimentation process. This is the fun part! "I have too many art supplies," said no one ever.

Pens

Drawing pens should feel good as they dance on paper. You may find that you want to change pens depending on the type, technique, and style of your drawing. Good! Do that! Make the experience yours.

PEN TIP SIZES

Pen tip sizes should be appropriate to the scale of your illustrations. For example, if you are drawing very small, you won't want to use a larger tip like an 08 (.5mm) because details will easily get lost. On the other hand, if you're drawing a larger piece, a finer tip may cause your drawing to look unfinished due to the thin lines—unless you opt for a much more detailed piece. Using the wrong size tip for your illustration can make you cringe at your work, even if the illustration is actually quite lovely! Sometimes it just needs a different size tip/nib/point to look complete. I recommend an 03 (.35mm) or 05 (.45mm) to start. This size is right in the middle but will allow for finer lines in detail work. From there, you'll soon discover whether you'd like your lines to be thinner, thicker, or right where they are.

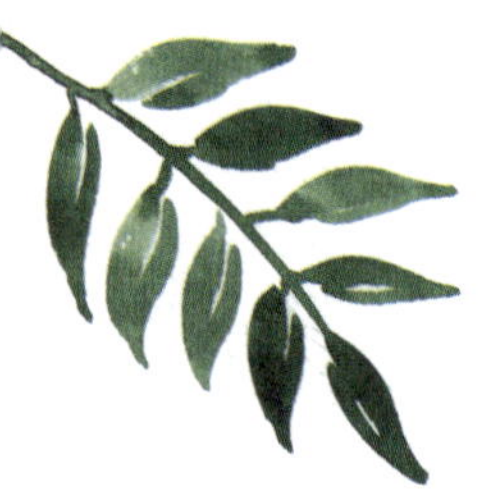

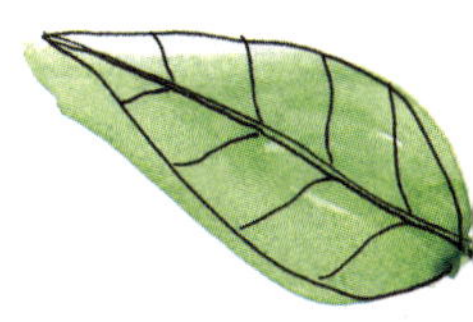

When you use a particular size pen tip intentionally, you're doing it to create a specific effect. Notice how the same illustration using different tip sizes gives a different appearance? Bolder lines will give you more of a doodle effect, while fine lines encourage more detailing, leading to a more sophisticated-looking illustration.

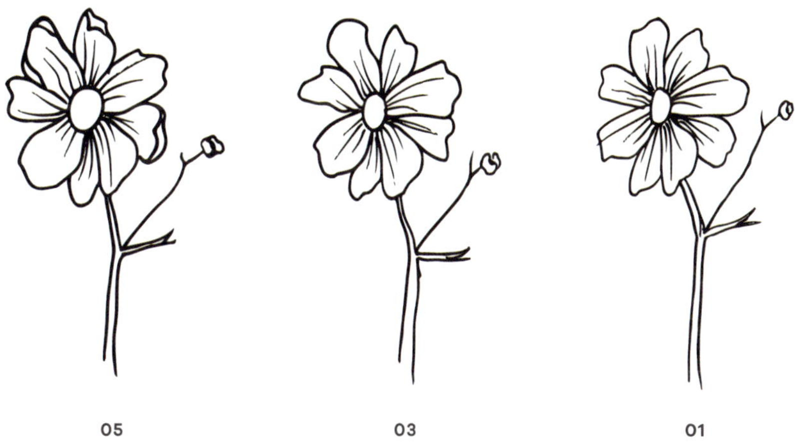

WATER-BASED PENS

Tombow MONO Drawing Pens produce strokes on paper like whipped butter on toast. They're smooth and satisfying. These pens have black, water-based ink and you can find these gems in three sizes: 03, 05, and 08. Remember when I told you those were the best sizes? Yep. They are. Note that because the ink is water-based, you will not be able to use water media over your illustration without the ink bleeding. (If that's your thing, though, you do you!) You can, however, add ink on top of watercolor once it has completely dried, so it's not a deal breaker. If you don't plan on using water-colors, these pens are a straight-up YES.

Why use archival pens? The main reason I use them is because it's likely that I'm going to apply watercolors to my illustration. Water media can be applied on top of this type of ink because it's not water-soluble and won't bleed. The other plus is that archival ink will make your illustrations last a lifetime.

Archival pens use ink that is fade resistant, permanent, and doesn't bleed, even through thin paper. They are chemically stable and durable, and they also don't stink like other permanent markers. Bonus!

I have two sets of favorites for this type of pen. First, I have my own line called MONOLINE Studio by The Pigeon Letters, which feature a small window that allows you to see the tip through the pen cap. Unlike other pens in its category, the tips have a slightly rounded edge that forgives our hands when they want to draw at more of an angle. Sakura Microns are another solid choice. Both of these brands come in a variety of sizes so you can focus on small details or get more playful with bolder lines. My go-to sizes are the 03 (.35mm) and the 05 (.45mm). I find them to be the perfect size for my illustrations. These pens are meant to be used with light pressure, as the ink flows with ease and you don't want to damage the tips.

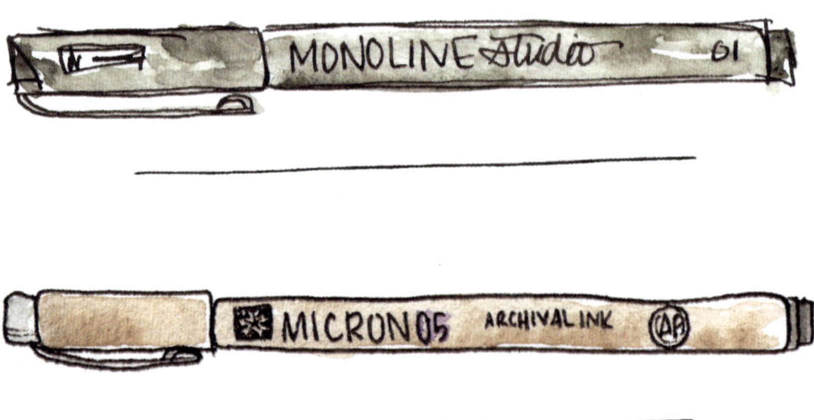

FOUNTAIN PENS

The pens I've mentioned thus far are disposable and not meant to be reused. If you're attracted to the idea of a refillable pen, there are some great options out there. One of the most commonly used is the Lamy Safari fountain pen. It's lightweight, and the ink flows nicely. It even has a little window displaying your ink level, so you know when you're getting close to needing to fill it. (I love these tiny windows in pens!)

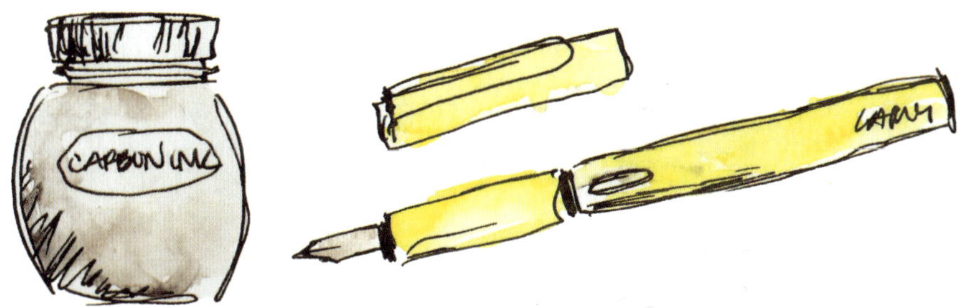

Fountain pens can be filled two ways: with cartridges or converters. Cartridges are disposable pre-filled ink containers that are inserted into the pen. Converters allow you to fill the cartridges with any ink of your choice. I like Platinum Carbon Ink—it's permanent, so I can use it with water media. I have a helpful video on YouTube that will take you through how to fill the converter with ink because it can seem a little overwhelming the first time you do it. If you don't mind a slight learning curve, this can be a great way to go.

You can get varying line thickness from some pointed pen tips by adjusting how hard you're pressing down to achieve thinner or thicker lines. This fact alone is a win for those of us who want to keep our load lighter when we're out and about.

Water-Based Brush Pens

Allow me to introduce to you one of my best friends, the Tombow Dual Brush Pen. These pens are so versatile that sometimes I wonder if there's anything they *can't* do. Okay, that's extreme. There's plenty they're not capable of, but within the realm of what they're made for, they're like finding a gold mine—a very accessible, price-conscious gold mine.

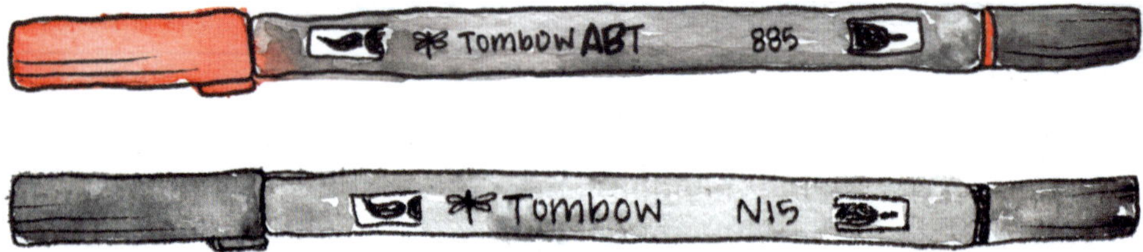

You can use them as watercolors because they're water-based pens! Although there are plenty of brush pens out there, the flexibility, durability, and color selection of Tombows can't be beaten. They can be found individually or in curated sets, both online and at your local art store. I'll go over a few tricks for using this kind of pen, that you may or may not be aware of, when we dive in to creating (see page 79).

Watercolor Paints

I want to highlight some of my favorite watercolors for quick reference. You'll find watercolor paints in two forms: tubes and pans (sometimes known as cakes). There are a ton of options for these colorful art companions, but the good news is there's not a right or a wrong choice here. It comes down to personal preference. If you grab tubes, you'll get to explore a higher-quality product, mixing colors and even building your very own customized palette.

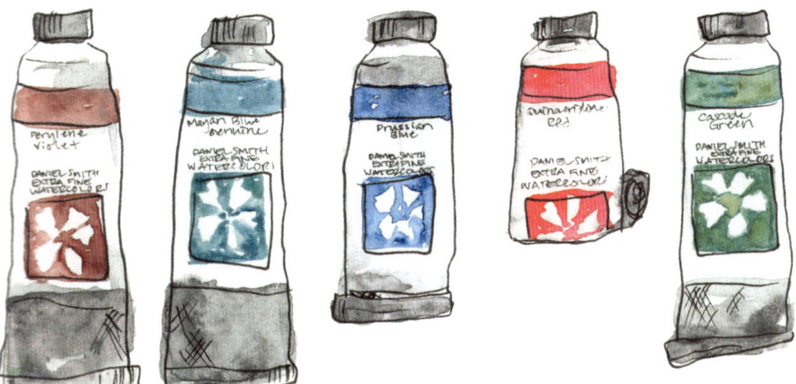

Some advice: If you choose to make your own palette, write down the colors you use to fill the wells so you'll know which combination to use when you refill them. And if you have to take a break while you're in the middle of a painting, and you've mixed a couple of shades together, make a note of the colors you mixed so you know what shade to use when you return. It can also be helpful to create swatches of the pure tube colors in your palette.

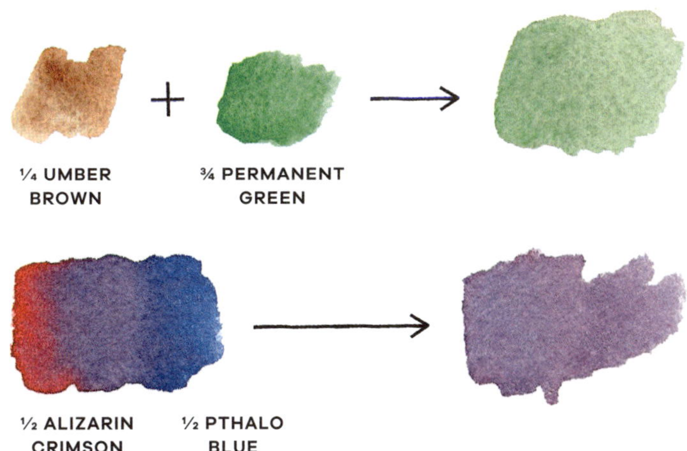

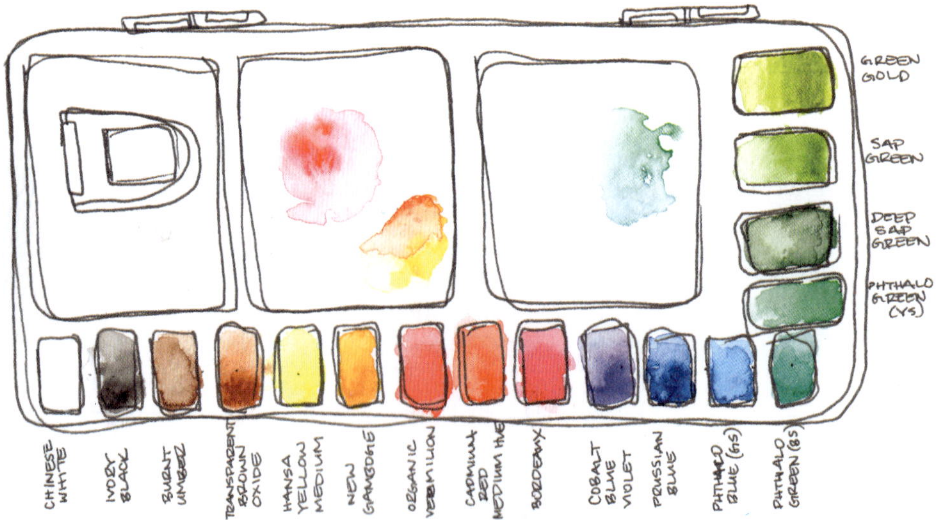

PAN SETS

Palettes filled with watercolor cakes can be found in all price ranges. You can get them as cheap as $6, I say "cheap" instead of "inexpensive" because they're low-quality and you get what you pay for. The consistency is poor and the texture is chalky. Have you ever tried using ink over watercolor only to find the pen skipping over sections and not working properly? Hint: It's not your pen. You'll see the labels "student grade" and "professional grade/artist grade" on watercolors, which indicate their quality. Student-grade watercolors don't have as many color options and they contain fillers that give them a less-than-desirable chalky texture. They also don't mix as well as higher-quality pigments. Professional- or artist-grade watercolors are highly pigmented, much more concentrated, and flow better while painting because their pigment isn't diluted with binders. You want your work to last a lifetime, and you typically won't get that with most student-grade materials.

There are, however, some excellent, inexpensive pan sets that will last a long time. The first worth mentioning is the Sketcher's Pocket Box by Winsor & Newton. This palette is small enough to fit in your pocket and has twelve half pans. The paints are dense and highly pigmented, which give you a lot of bang for your buck. They're very smooth and look beautiful when applied transparently or in layers.

If you're looking for convenience, the Sakura Koi thirty-color watercolor palette will fit easily in smaller art bags. You can also get this set in twelve-, eighteen-, twenty-four-, thirty-six-, or forty-eight-color palettes, whichever is the best option for your needs. Inside, you'll find a leakproof water brush, a sponge, and a removable tray that can be attached to the side or the back of the palette and used as a mixing area. You can grab this palette and watercolor paper and be set, needing nothing more. Can't argue with convenience!

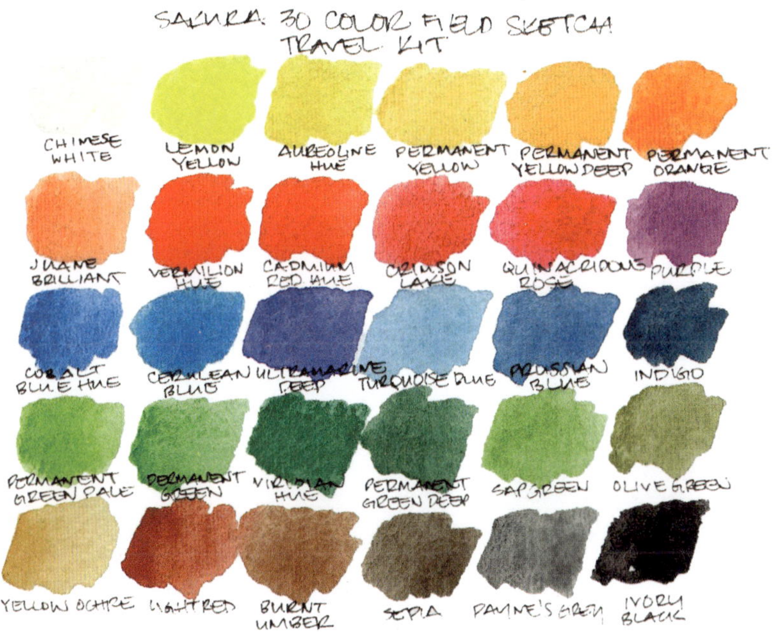

TUBES

The topic of watercolor tubes could be an entire chapter itself, but let's not overcomplicate things. If you're investing in tubes, you're probably moderately serious about getting into watercolors. If you've already dabbled and you want to find some good gems to help evolve your craft, you can't go wrong with Daniel Smith or Winsor & Newton artist-grade paints. Each color will list what level of quality it is along with its **transparency** (transparent, semitransparent, or opaque), **lightfastness** rating (how much the color fades with exposure to light), and **granulation** (texture caused by some pigments), all of which factor in the price.

DANIEL SMITH

EXTRA FINE™ WATERCOLOR
Peggy Dean

PEGGY DEAN PALETTE

Wet a brush and begin testing some of
our exciting colors.

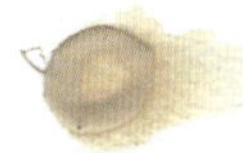
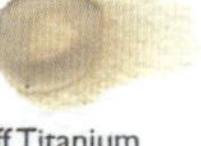

Buff Titanium
Series 1   284 600 009
I • 1 • Y • ◑

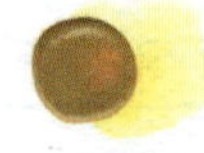

Indian Yellow
Series 3   284 600 045
I • 2 • N • ○

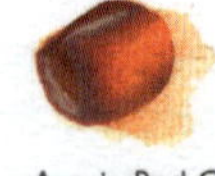

Aussie Red Gold
Series 2   284 600 234
I • 2 • N • ○

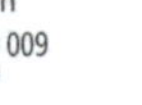

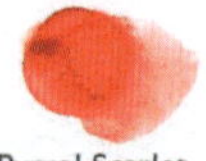

Pyrrol Scarlet
Series 3   284 600 085
I • 3 • N • ◑

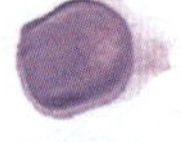

Wisteria
Series 2   284 600 231
II • 1 • N • ◑

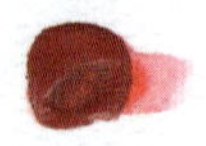

Quinacridone Red
Series 2   284 600 091
I • 3 • N • ○

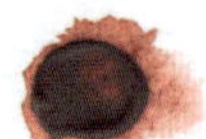

Garnet Genuine
Series 4   284 600 205
I • 2 • Y • ○ Ⓟ

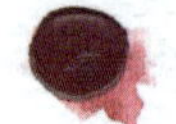

Quinacridone Violet
Series 2   284 600 094
I • 4 • N • ○

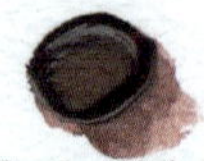

Perylene Violet
Series 3   284 600 201
I (NR) • 3 • N • ○

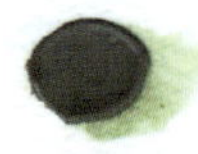
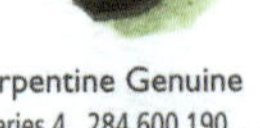

Serpentine Genuine
Series 4   284 600 190
I • 1 • Y • ◑ Ⓟ

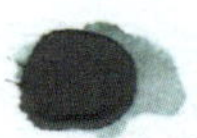
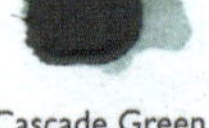

Cascade Green
Series 1   284 600 142
I • 3 • Y • ◑

Diopside Genuine
Series 3   284 600 210
I • 2 • Y • ○ Ⓟ

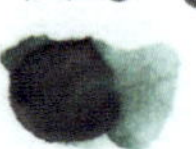
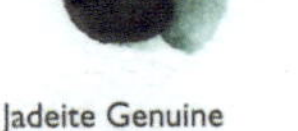

Jadeite Genuine
Series 4   284 600 195
I • 1 • Y • ◑ Ⓟ

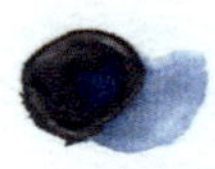

Prussian Blue
Series 1   284 600 082
I • 3 • Y • ◑

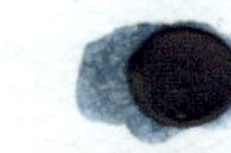

Mayan Blue Genuine
Series 3   284 600 211
II • 2 • Y • ○ Ⓟ

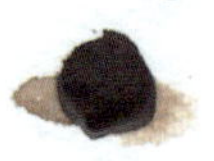

Burnt Umber
Series 1   284 600 011
I • 2 • Y • ◑

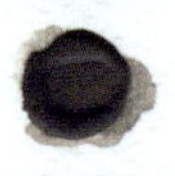

Van Dyck Brown
Series 1   284 600 110
I • 1 • Y • ◑

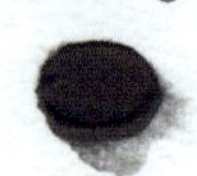

Lunar Black
Series 1   284 600 049
I (NR) • 2 • Y • ○

*The Color Key Information is on the back of this card. This paper is
unsized and is used to bring the Color Dots to you. Paint-out the
Color Dots on your favorite watercolor paper and enjoy!*

999001047
Rev. Date 01/18

When you're ready to invest in tubes, how do you choose between brands? These two companies are both solid choices, with great selection and quality pigments. Winsor & Newton also offers other art supplies for creating such as paintbrushes, markers, inks, charcoals, and more. Daniel Smith, on the other hand, has a strong focus on pigments in paints and inks, which are the only products they offer. I like the exclusivity and focus; something about that screams quality to me. Daniel Smith is a natural choice to start with because they also offer a sample dot chart featuring all of their 238 colors. Not only will you be able to sample their colors, but you'll be able to create several paintings with the chart, as the colors are so heavily pigmented that a little goes a long way.

If you want to start even smaller, try my eighteen-color Daniel Smith x Peggy Dean Dot Chart, which you can grab at thepigeonletters.com.

Water Jars

Rinsing your brush with water is necessary throughout your painting process. Grab an extra jar so you have two—one for cool colors and one for warm colors. This way, you won't run the risk of your paint colors being skewed by murky browns (because warm colors and cool colors turn brown when mixed). Another option is to designate one jar for dirty water and another for clean, clear water. You can rinse the paint off in the dirty jar, then visit your clean jar for extra measure. (I opt out of this method because I tend to get my clean jar dirty quickly, but it may work for you.)

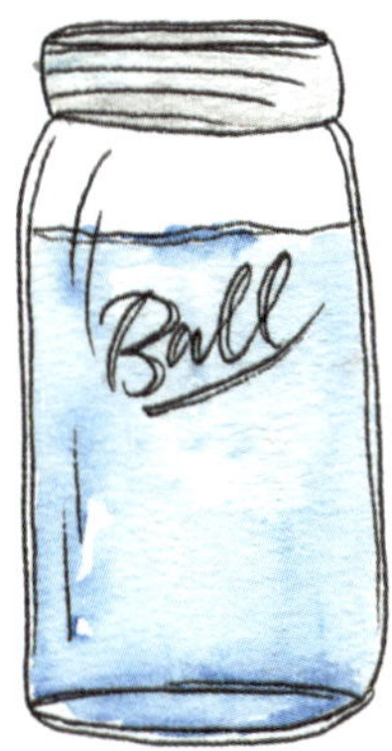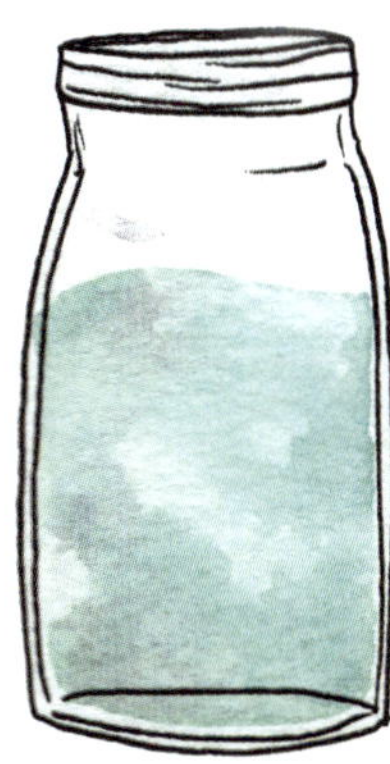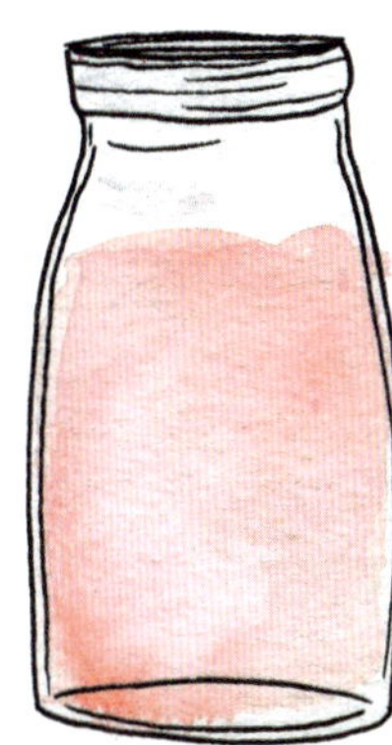

Paper

I've said it before, again, again after that, more agains, and I'm going to say it now. Paper can make or break your art pieces. The reason specialty paper exists is because it's made for what you want to accomplish. This is another aspect that can be overwhelming, and I don't want to overwhelm you further. To this day, I'm still discovering new options and sifting through what I'm using. By no means are my paper preferences the best answer, but they're what I like the most.

If you're wondering about the paper weight thing, allow me to explain. Most paper will show its weight on its packaging. The weight is measured in pounds (lb) or grams per square meter (gsm), such as 140lb or 300gsm: this number designates the weight of a ream of that paper. A **ream** consists of 500 sheets of paper. When you see a higher weight on paper packaging, it means that the paper is thicker. Drawing paper is usually lighter, 60 to 80lb, since heavy-weight paper isn't needed to support drawing pens and pencils. Mixed-media paper weighs in at 90lb, while watercolor paper is the thickest at 140lb and 300gsm. These papers hold up better when water is applied to them because they're much thicker.

PAPER FOR DRAWING

Nine times out of ten, I use **mixed-media** paper for drawing. It's an easy choice to grab if you're not sure what you'll want to use the paper for. Sometimes you may feel like drawing, and sometimes you might want to paint. Mixed-media paper works well for me because I often apply water media later, and I want to make sure the paper will hold up. This won't give you a silky-smooth, crisp drawing, but it will offer support for add-ons. Strathmore offers a variety of mixed-media paper options, including tear-away pads, spiral notebooks, and even journals.

If you know you're not going to be adding wet media, Bristol board paper is thick and smooth, with a weight of about 100lb. Both Canson and Strathmore have generously packed pads of Bristol paper. For a thinner weight at 80lb, Hahnemühle has paper that feels so smooth when your pen glides on the surface.

WATERCOLOR PAPER

Although I mentioned using mixed-media paper for drawing with watercolor, if you *know* you're going to be using watercolors and you want to ensure quality in your piece, you'll want your paper to be at least 140lb/300gsm watercolor paper. My favorites are Hahnemühle Harmony and Legion Cold Press Aqua Paper, which come in several sizes on blocks. Note: Watercolor paper on blocks is your friend. It is glued on multiple edges to prevent the paper from warping as you paint!

Cold press paper is ideal for watercolors because it helps maintain the natural texture and granulation that watercolor pigments produce. *Cold press* means that the paper has a textured surface, which keeps the water in place. If you see watercolor paper that says *hot press*, that means it has a smooth surface. I don't actually know of any watercolor artists who have a preference for hot press paper. Cold press is the way to go!

Brushes

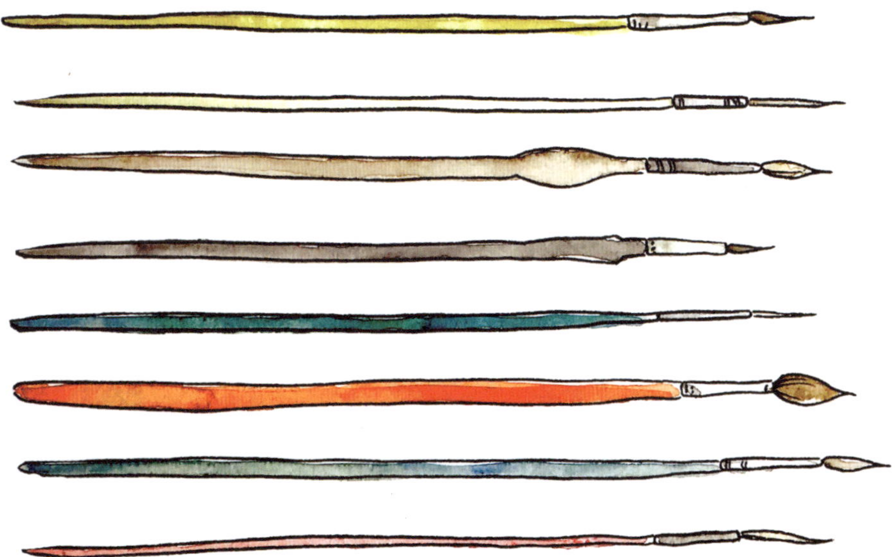

If you opt to add watercolor to your artwork, knowing which brushes to use will help. I'm going to make this easy. For an affordable option, remember these details: round brush, pure synthetic, size 4 or 6. This will help you not have to overthink when you start browsing hundreds of brushes. I'm not kidding. Try looking them up and knowing what to decide. It's hard, even when you've already made up your mind ahead of time! I recommend round brushes because they're versatile and you can use the full belly of the brush for broader coverage and the tip of the brush for thinner strokes. Synthetic hair keeps your price point down and operates well (plus it's cruelty-free).

Sizes 4 and 6 are great for small to medium coverage. I recommend those sizes if you're going to go out and purchase only one brush. You can review other sizes and see if there's a different one you prefer.

If you head over to Amazon, you'll find a steal of a deal on Loew Cornell Round Brushes in a pack that includes four sizes. If you want premium-quality brushes, The Pigeon Letters has a line of round brushes as well: Studio Round Brushes—a no-frills, professional-grade, pure synthetic set. "Pure synthetic" means cruelty-free (no fur of any kind)! Not only are these quality, made-to-last brushes, but they're manufactured in the United States and a percentage of proceeds goes to the sustainability of forests and wildlife. You're diving into a book all about nature, so let's give back while we're at it.

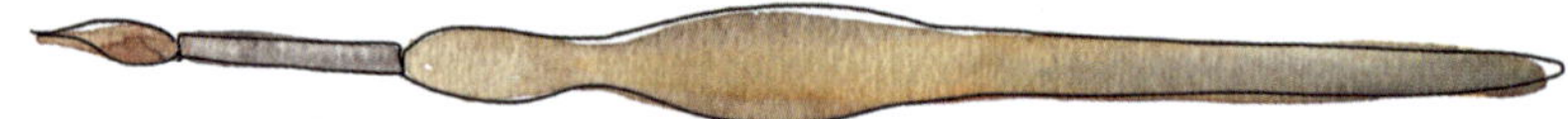

It's also worth mentioning that the Pentel Aquash Water Brush is a treat while traveling. It's basically a water tube with a pointed brush tip that you can control by squeezing it. Water moves through to the tip of the brush at your command, and it's leakproof, so you can throw it in your bag without worrying about spilling.

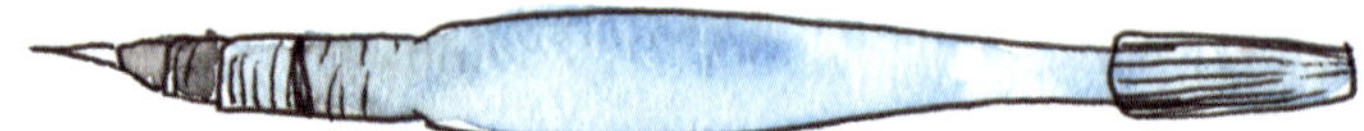

You want your brushes to be your best friend for a long time. Paint brushes are an investment and they can last for years if you care for them properly. Don't soak brushes in water. This includes accidentally leaving them in a water jar, which will bend the fibers. Always store brushes upright. If they're stored point down, the bristles will bend, and if they're bent for a prolonged amount of time, there's no going back. The pressure will keep them bent or spread out, ruining their shape and rendering them useless.

I also don't recommend brush cleaner. It's toxic and unnecessary. Don't let paint dry on brushes when you're finished using them. Water is the optimal cleaning agent and will do the job perfectly. Just thoroughly rinse your brushes in water when you're done using them and gently massage the bristles to release the paint, exposing the inner bristles for a thorough rinse.

In conclusion, I'm going to contradict all of the information I just provided by saying this: To get started in drawing, simply pick up a ballpoint pen and a piece of scratch paper. That's right. I challenge you to work with what you have. Don't overthink this stuff. You got this.

COLOR THEORY

Did you know there are entire books just about color? I highly recommend *Color: A Natural History of the Palette*, written by Victoria Finlay, if you want to learn the history of where color sources came from and how they have been used through history. There's so much that we can soak up about the magic of color. I'm going to skim the surface of a few basics that will be helpful in your painting journey.

Primary Colors

What are **primary colors**? They are the three main colors that all other colors can be derived from through mixing different ratios together. These colors are red, blue, and yellow.

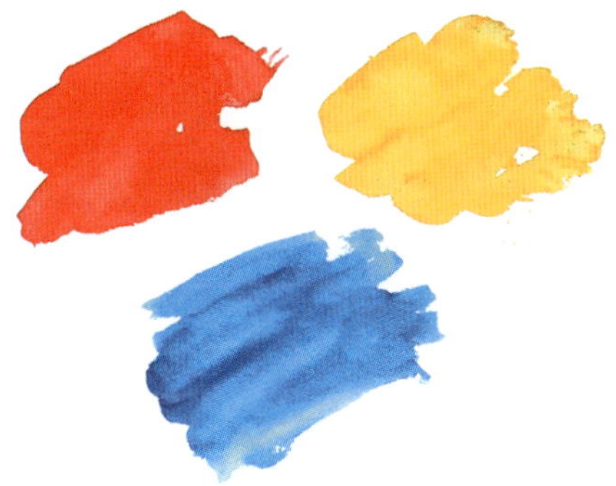

Secondary Colors

Secondary colors are created when two of the primary colors are mixed together in equal amounts. These colors are green (mixing equal parts of yellow and blue), purple (mixing equal parts of red and blue), and orange (mixing equal parts of red and yellow).

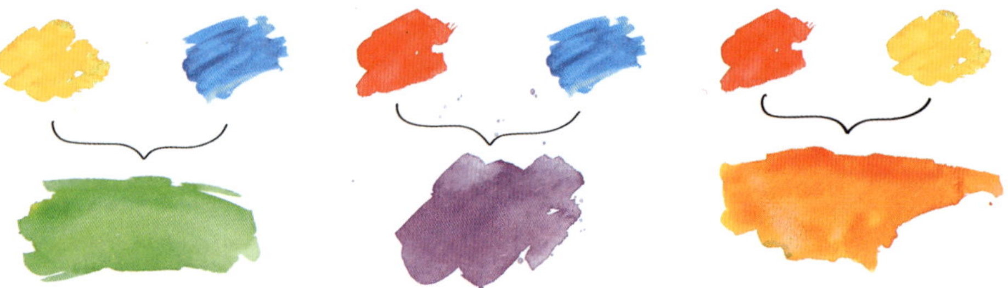

Contrasting Colors

Contrasting colors are opposite each other on the color wheel and are also called **complementary colors** because they look great when placed next to each other. Contrasting colors are considered the most harmonious. When contrasting colors are mixed together, they cancel each other out, creating a neutral brown or gray. This is good to know when you need to create brown, right? Contrasting colors are purple and yellow, red and green, and orange and blue.

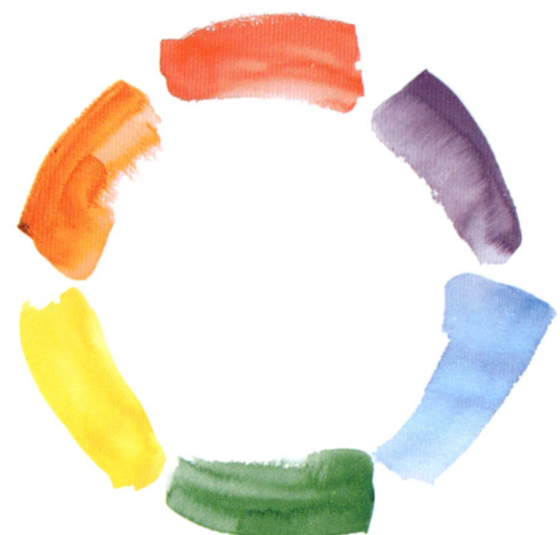

Hue and Value

Hue is simply color. Think of any color in existence: it's a hue. Taking different ratios of color and mixing them together can create an abundance of colors, probably more than we can think of. Experts say that we see about 10 million colors. It's crazy to think that they all stem from three primary colors. To put a "hue" in terms we can better understand, let's use the color red. With red, we can create red-orange, pink, magenta, and more. These colors are what dreams are made of. You now know that purple (a secondary color) is created when blue is added to red. We can also make warmer reds with yellow undertones, creating oranges (another secondary color). Because there are so many varieties of oranges, additional colors and different ratios can be added to create even more hues. Hues can be adjusted for any color. Yellows can be warmer with a dash of orange, or greener and brighter to create more of a neon color. Knowing about hues will help you determine the perfect color palette for your taste.

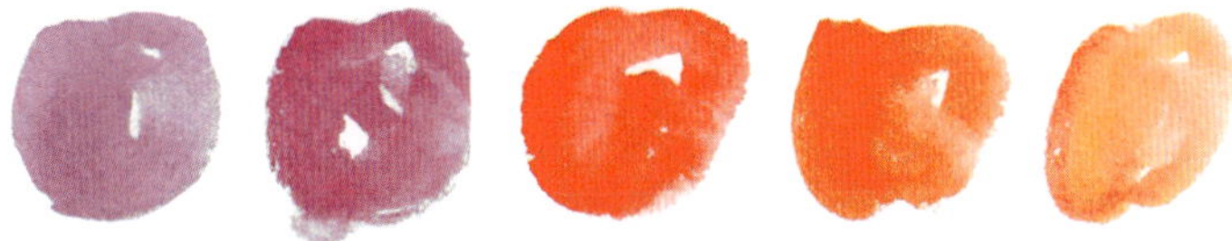

Value refers to the lightness or darkness of a color. If we remove color and focus only on a gray scale, we simply see the color in all of its stages from white to black. When we add white to colors, they begin looking more pastel, which is lightening the value. When we add black, we're darkening the value. Note that making these changes will reduce the **saturation** of the color as well, meaning the vividness of the color itself. In the case of watercolor, saturation can be adjusted by paying attention to the paint-to-water ratio you use. We'll get more into this soon.

Mix It Up

One of my favorite parts of illustrating flowers with color is deciding what color combos I want to include. Color combinations add emphasis to the moods they invoke.

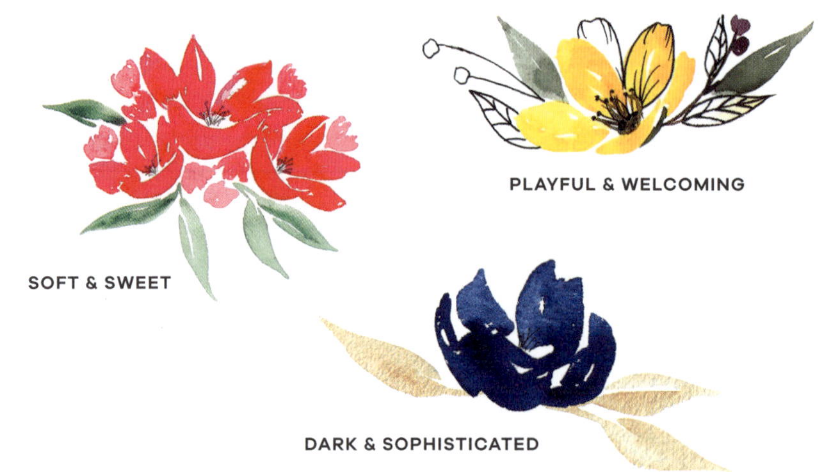

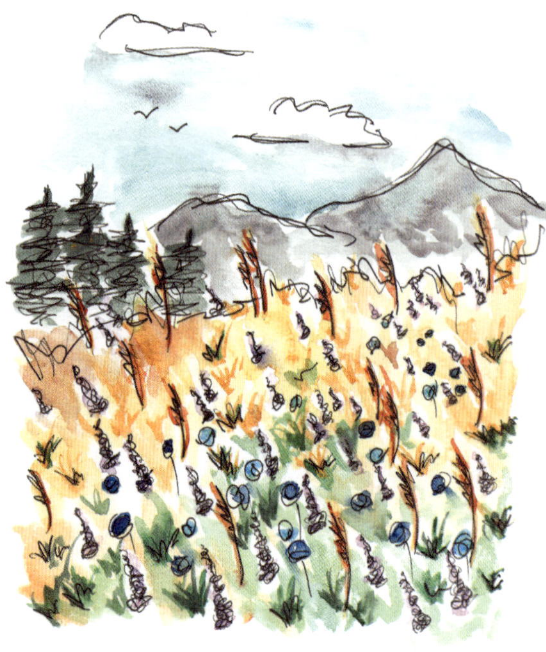

Ah, a field of wildflowers. There's something about this airy stretch of land that makes me want to run to the center and stretch my arms as wide as they can go, with flowers in my hair and a white linen dress flowing with the wind (that could also be the Disney kid in me). There are so many colors to be found among wildflowers, and you have the freedom to pick and choose which ones you'd like to include.

Colors in Nature

Thinking of colors found in nature, what immediately comes to mind? This might vary depending on the terrain and climate where you live. Having been born and raised and currently residing in the Pacific Northwest, I always default to deep forest greens in layers of different opacities as they submerge into misty fog.

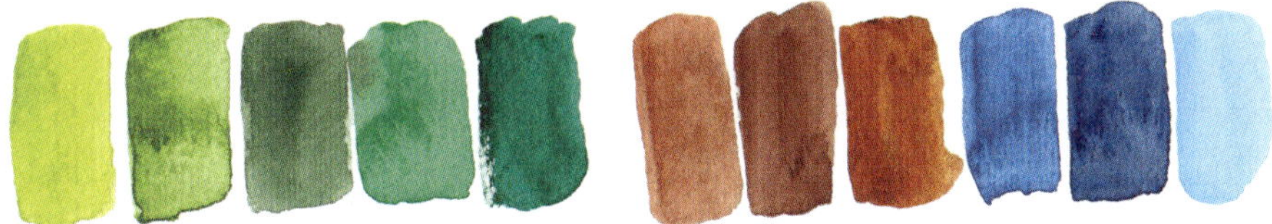

Exploration of color can get you excited about drawing things you may not have thought of. For example, one of my absolute favorite colors happens to share the name of its flower: poppy red. Look at the richness of that warm red with an undertone of orange. It's such a unique color.

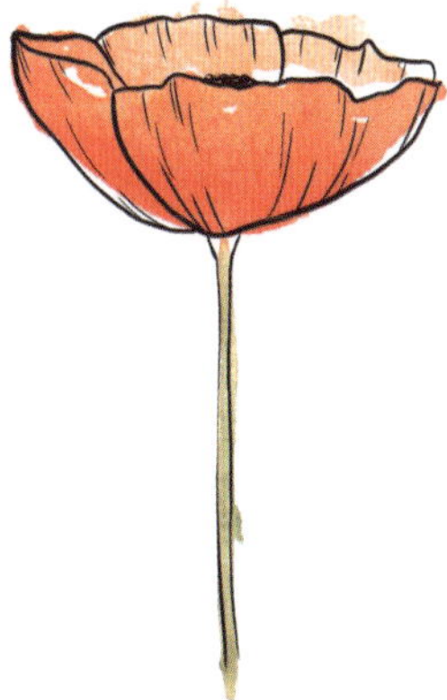

You might see fields of purples, oranges, and yellows or rich reddish browns with pops of green here and there. There are three main color groups in botanicals: greens and browns, reds to blues, and yellows to red-oranges.

Let's explore the colors of nature together, shall we?

Green

Green is considered the most relaxing of all colors. This might come as a surprise to you, since many people assume that blue is the most relaxing. Green is seen as the most relaxed color because it's the most restful for our eyes. It acts as a bridge between warm colors and cool colors, which suggests stability. It's soothing to pain and associated with optimism. Green produces an overall balanced, healthy, happy, fresh feeling. It's also the most common color found in nature!

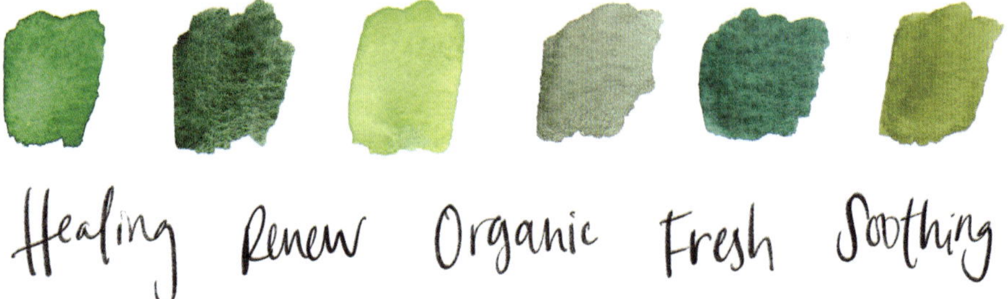

Blue

Blue may not be the top relaxing color, but it is a close second. It's calming, serene, and quieting. It's also thought to be the world's most popular color, and one that creates a sense of security. Blue is actually the rarest true pigment found in nature. It's hard to believe, considering the sky and the ocean are blue—except that they're not really! Blue light travels in shorter wavelengths and tiny molecules scatter the wavelengths more than other colors, so we think we see it more. Crazy, right? Oh, science.

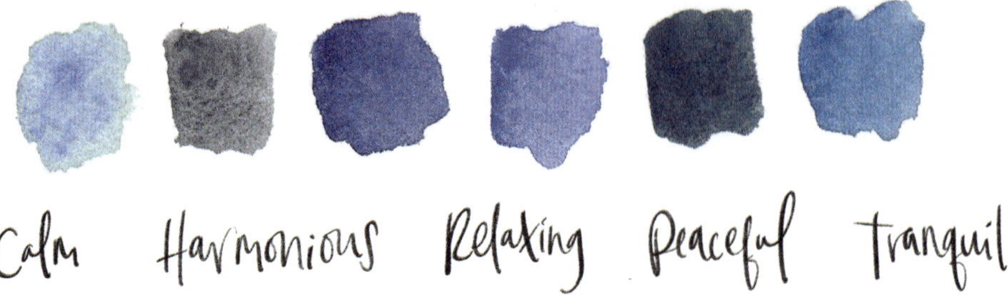

Brown

Brown is associated with the earth, specifically the ground. We think of soil and trees that are deeply rooted, therefore it leads to a sense of stability. Although brown is often dismissed as a dull color, there are some beautiful warm shades of brown to be found among desert mountain ranges. Some browns can be so rich that they look almost red.

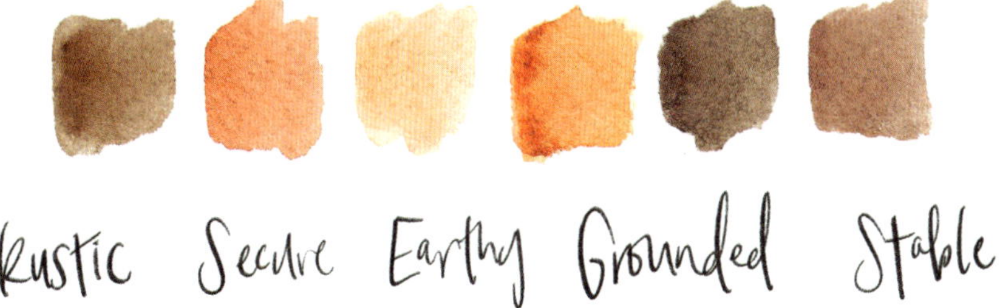

Red

Studies have shown that red is considered the most intense of colors; it is a color of passion, aggression, and impulse. It raises energy levels and stimulates action. As mentioned before, the poppy welcomes us with its warm and playful undertones, and birds such as cardinals and macaws demand attention with their bright red hues. You can find the deep, romantic red hues in roses, peonies, and so many other flowers.

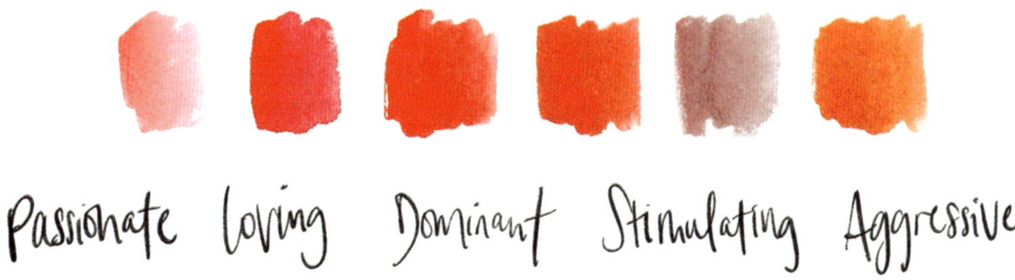

Orange

Orange is also warm in color, so it also spurs ambition, but it's softer than red, so it brings out a little milder enthusiasm. It's a friendly, social, and joyous color. Some of my favorite oranges pop up in lilies and monarch butterflies. Can we also talk about a glorious sunset?!

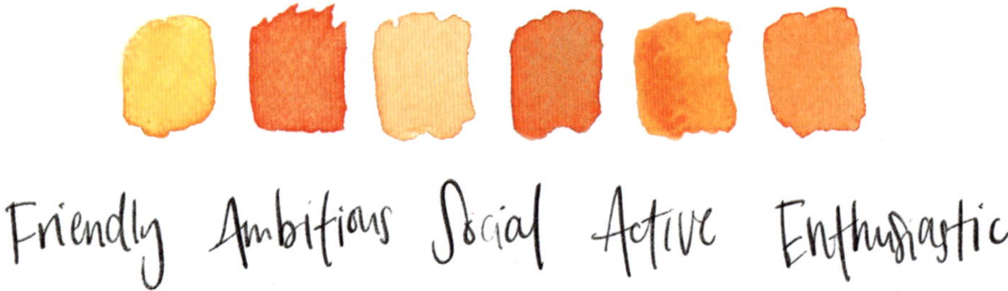

Yellow

Yellow is the perfect accent color. It gives off a happy, friendly, and even playful vibe when dashed among other colors, like morning sunlight glittering on the surface of a lake. There's also the sunflower, which faces the sun to bloom. Does it get happier than that?

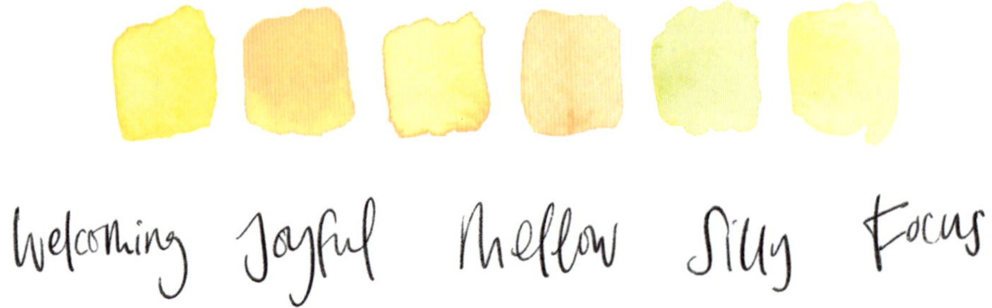

Purple

Purple goes way back in time as a color symbolic of royalty. That's not far off from our modern-day association with originality, sophistication, luxury, and elegance. It's also thought to stimulate creativity and imagination. Lavender and lilacs are among so many lovely purple flowers. Purple starfish bring elegance to their colorful companions under the sea. It also gives us the magic hues to behold in distant mountains at dusk.

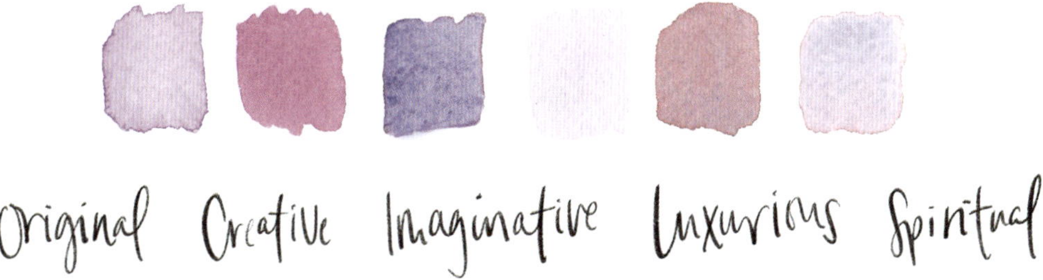

Pink

Pink is a soft, youthful color that is associated with caring and compassion and is a sign of hope. It's a color of innocence and sweetness. The peony is the first flower that comes to mind for me when I think of delicate pink flowers. Then we have bolder hues in camellias, flamingos, and the colors that are captured in clouds at sunrise.

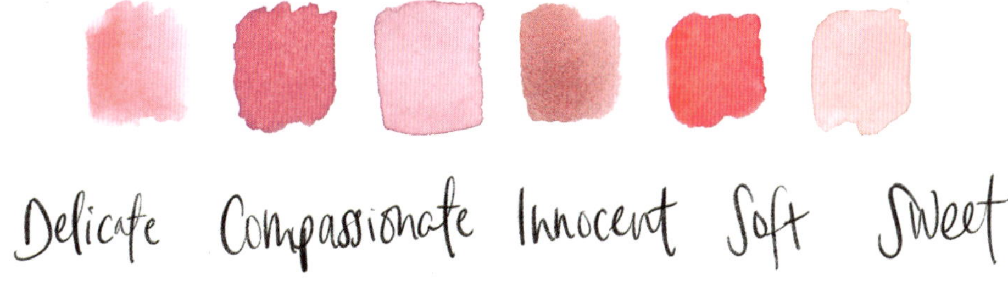

Part One

LET'S GO! LEARN BASIC DRAWING TECHNIQUES

Nature begs for imperfection. It's as raw in form as it gets, which you'll notice in your illustration styles as you experiment. Throughout this book, we'll be focusing on a handful of elements:

SHAPE

Learn to draw in shapes to execute your final illustration.

SPACE

Learn how to properly space shapes and lines, and when negative space works to your benefit.

SIZE

Learn how viewing objects from different perspectives affects their size in the illustration.

MOVEMENT

Learn how imperfect lines add character and how swift motions enhance energy.

DETAIL

Learn what to enhance and, equally important, what to leave out.

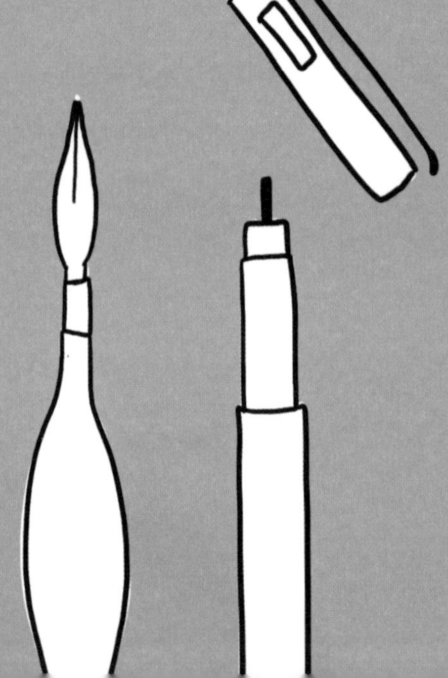

SHAPES AND CURVES

In the following exercises you'll draw the same shape using varying styles of contour drawing to show you how changing small elements can dramatically shift the effect of an illustration. Each of these doodles begins with a slightly curved line, and the differences occur in the leaves and stems. As we begin, remember that nature is imperfect. If your lines are shaky or uneven, or if you find that you're not creating equal balance, embrace that. Learn to accept the imperfections as enhancing the beauty in your work, not "messing up." Since nature isn't perfect, there's no reason your illustrations need to be!

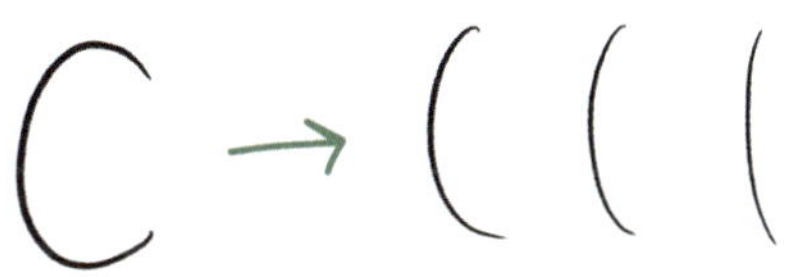

C-CURVE We'll be using C-curves a whole lot throughout this book. These lines can be slightly curved or dramatically curved depending on what's being drawn. It's exactly what it sounds like: a curved line.

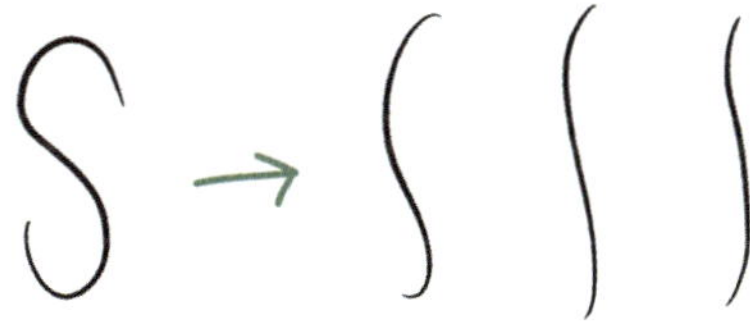

S-CURVE Just as we'll be using the C-curve in abundance, we'll also put plenty of focus on S-curves. Think of it as a lazy *S*, as if you didn't feel like putting the effort into really curving it, so you end up with a wavy line.

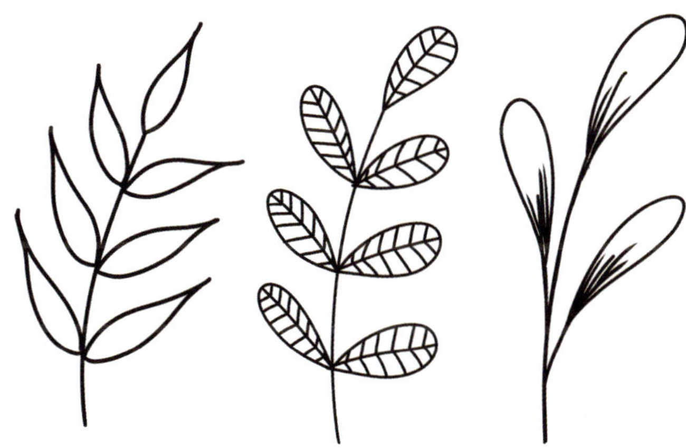

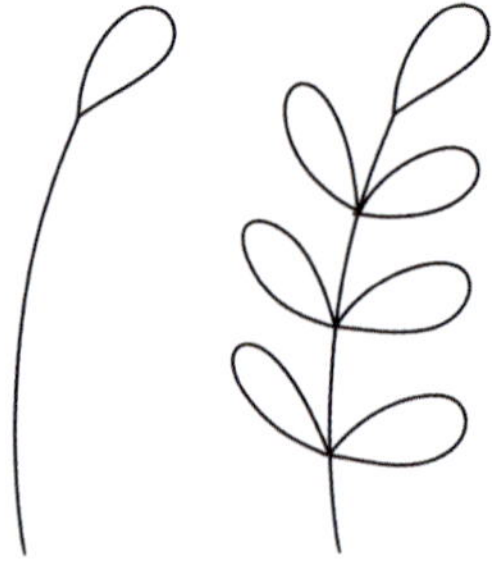

STEP 1 Draw a slight C-curve to form the stem.

STEP 2 Draw a leaf that begins with a straight line coming off of the top of the stem, curves at the top, and comes back down in a straight line and connects at the point where you began the line.

STEP 3 Continue drawing these leaves on each side of the stem until you have three or four on each side.

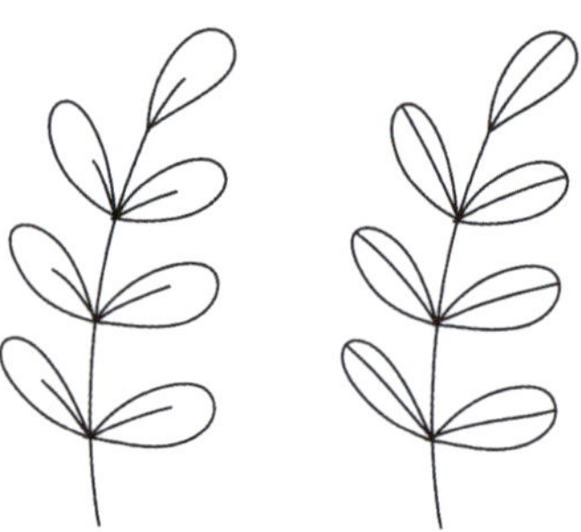

This style can evolve by adding lines in the center of each round leaf. You can choose to add a line that starts at the stem and only reaches halfway through the leaf, or you can choose to draw a line that reaches the whole way through the middle of the leaf. Although alike, the first looks as though it has slightly more shape, while the second version looks flatter. Both options are great depending on the illustration style you're going for.

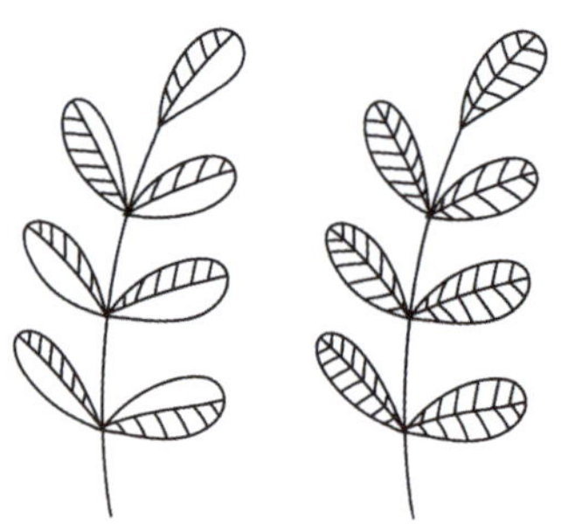

Evolving this style even further, add line work by drawing veins in the leaves. You can opt for a more playful version of this by choosing to add veins to only one side of the center lines or on both sides.

STYLE 2 | Simple Thin Leaves

Next we'll work on a leaf shape that begins with a straighter line than the previous curved leaves. This shape will loop tightly around and return to its starting point with another, straighter line, connecting at a sharp point. This style will have more leaves coming from the stem and they will be much skinnier due to the narrow leaves created from the straighter lines and the tighter curve at the tips.

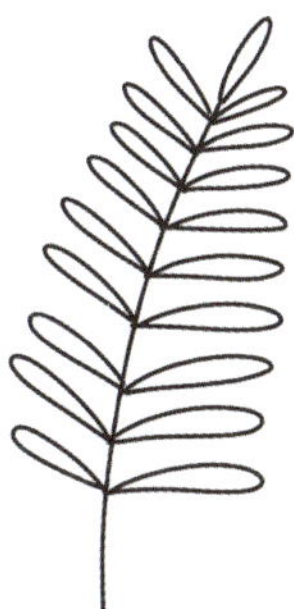

STEP 1 Draw a slight C-curve to form the stem.

STEP 2 Draw a leaf at the top of the stem that begins with a straighter C-curve, tightly loops around at the top, and comes back down in a straight line and connects at a point.

STEP 3 Continue drawing these leaves on each side of the stem until you have leaves filling each side.

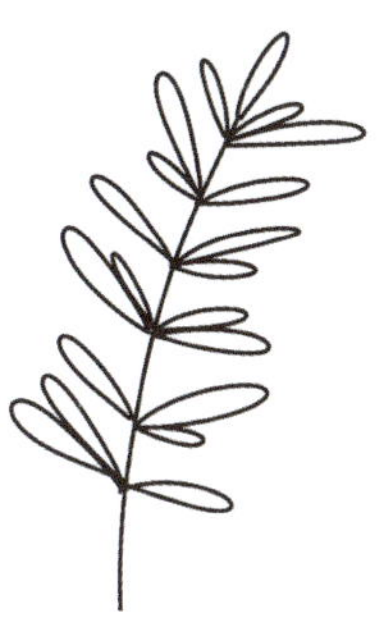

Try doing the same thing again with the leaves at the same width, but this time alternate the lengths, connecting a few at the base as you go. See how the same style can give off a different look just by tweaking one or two details? Let's keep going, but tweak the overall leaf shape a little more.

STYLE 3 | ## Simple Teardrop Leaves

This time we're going to add a soft start with an S-curve that moves inward first, then out and around, looping back to an S-curve that mirrors the other side. This shape is best described as a teardrop. In this first example, the style almost looks like it has tiny stems coming off of the main stem.

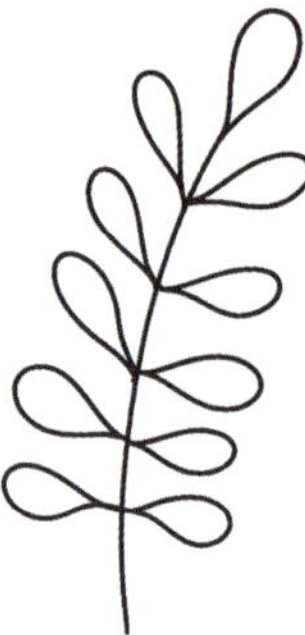

STEP 1 Draw a slight C-curve to form the stem.

STEP 2 Draw a leaf at the top of the stem that moves inward, curves outward on the side of the leaf, around at the top (S-curve), and back down in another S-curve and connecting at a point on the stem.

STEP 3 Continue drawing these leaves on each side of the stem until you have four or five on each side.

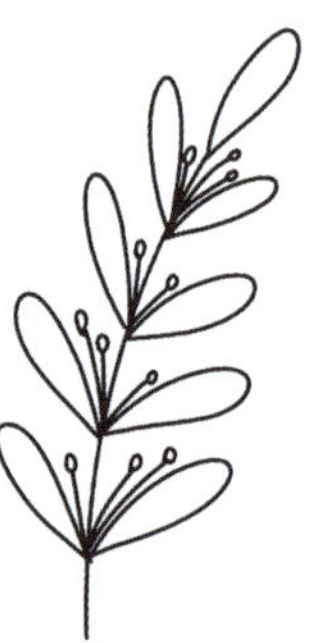

Using any of these leaf style examples, add extra details by drawing a short line from the stem near a leaf and adding a tiny circle at the end. Place them along the stem.

Pointed Leaves

Time to turn a new leaf! (Sorry. I couldn't help myself.) Now let's learn to include petioles, which look like tiny stems branching off of the main stem. They're what connect a stem to a leaf.

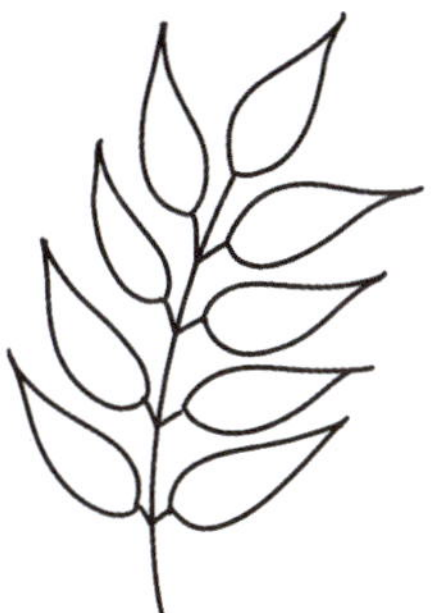

STEP 1 Draw a slight C-curve to form the stem, then add petioles along each side.

STEP 2 Add leaves with S-curves that move outward and into a point at the tip on each side.

Try this same leaf style without petioles, extending the length and decreasing the width of each leaf.

Blend both of these styles on the same stem. In the areas that might overlap, envision where the line of the leaf behind another one would usually be, then when it's visible, continue the real lines to complete the leaf.

Look at all the different varieties of leaves created from the same basic idea! This exercise is the perfect example of how you can create new styles of natural elements by changing very simple details. As we get further into our nature drawing exploration, we'll visit some more realistic versions as well. By then, you'll be grasping this concept more naturally.

CONTOUR DRAWING

One of the ways to explore styles is to put pen to paper. You might find that you enjoy branching off into other drawing styles, and I invite you to explore those options. Thus far, we've briefly explored **contour drawing**, a technique that essentially focuses on the outlines of objects.

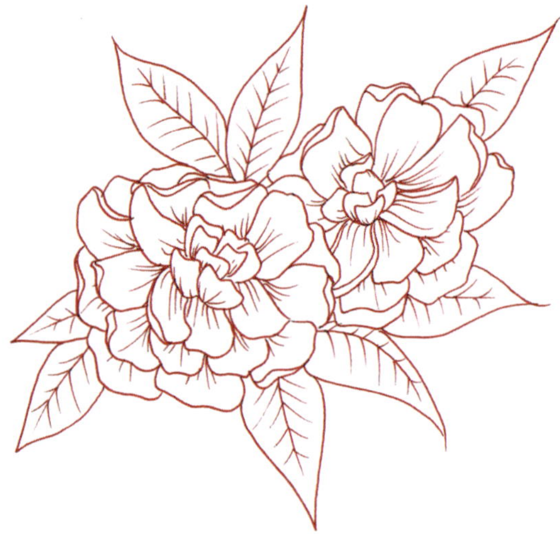

Contour here means "outline." Contour drawing is a great place to start when you open the door to your drawing adventures. **Blind contour drawing** is also a good place to begin, and it is what it sounds like: you work on drawing the outline of an object without looking at the paper and without lifting your pen. This exercise has several benefits. It demands hand-eye coordination while forcing you to keep your eyes on the object you're draw-ing. As you're looking at the object, you are learning how to see it in shapes and lines. You find distinct features that you may not have noticed if you were focused too much on the drawing itself. Rather than an exercise in drawing, this is an exercise in seeing.

Let's start with something simple and focus on natural items (since we're going with a nature theme in this book and all). This could be a houseplant in a pot, a seashell, a piece of driftwood, a vase with flowers, or a tree out-side your window. This step is easy. Find your subject. When you've found the perfect item, let's continue.

Place an object in front of you. It's important that this be a still-life object, meaning it will not move. (So don't grab your cat. Not only will the little guy move but he'll probably knock your pens on the floor and sit on your paper, which is adorable but not helpful.) As long as it's inanimate, it can be anything. My very first blind contour drawing was my own face in a mirror, which turned out to be what some would call a masterpiece. I say that with great sarcasm. The second blind contour drawing I did was my hand. You're probably wondering why I'm contradicting myself when I just said not to use an object that moves. Listen, I'm just telling you what I did, not that it was the best move. (Also, we have more control over our bodies than we do the cat's. So there.) The third blind contour drawing I did was a chunky combat boot, and the next was my fireplace.

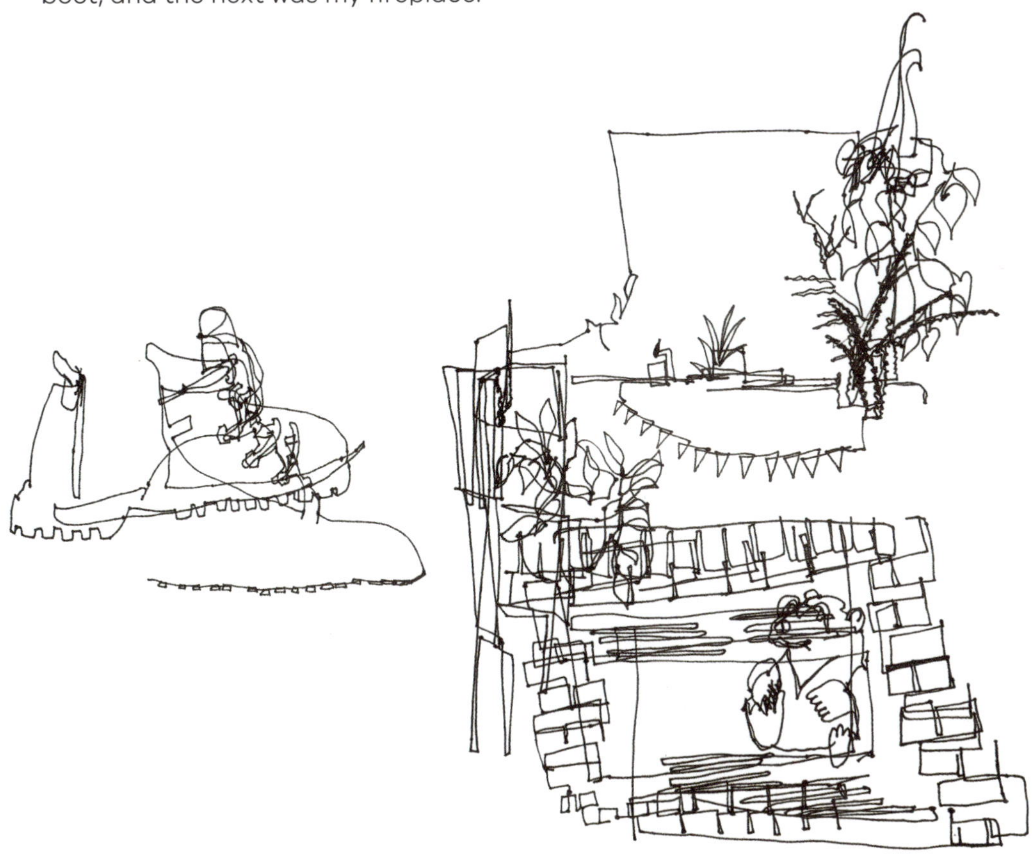

Before beginning to draw, with your item of choice in front of you, try to break it down into shapes. For example, in my plant (below), I see that I've got the plant holder/pot, long lines for stems, and oblong shapes for leaves with pointed tips. I'm also noticing detail on the plant holder that I'll include (which definitely won't look like it's supposed to, but that's the beauty of blind contour drawing!).

After you've visualized your object in broken-down shapes, notice its size and the size of each shape in relation to the others. This will help you figure out where to start on the paper. Knowing that a little over half of the plant is in the stems and leaves and the other part is the plant holder, I know I'm pretty safe to start my drawing in between these main areas by beginning in the middle of my paper.

Here's the kicker: Once you set your pen down on your paper in your starting position, you're going to look up at your object and not look back down until you're finished. So place your pen down on your paper, look up at your object, and begin drawing what you see. Use shapes as reference. It's okay to trace back over what you've already done. Whatever you do, don't lift your pen and don't look at your paper.

After you think you've completed your drawing, you can set your pen down and look at your masterpiece! Chances are that your first reaction will be to laugh. You might see some major disproportions or a random feature that's spaced way off the object. That's okay! You just drew blindly!

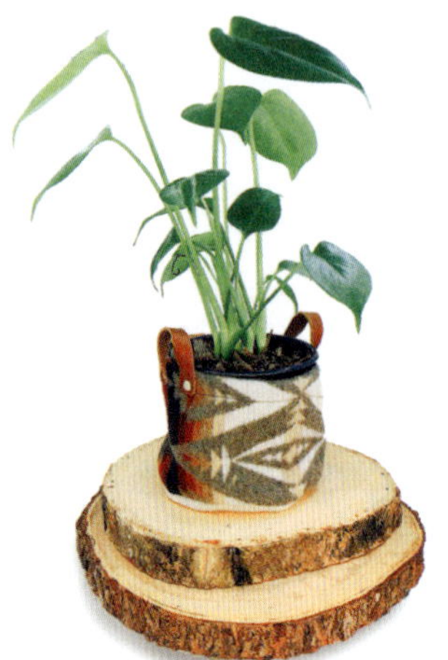

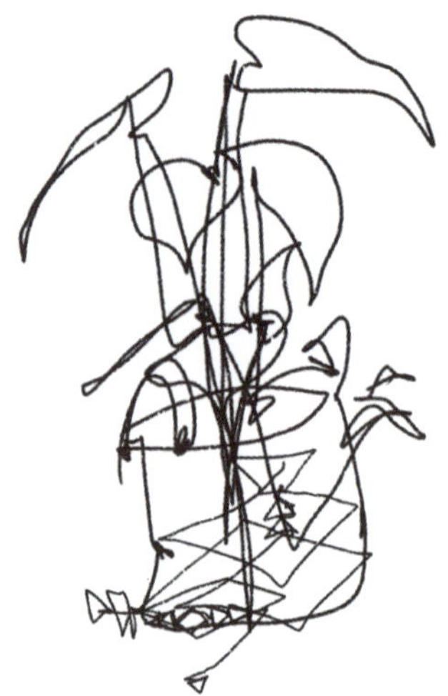

Once you've finished your blind contour drawing, draw the same object in contour style (with focus on outlines), but not blindly. Now you can look at your paper as you draw. Whether you lift your pen is up to you. In my example, I decided to keep my pen on the paper until I was finished. It's interesting to see the way we pick up information this way. You'll probably notice details that, without having first drawn the object blindly, you might not have noticed. You're welcome (even though I totally didn't come up with blind contour drawing, which was first introduced by artist Kimon Nicolaïdes in his posthumous book *The Natural Way to Draw* in 1941, but still).

With the same item you chose for your blind contour drawing in front of you, revisit the visualization of its shapes.

As you draw, break down each shape. For my plant, I start at the plant holder, drawing a soft square shape. Since I'm not lifting my pen, I can travel inside the plant holder for some designs, then travel upward for the stems and leaves.

If you choose to lift your pen, try hard not to focus too much on the details. Instead, draw the shapes you see. Visualize the ratios. Notice that my contour drawing's ratios are much more accurate to the object than my blind contour drawing since I've made the stems of my leaves longer. These are things to pay attention to now.

You're most likely finished before you feel finished. Don't overdo it! It looks amazing. Promise.

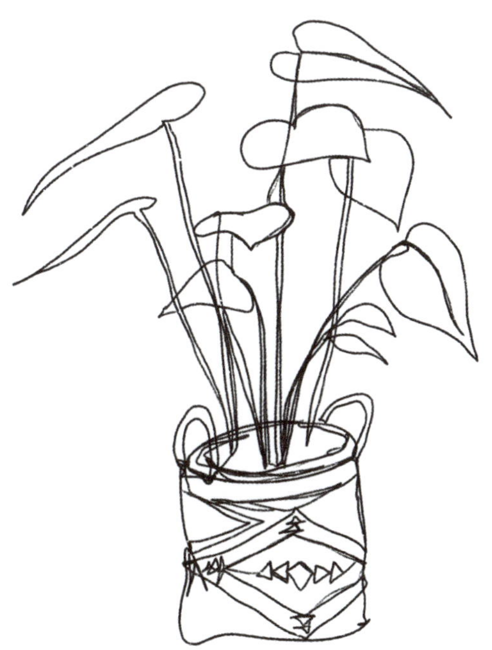

LOOSE SKETCHING

Loose sketching takes details we see and demands quick, loose strokes to capture a scene in a short amount of time. Sketching is often done with pencil before an illustration is fine-tuned. In this case, we won't be applying pencil because I want to challenge you to embrace imperfections by not being able to erase. Work with what you have—a ballpoint or felt-tip pen will do the trick. This will help you learn faster as you make mistakes. You'll create muscle memory by tweaking perspectives in the way they should appear. **Gesture drawing** is a form of loose sketching that is often applied to action and moving figures. It is an acquired skill of remembering motions that you see and sketching them quickly from memory. This will be beneficial when you're mentally snapshotting movements in animals. It's like taking a picture with your pen and paper, quickly recording the information you see. Have you ever heard of or participated in a one-minute writing challenge, where you sit down and write out everything that comes to mind? Try doing that with sketching what you see. It's so interesting what comes out of it. Just as with any art style or medium, there are techniques to pick up that will help you to create pieces that are reflective of your intention, but this raw loose sketching will most likely surprise you when you see the organic character it gives your artwork.

I like to apply this technique to urban sketching, overlapping my lines to produce the main effect that I'm going for. The overlapping lines not only correct lines that I'm not the happiest with but they also add a unique character to my illustrations. I don't like to strive for perfection, or even accuracy. I like to incorporate unique energy into my drawings.

There are a few wrist and arm motions that will assist you in executing these styles. To switch to loose, smooth lines, instead of gripping your pen close to the tip and guiding it with your hand or wrist, adjust your grip a little farther from the tip of the pen and use your elbow to guide your strokes. You'll feel less tension in your wrist, and your lines will be smoother and longer.

 # Loose Strokes

In the first example below, the lines are bolder and more wobbly. They were created primarily with tension and grip from the hand (fingers and wrist). The second example features smoother, wispier lines. They were executed with a lighter grip on the pen and sweeping motions using more of the elbow.

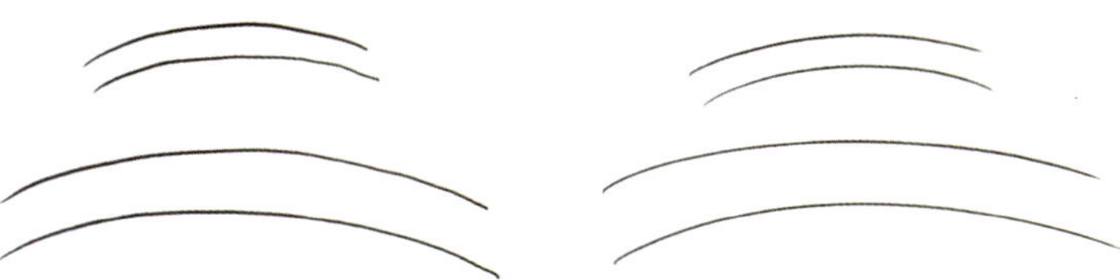

Let's draw a square and a circle the way you normally would. Then, try loosening your grip and letting your pen glide quickly without much care. Overlap your lines once or twice. Your shapes now have a little energy!

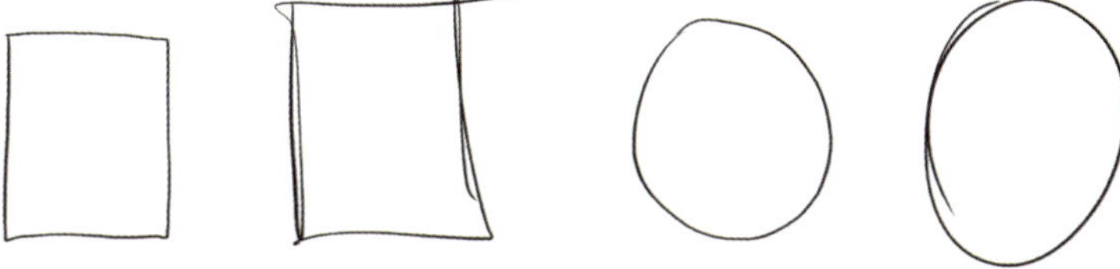

Loose Sketching with Trees

The imperfections of loose sketching portray energy, character, and emotion. This style is meant to be executed with less thought, more action. Think of it as your eyes and hands working simultaneously to create a snapshot, quickly recording on paper what you're seeing. Let's go over some simple examples of detail in a loose sketch.

Trees are found everywhere, so I've included a collection of examples here. You'll find that very simple variations will capture the different essences of trees with little effort. In even a very simple illustration, these loosely sketched trees can represent many different types of trees.

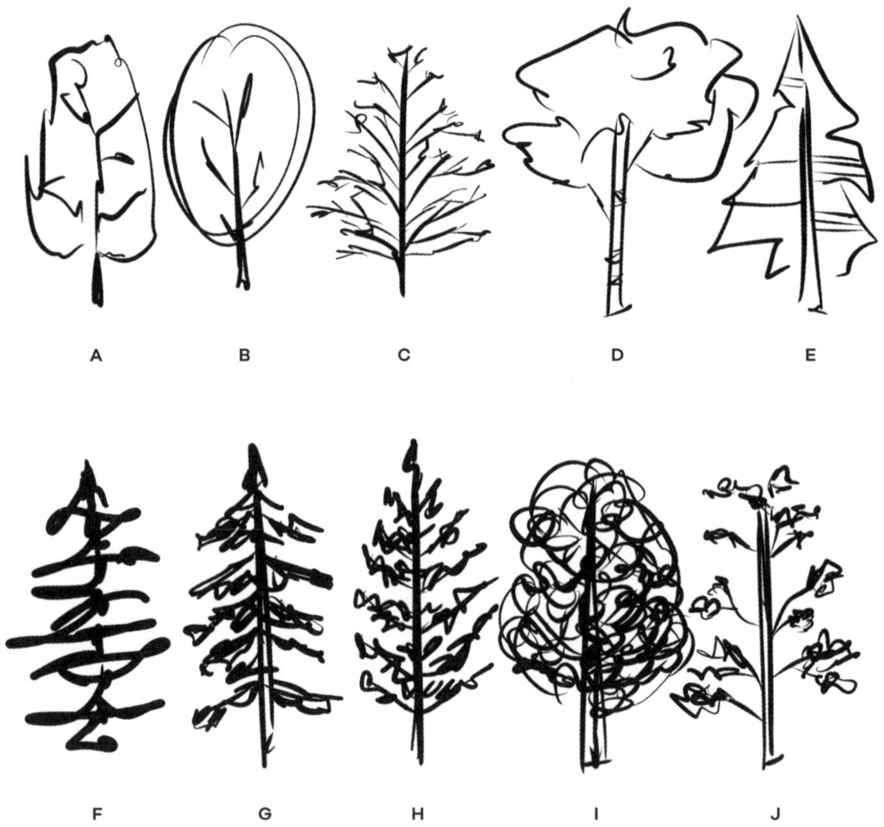

The lists below include just a sampling of the many trees these sketches could represent.

(A) Columnar English oak, Lombardy poplar, linden

(B) Ash, boxwood tree (shaped), basswood

(C) Contorted filbert, cherry (leafless), yew

(D) Honey locust, maple, beech, walnut, elm

(E) Pine, hemlock, cedar, blue spruce

(F) Larix, Douglas fir, red cedar

(G) Siberian fir, sugar pine

(H) Larch, spruce, tamarack, Norfolk pine

(I) Aspen, alder, hornbeam, chestnut

(J) Yucca, banyan, birch, cypress

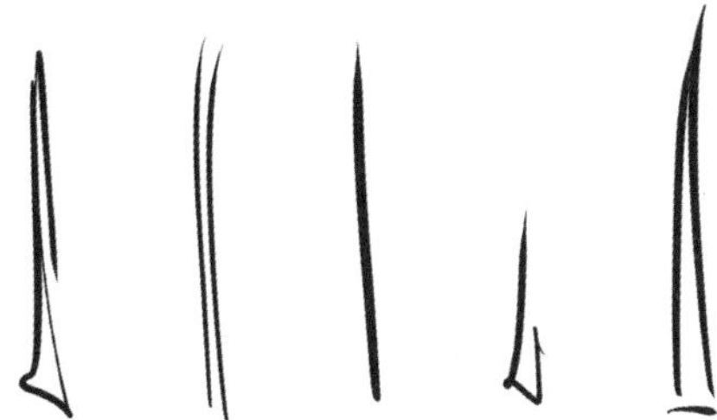

When loosely sketching tree trunks, use quick lines that don't have much structure. They can also be straight lines. They can reach up to the height of the tree to show it branching off, or they can stay low so you can focus more on the fullness of the tree.

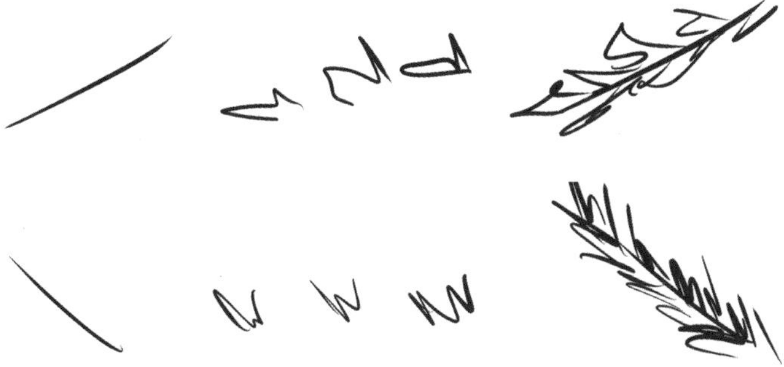

Depending on the tree, you might find that its branches droop a bit, hanging toward the ground. Some branches lift toward the sky. Some spread out from other branches, reaching outward.

Adding branches takes just as little effort. Use those loose, quick movements throughout. In this process, you'll probably notice that you have a little hand motion or two that develops as a habit in your sketches. Mine is a break in my lines where I abruptly stop to create a very small notch in the line before continuing. Character can be found wherever your pen wants to guide you.

Leaves can look sparse or full. I find that smaller scribbles on fir trees well represent their pine needles and cones from a distance. It's a detail so small that it's assumed, and therefore it's effortless. Fuller trees could have little detail or a lot of detail. Building up these trees is simple. Loosen your grip and allow your pen to make abrupt changes in its flow or direction. Begin straight down, then drag your pen quickly side to side. Repeat this motion, getting wider as you reach the bottom. Once you reach the bottom of the canopy, add a small vertical line that signals the beginning of the tree trunk.

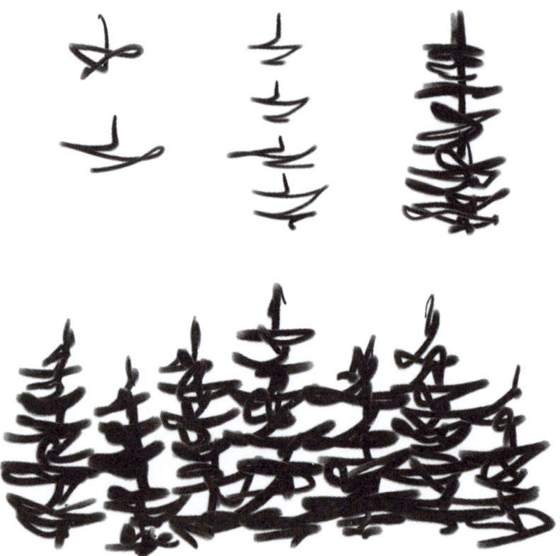

MARK MAKING

Mark making is a term that describes the texture we add to illustrations with the use of particular line work that adds depth and details. This technique can be executed with various line styles, including hatching and cross hatching, circles, horseshoes, scribbles, you name it. This will come in handy when you want to add detail without adding the actual details. So many times we try to make our illustrations too literal when they don't need to be! These techniques exist for a reason—they work. We'll be using a daisy as our subject as we walk through some mark making.

To the beginner, the flower can be a tricky little guy. For one, we're taught from a young age that petals are these bubbly objects that are attached to a circle that acts as the center of the flower. A lot of us never really progress past that. Don't get me wrong, this style can be a lot of fun and can make for some adorable illustrations. Keeping a doodle aesthetic in mind, we can greatly enhance it by learning to make slight adjustments to these go-to shapes; small details such as a tiny V at the tips of the petals, changing the width and length of the petals, and looking at the proportions between the center and petals.

When I teach people about botanical illustration, the first flower I jump to is the daisy—the Gerbera daisy in particular. We don't bother working on elements and techniques. We don't worry about mark-making details. We just jump right in with a live flower and a pen. Here's why: The daisy is a recognizable flower. Ask most people to draw a flower and it will probably look something like this. We already feel a sense of comfort in executing these basic shapes, so fine-tuning our skills to more accurately match what we see is easier than you may realize.

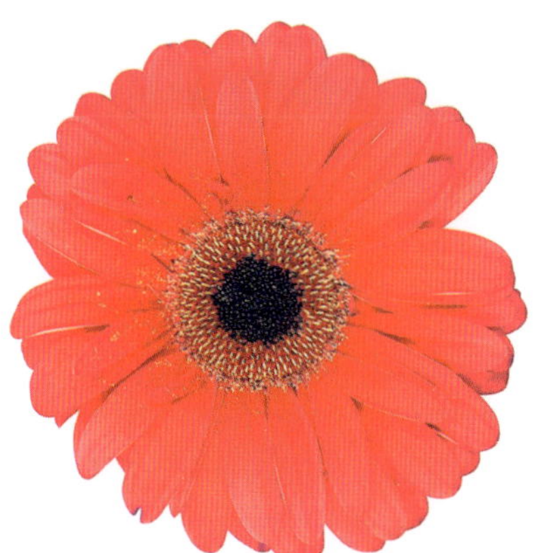 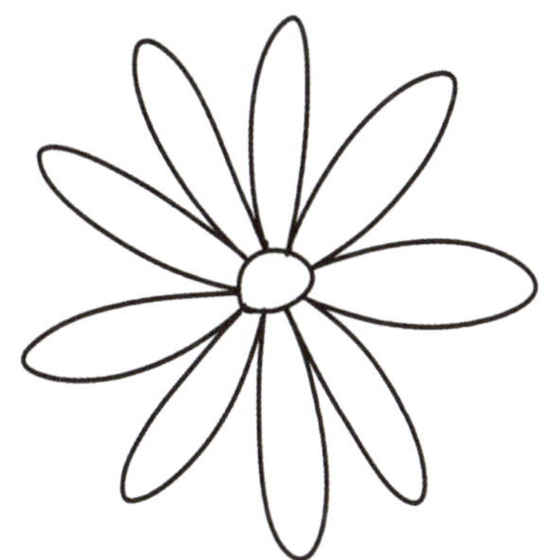

Let's start by looking at it head-on. The key to drawing live flowers is to imagine them as pictures. You'll find that it's a little trickier to visualize the elements we're going over when the object is three-dimensional, but the same will apply, so don't psych yourself out when you grab a real flower! Just remember the rules that follow.

Three main features of the flower stand out: the center, the petals, and the details. "Detail" sounds like a loaded word, doesn't it? Don't worry, I'll break down the details as well.

Drawing the center of a flower can be achieved with mark making. This is a small part of your illustration, so there's no need to put too much effort into the center unless you're drawing on a larger scale. Speaking of size, remember in the materials section when I mentioned that the size of your pen tip relates to the size of your illustration (see page 10)? Keep that in mind! Small details can get lost with a broad tip if your illustration is on the small side. I recommend starting by drawing a flower about the size of an actual Gerbera daisy using an 05 tip. This should make it easier for you.

The marks you make to create the center can represent the real thing. I typically go about the center in one of three styles, below.

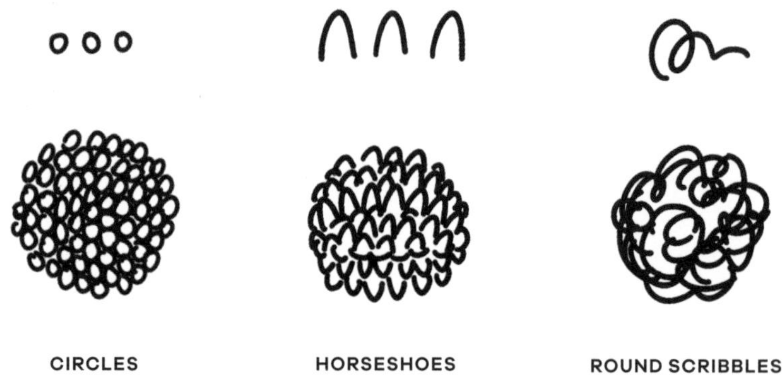

CIRCLES HORSESHOES ROUND SCRIBBLES

Remember: You're not out to win an award for the best realistic illustration. These techniques will merely expand your skillset and help you get creative with how you translate onto paper the information you see in the world.

A general rule of thumb when it comes time to attack petals is to see the center of a flower with the petals opening up from its core, which sits within a circular shape. The petals are often oval shapes, with more definition toward the inside. This gives the illusion that they're being tucked into the center. They can be drawn with small ridges, featuring texture at the tip. They can also be drawn with folds.

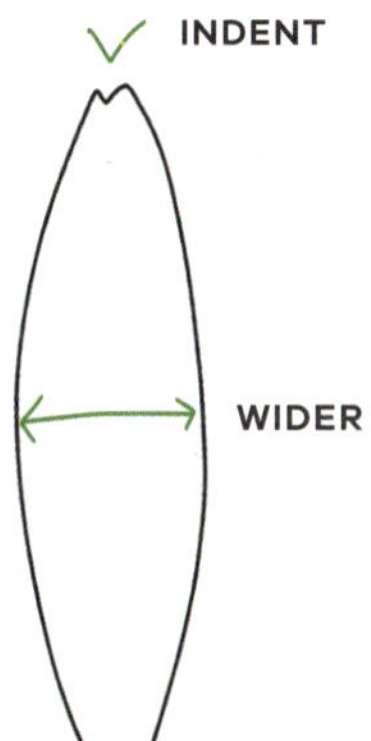

STEP 1 Draw the center of your daisy with circles, horseshoes, or round scribbles.

STEP 2 After drawing the center, it's on to the petals. First, think of the tip and the base. A daisy's petal is about the same width at each end and broadest in the middle.

To achieve this look, draw a C-curve from the bottom toward the top. You'll want this line to be about 1.5 times as long as the center's width. When you reach the top, rather than simply curving over and coming back down, add a small indent. Believe it or not, these tiny details can bring out a ton of character. You'll then travel back down with another C-curve, leaving a small space at the base.

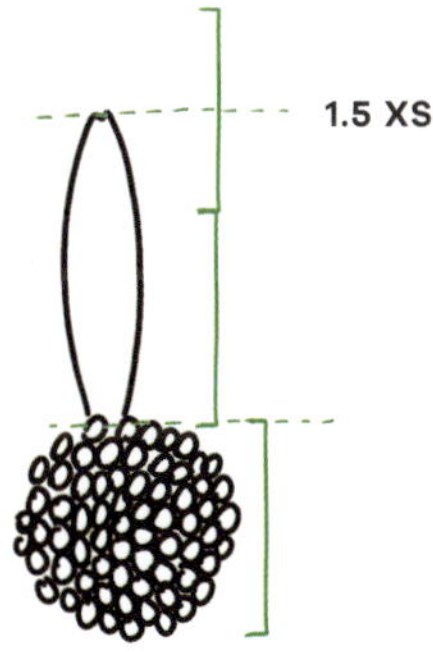

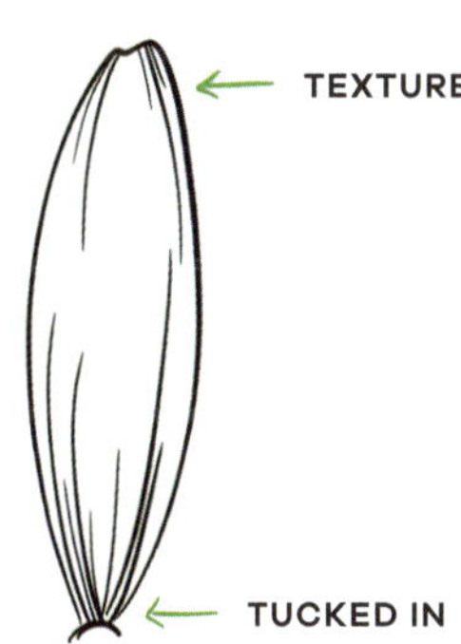

Congratulations! You've executed your first petal. Now do that seven hundred more times. Kidding, but you will need to repeat this around the center until you create the full flower. A common issue people have when drawing flowers is symmetry. Nobody wants one side of the flower to look wonky and misshapen. The trick to the best consistency in your petals is to jump to the other side for the second petal. I'd also be sure to offset it a little so it's not directly across from the first petal you drew. Sometimes it's okay to have petals perfectly placed like that, but I like to suggest getting into the habit of offsetting your petals for a more realistic look. Turning your paper may help you as you place your petals.

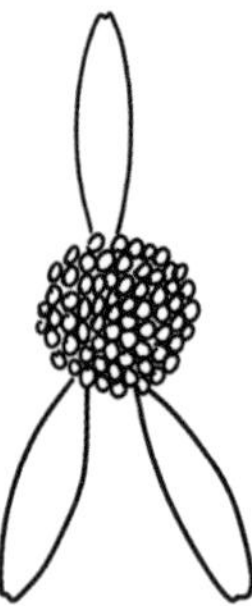

Draw another petal near the first, which will act as another guide. From here, just fill in the empty space. There will be areas that petals won't fit. I even recommend starting closer to a petal than you should so it won't! This will force you to create an overlapping effect. Just stop the line when you reach the petal next to it, then hover over where the line would be, and if you find that it needs to be added toward the bottom as well, continue the line through to the base.

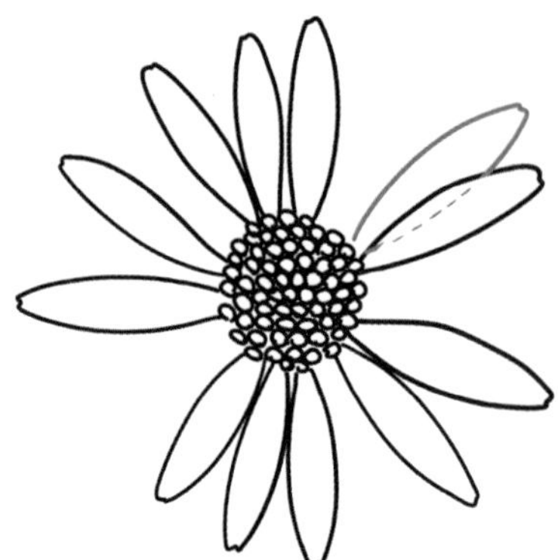

You could be finished with your base shape and move on to details at this point, or you might want to enhance it more by adding "peek-a-boo" petals in the back, creating a layered effect. If you opt for this, do so using the same overlapping method.

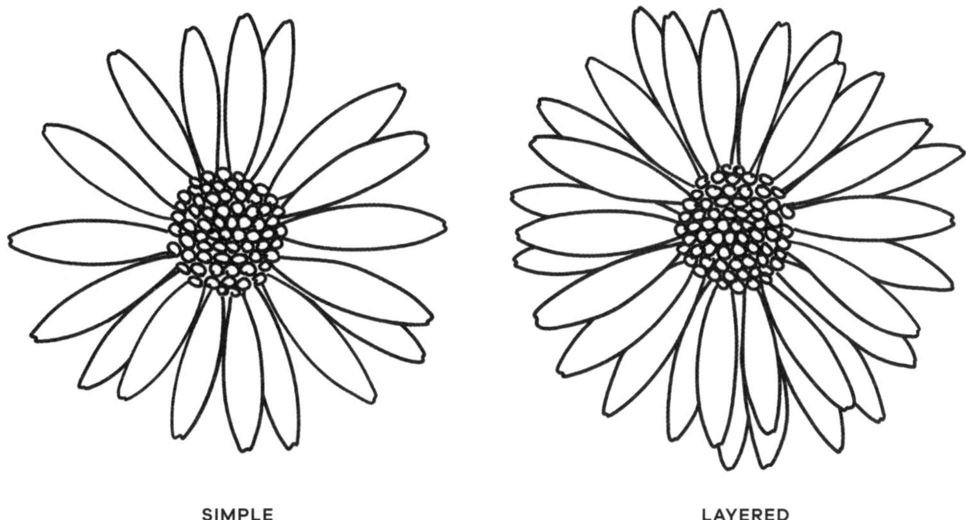

Line Weight

On to the fun part! You'll see your flowers really come to life when you add details.

We'll start with lines in your petals. Another reason I start with the daisy is because its lines are precise and uniform. There are enough to see definition and movement, but not too many to confuse you in the learning process. You can choose to create lines that vary in **weight**, or thickness, or you can draw lines that are the same weight throughout.

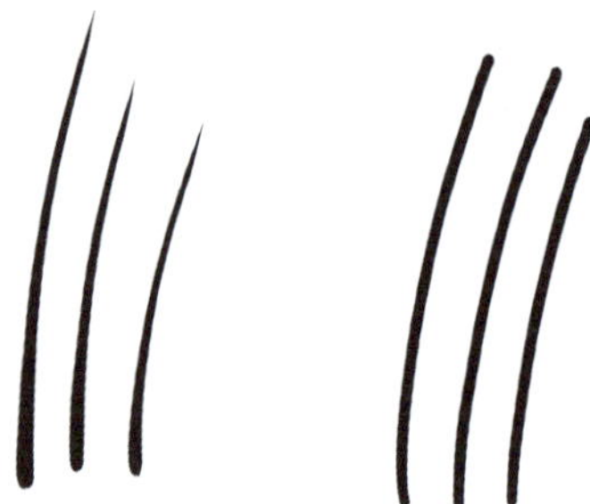

I like my lines to vary in thickness because I like the look of the "fall off," where the line tapers and gets lighter as it ends. It's usually toward the center of daisy petals that the most light hits the flower, as that's where the petals project forward, so drawing lines that fade more toward the center, with the broader part of the strokes at the ends, will create the appearance of depth. See how that gives the illusion of movement?

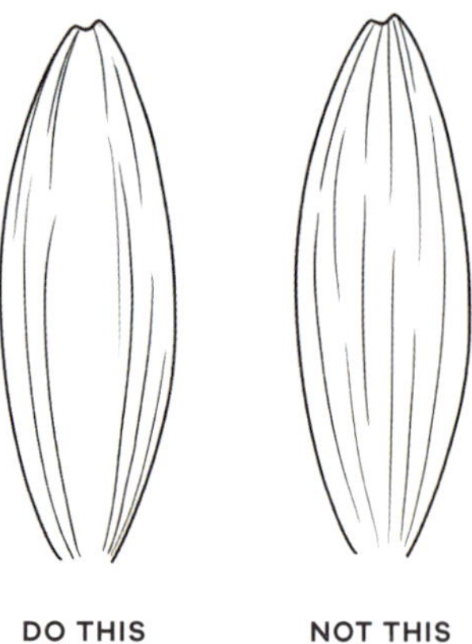

To achieve the tapered look, just set your pen down, slightly drag it, then flick it outward gently in the direction that you want the line. This flicking motion will lift the pen just enough to make the end thinner and lighter.

You also have the option of switching your pen to a thinner tip so your line work appears more delicate. I encourage you to practice on a piece of scratch paper with different types of pens and different tip sizes so you can get a good idea of how this will look in your petals.

When drawing lines in your petals, you want them to travel with the petal's natural shape. The sides are curved more, so the lines should follow the curve of the sides of the petal, getting slightly straighter as they move toward the center.

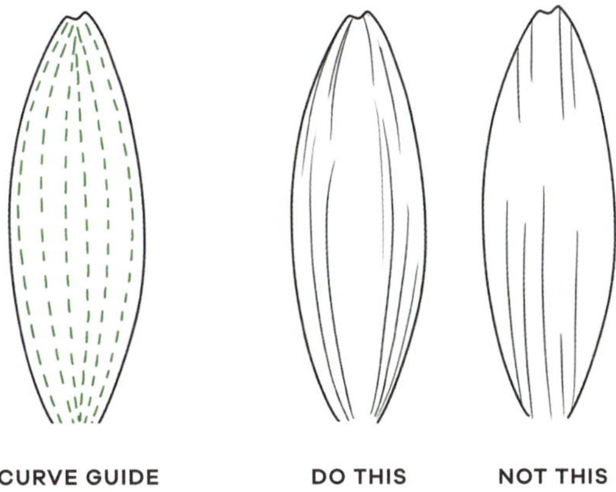

You can further enhance the center by considering the light and dark areas. Rather than mimicking this exactly on paper, however, I typically do my own version of adding depth. Darker areas add depth and can create movement, and the same goes for line detail. I don't add any of these details until I'm finished with the main structure of my drawing, however.

Now for the finishing touches. Remember that depth I just mentioned in the center of your flower? You know, the one that makes it look like your petals are being tucked in and held? Let's make it happen. To achieve this effect, keep in mind that darker areas add depth, and mark making adds darkness. This trick is so easy that I get giddy sharing it! Here's all you do: Simply draw the exact same marks that you used to create the center around the edges of the center. That's it! Look at the difference! BAM. Because of the line work you've already included, adding this depth will create the perfect illusion of the petals being hugged in place. Last, you can always add a bit more depth in the middle of the center by doing the same thing. A little extra dimension never hurt anyone.

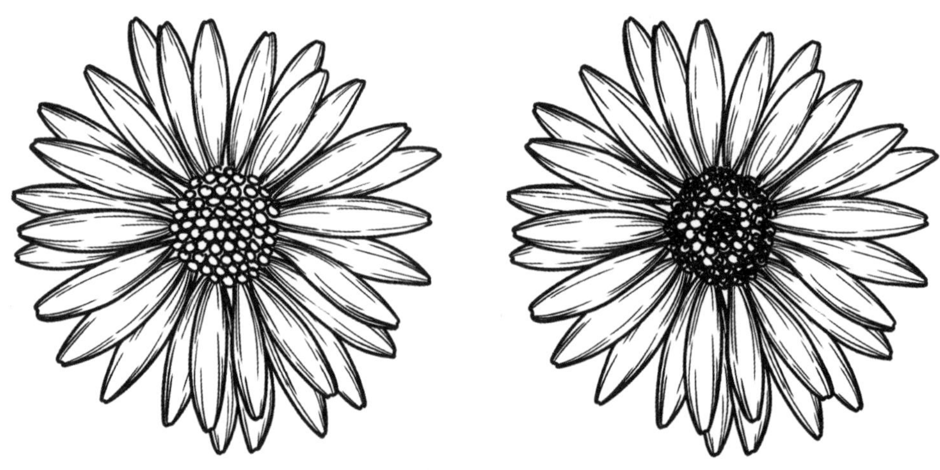

Shading and Shadows

When you get into shadow and light, there's a simple rule that will help: The more line work that is added, the darker it will appear, which is what creates depth. This will continue to come up in your illustrations. Light direction matters as well.

For an example, mountain ranges look more believable when the bulk of the details are isolated to one side, giving the illusion that the sun is bouncing off of one side while the other is in shadow.

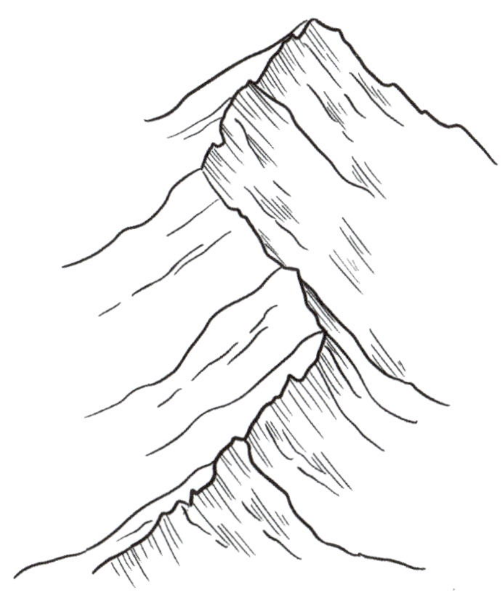

Think about it this way—let's say you took a flashlight to an object; it's obvious where the light hits it directly, and it's also obvious where the shadows are. In nature the sun acts as our flashlight, so simply leave the areas that the light would hit as blank space and add details in the areas that would have shadows. If you want to get fancy, keep in mind that shadows are darkest where they lie closest to an object (as at the tip of this mountain range) and fade the farther away they get.

Hatching

There's not a ton to know about **hatching**. It's simple straight lines, repeated in very close parallel to each other. You can decrease the depth of an object by spreading the lines out a bit more; which gives the illusion of a change in the value, or how light or dark something is.

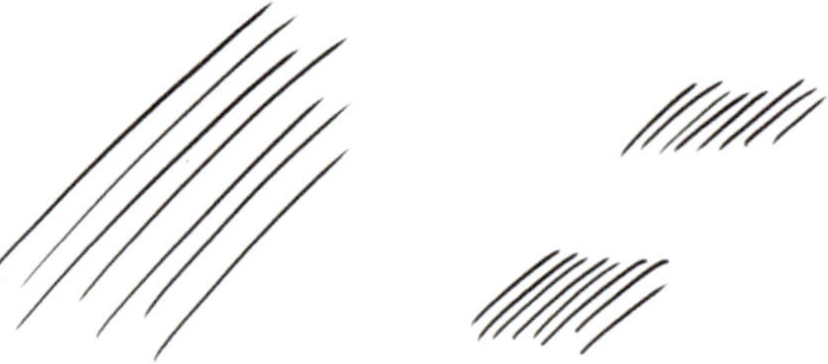

When you draw parallel lines in close proximity to one another, they appear darker. When they're farther apart, they appear lighter.

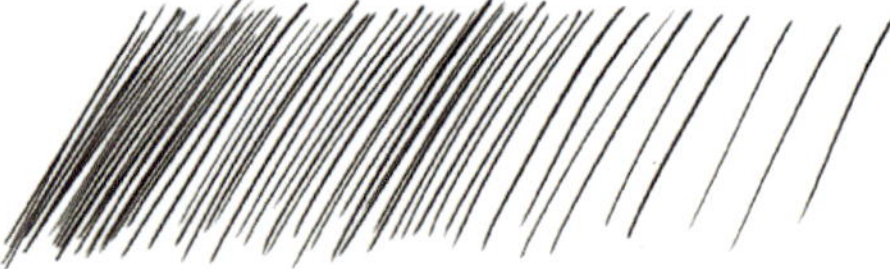

Practice Hatching

Practice hatching by drawing parallel lines that vary in spacing. Then, put your practice to work by creating a hatching blob! This is a cylindrical shape made up of small sections of a variety of hatching marks with different directions, spacings, and thicknesses.

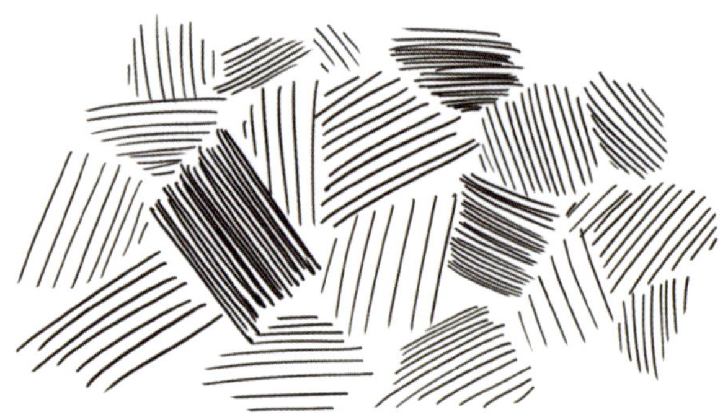

Cross Hatching

Cross hatching is an extension of hatching. It builds off of standard hatching by adding a second set of parallel lines that sit on top of the first set, usually perpendicular, but they can be placed at any angle. The point is that the two sets are intersecting. This is another technique that is ideal for adding shadows or depth in illustrations.

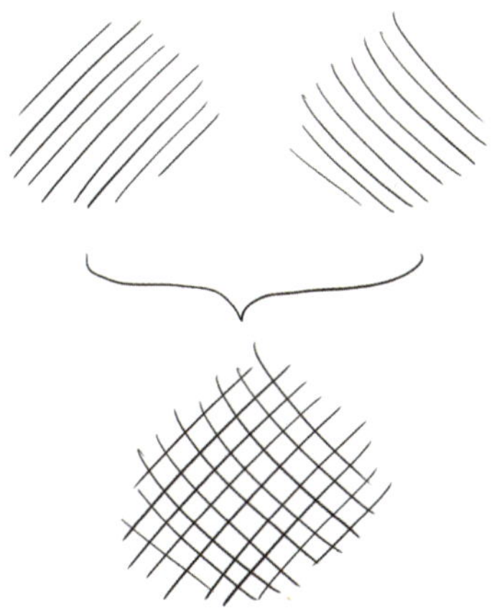

Practice Cross Hatching

Practice this technique just as you did with regular hatching. Play with spacing between lines to see how it can vary the illusion of depth.

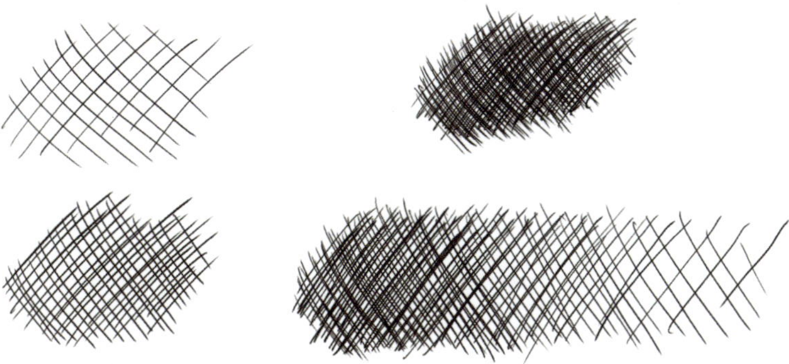

Now practice varying the angle of your cross lines. They don't have to be at a perfect angle of 90 degrees to your first set of lines. You can angle them in the middle of that at 45 degrees, or less.

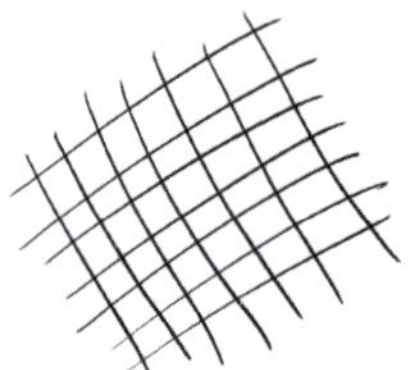 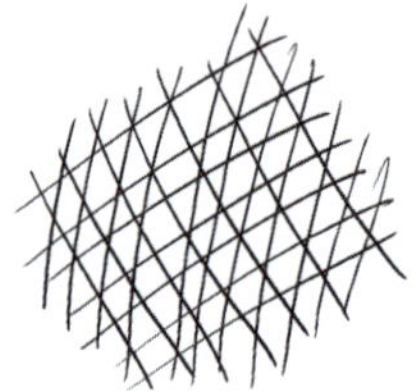 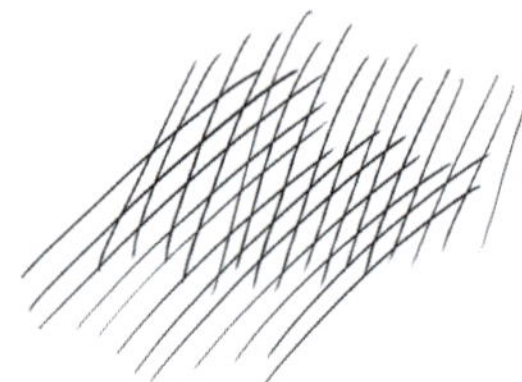

Practice Shading

Continue your hatching practice with a loose sketch of a tree. Draw your tree first. We'll then assume the shadow of the tree by envisioning that the light source is coming from the top left, which means the shadow will be on the bottom right. Shadows are darker closest to the object, and they fade lighter as they gain distance. Draw small hatching marks very close to the tree trunk. As you get farther away, begin adding a little more length to your lines and a little more distance between them. As you get to the end, space them out even more.

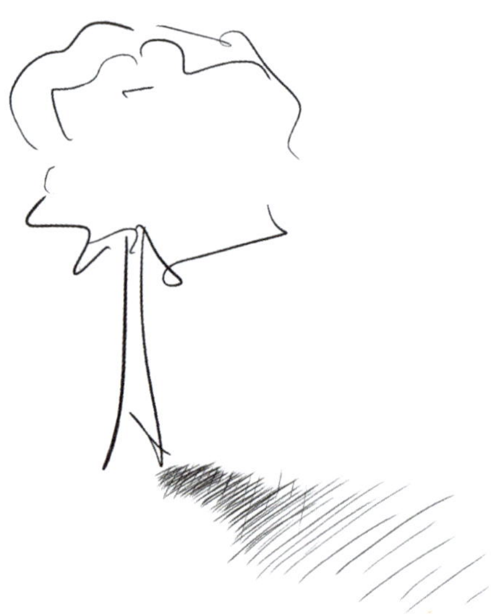

Stippling

There's nothing quite like artwork that has been executed by **stippling**. This technique involves filling in an area with nothing but dots or tiny specks. Placing these dots very close in proximity will create a much darker value, while separating the dots will show a much lighter area.

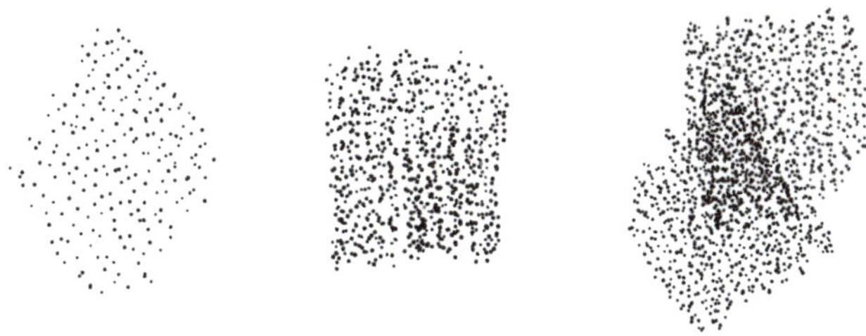

Practice Stippling

Practice stippling in shapes. Try spacing your dots evenly, then experiment with overlapping more dots to add depth. Below, I've drawn a circle with evenly spaced stippling. Draw a circle as I have, then layer additional stippling on one side. The more you add to a particular section, the more depth you'll see, and it will morph into a shadow before your eyes! This is a great technique for drawing the centers of flowers or clouds.

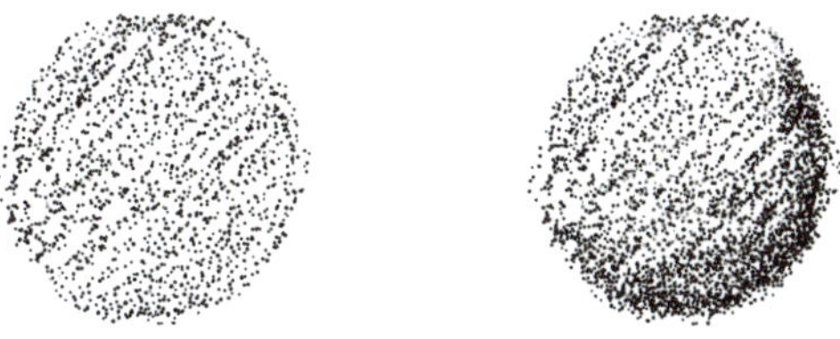

As you practice, don't think that your mark-making skills need to be confined to hatching, cross hatching, and stippling. These are just some examples, but you can really get creative and come up with some of your own unique go-to marks. Take out a piece of paper and separate it into nine squares. Fill those squares with some of your very own marks. The more you experiment, the more your style will develop organically.

SPACE AND PERSPECTIVE

Perspective will pop up quite a bit as we get into landscapes and look at how to accentuate depth for individual objects. Don't let the idea of how to properly size objects intimidate you. One of the main things to recognize is that we want to emphasize the foreground and minimize the background.

So much of this earth consists of beautiful rolling hills, snow-capped mountains, and deep-red canyons. We'll go over some techniques for adding depth to landscapes by applying line work where natural ridges and rock formations lie. When you're illustrating a landscape, you will want to show distance. This can be accomplished in several ways.

The first method is the easiest: The nearest objects should be bold and detailed and the objects farthest away should be lighter, with fewer details. You can enhance the foreground by making bolder, darker lines. This is done by applying more pressure with your pen or using a pen with a bolder tip. Then you will use less pressure, or a pen with a smaller tip, on the objects in the background, which creates soft, light lines and gives the illusion of fading into the distance. You can also produce dimension in your illustrations by adding quick pen strokes (mark making) to add detail. Adding more detail to the objects in the foreground and less in the background will make the foreground objects appear darker and more prominent.

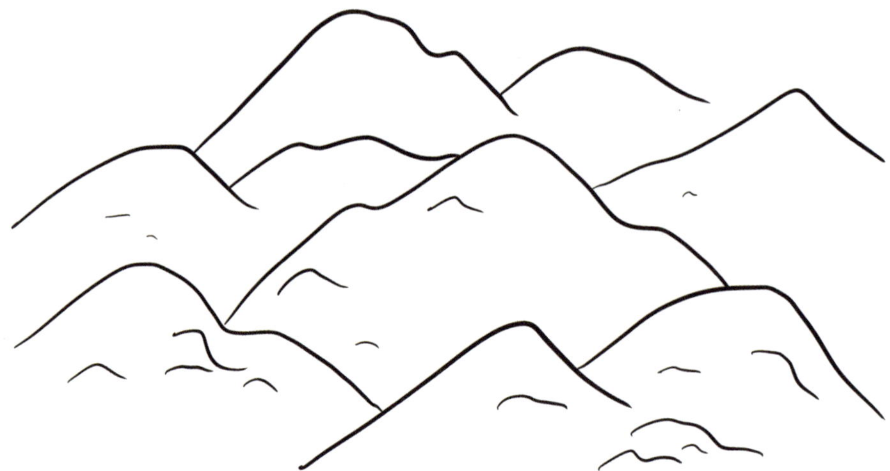

Practice Mountain Perspective

Mountains are a great study in perspective. They're big, beautiful, and can be drawn both realistically and a bit more playfully.

MOUNTAINS FROM THE GROUND

Let's begin by practicing mountains in one-point perspective, meaning we are seeing a flat image of only one dimension. In this case, it's the front of the mountains.

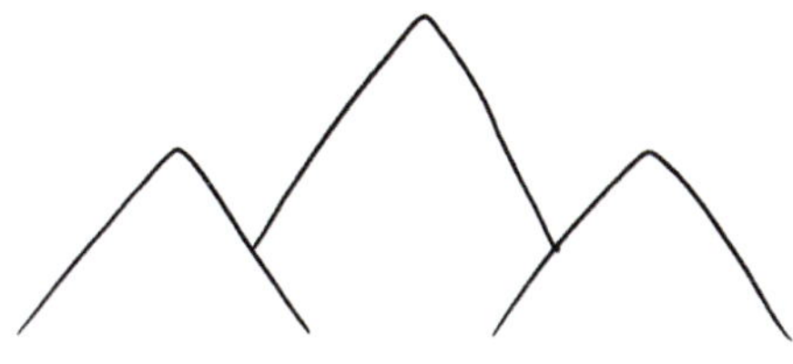

STEP 1 Draw three peaks using wide, upside-down V-shapes. Start with the two on the sides, then draw the middle a bit taller, connecting the ends of the lines to the smaller mountains.

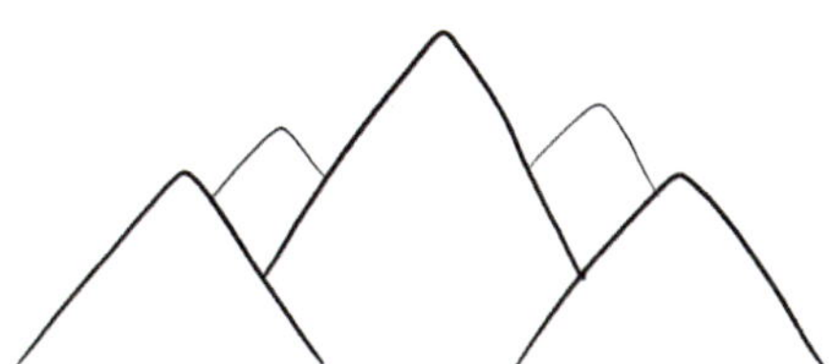

STEP 2 Using a thinner pen tip, or simply lighter pressure as you draw, add two more peaks in between both openings of the front mountain peaks. The lines should connect to the other mountains, to give the illusion that the front peaks are overlapping the back. This shows that the mountains being overlapped are farther away in the distance.

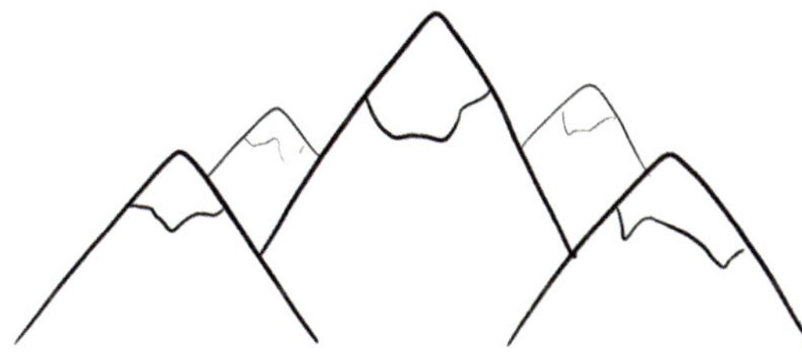

STEP 3 Last, using full pressure for the front mountains and lighter pressure for the back ones, add a jagged line to represent snowcaps toward the top of each peak. Simple enough, right?

MOUNTAINS FROM ABOVE

Let's take on a new perspective. In the previous example we were looking at the mountain range head-on. Now I want to show you what traditional drawing masters would consider a two-point perspective. We'll see two sides of the hills, as if we're looking at their peaks from above.

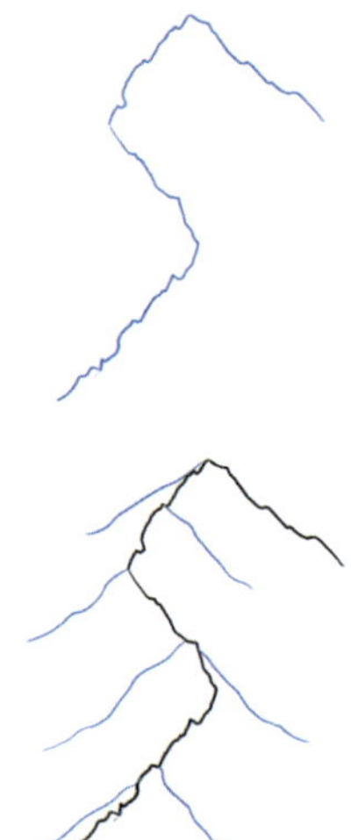

STEP 1 First draw a jagged line. You can think of it as a very jagged S-curve. Create many sharp dips in the line as you work your way through it.

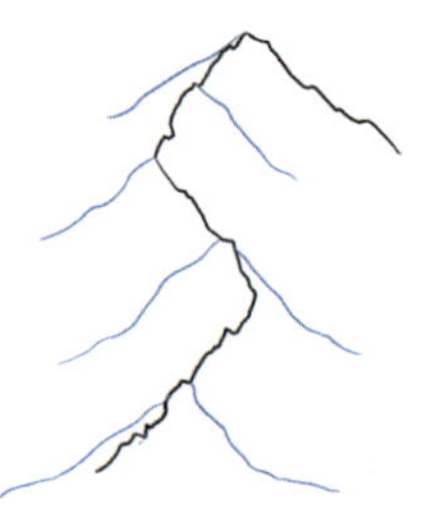

STEP 2 Next, find the main points where the direction changes and draw angled lines downward from each side.

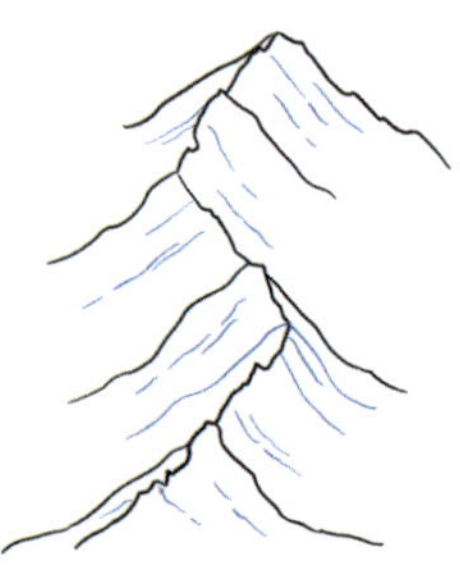

STEP 3 Now you want to add some detail. Just as you added lines in the previous step, draw lines at the same angles, only rather than traveling from the ridge all the way down, these lines should be shorter and with a few gaps.

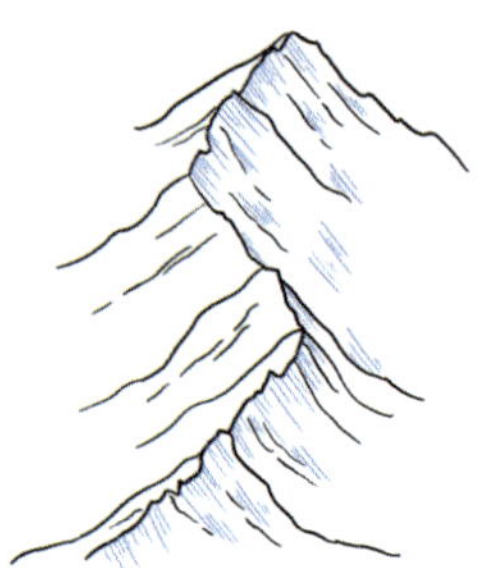

STEP 4 Finally, it's time to create some additional line work to show where the shadows are. Adding thin lines coming from the tops of one side of the range along with the lines you added for details will give the impression that the sun is shining on one side.

Practice Canyon Perspective

Canyons are mostly formed by erosion, but also by rivers and tectonic activity. Did you know that the red color in some canyons is caused by the presence of iron oxide and hematite? Did you also know that some paints are made from both of these minerals?! There's something really magical about painting with actual nature!

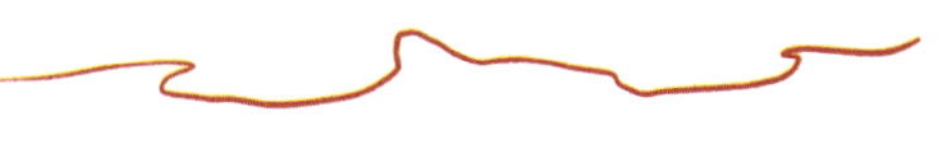

STEP 1 Draw a wavy line that sits above itself in small areas. For example, if you start from the left, you can dip your line down and to the left before continuing to draw it toward the right. Create a few of these types of dips along your wavy line.

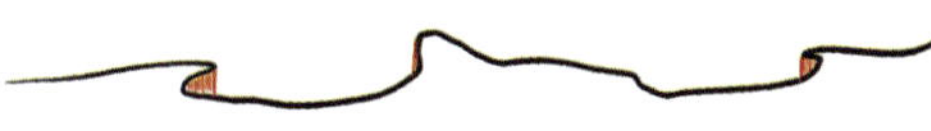

STEP 2 Wherever you see two lines on top of one another, draw a straight line down from the top of the curve and fill it in with some light shading. This is creating the edges of the inside of the canyon as if we're standing slightly above it.

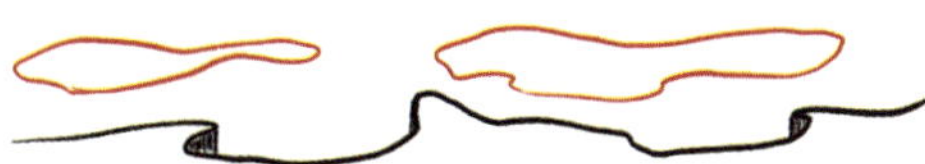

STEP 3 Draw a couple of flat, wavy ovals above the wavy line.

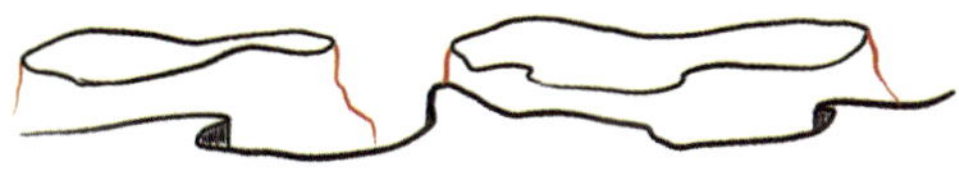

STEP 4 From the edges of each oval, draw a jagged line downward. These lines don't have to go straight down though. Instead, draw them at a slight angle. This will form the top of rock formations inside the canyon.

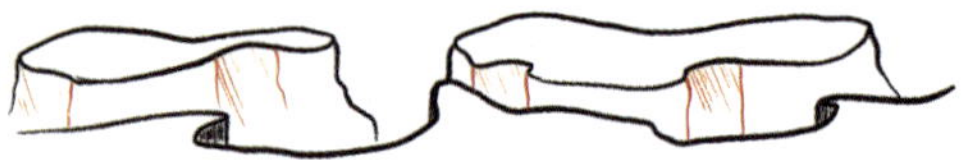

STEP 5 Look at your ovals and identify the areas where the bottom line bends toward the center. Draw light, jagged lines downward on each side of those bends and lightly fill them in with a hatching technique to produce depth.

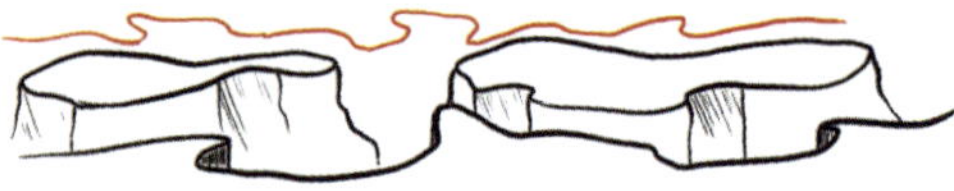

STEP 6 Create another wavy line across the top, very close to your ovals. Draw dips and bends as you did for your first line.

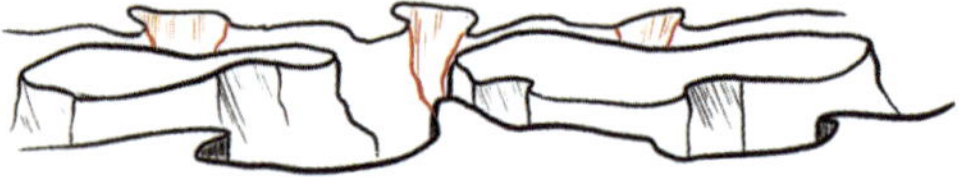

STEP 7 We're seeing the inside of this shelf rather than only seeing it from above. To add the inner sides like we did for the first line we drew, identify each area where your line bends upward. Draw two jagged lines on each side of these bends and use hatching to shade them.

STEP 8 Draw a horizon line above your canyon.

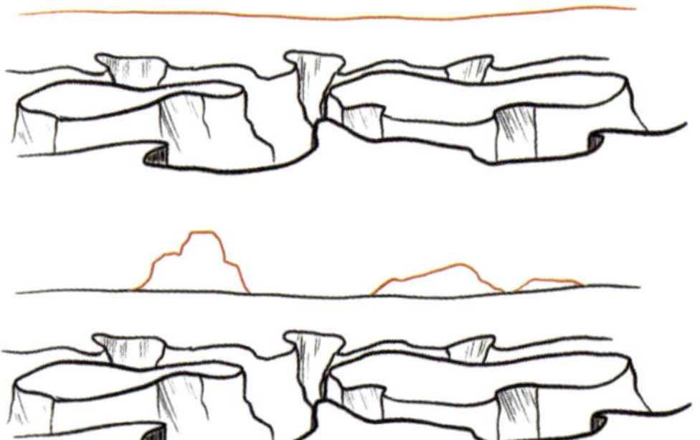

STEP 9 Add a few rock formations in the distance like you did with your mountains, only make your lines a bit more jagged.

 Rose Perspective
=======================

While there are more than a hundred species of roses, we'll focus on the obvious choice: the classic. No, this is not its official name. But isn't it applicable? The rose is a traditional flower that demands attention, and its various colors make it versatile and appropriate for any occasion. When we have a top view of the rose, we see its layers and layers of petals. Don't let this scare you. It's not as hard to draw as you might think.

ROSE FROM THE TOP

STEP 1 To begin, create the center with two little ovals.

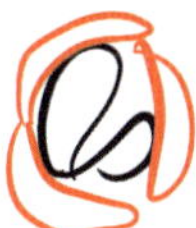

STEP 2 Then take the same loose oval shape and draw it thinner and longer, three times around the center. Drawing these shapes thinly gives the illusion that the petals are hugging the center tightly.

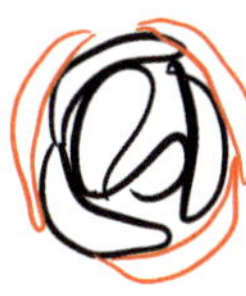

STEP 3 Repeat Step 2, lengthening the shape even more.

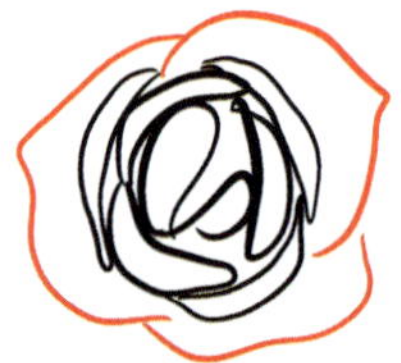

STEP 4 For the next three petals, rather than repeating the same shape, use S-curves to create petals and begin to open up. Simply draw some loose petals from the center, create points where the S-curves connect.

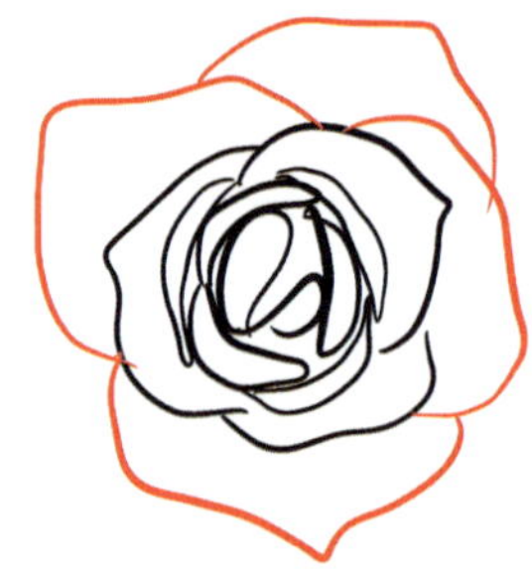

STEP 5 Create a few more of these petals opening up even larger. Don't overthink it and add too many. It's easy to keep adding more and more and more, but it's unnecessary. It probably looks phenomenal after just three to five more!

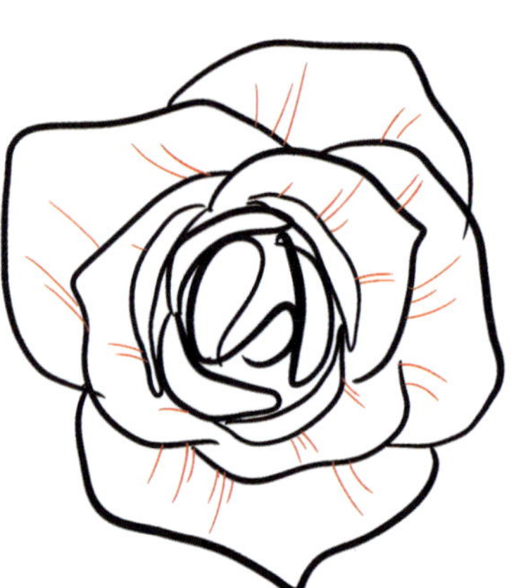

STEP 6 Add some light line details in the petals and be sure that each grouping travels the same direction. Lines that move from the bottom of petals outward, away from the middle, help the petals look like they're curved.

ROSE FROM THE SIDE

The side of a rose is less intimidating to draw than when it's face up. The outer petals hug the middle, and we can capture that effect with larger shapes.

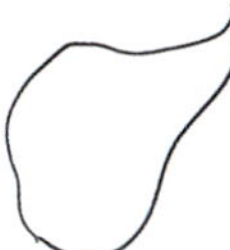

STEP 1 To start, draw a petal that presents the illusion that it is reaching around toward the back. Notice that the top left of the petal is directed inward with a soft C-curve, while the top right of the petal reaches a bit farther and comes up to a pointed tip. These small adjustments create movement.

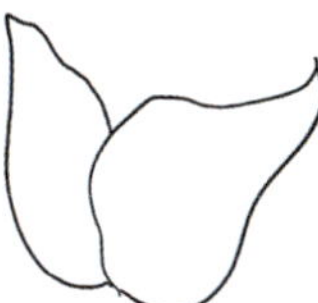

STEP 2 The next petal does the same thing, only the right side is tucked behind the first petal. Notice how the top left of this petal is in a point as well, but it's reaching outward rather than inward.

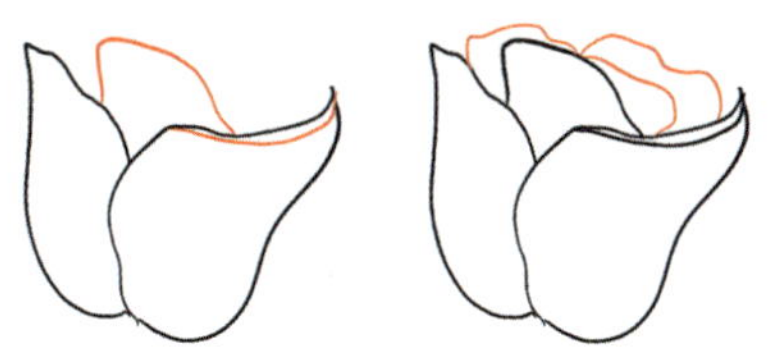

STEP 3 Now we'll build additional petals peeking from the inside and back. Add a line very close to the top of the first petal to suggest it's folding outward, creating even more movement. Use a wavy C-curve to draw the back petals and round out the rose.

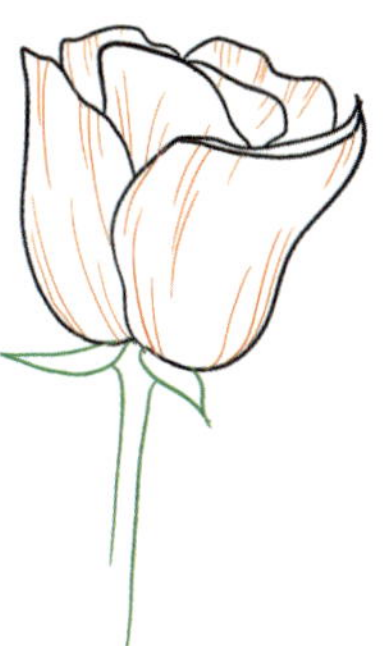

STEP 4 Add simple line work in the direction of the petals, along with small leaves and a stem at the base. That's it!

Angles

The daisy is such a great model: We must give it some credit—it holds its shape, it doesn't start slouching, it doesn't need breaks. Its color is phenomenal, it doesn't fight or move, and it's so very pretty. Because it does such a good job holding still, let's use it as an example to learn about angles.

I know, right when you feel like you executed a fantastic flower drawing, you turn the flower slightly to draw it at an angle and feel stumped. Everything you just learned flew out the window. But I'm here to let you know that it didn't, so don't fret! Just remember the key techniques. The primary focus here will be on shapes.

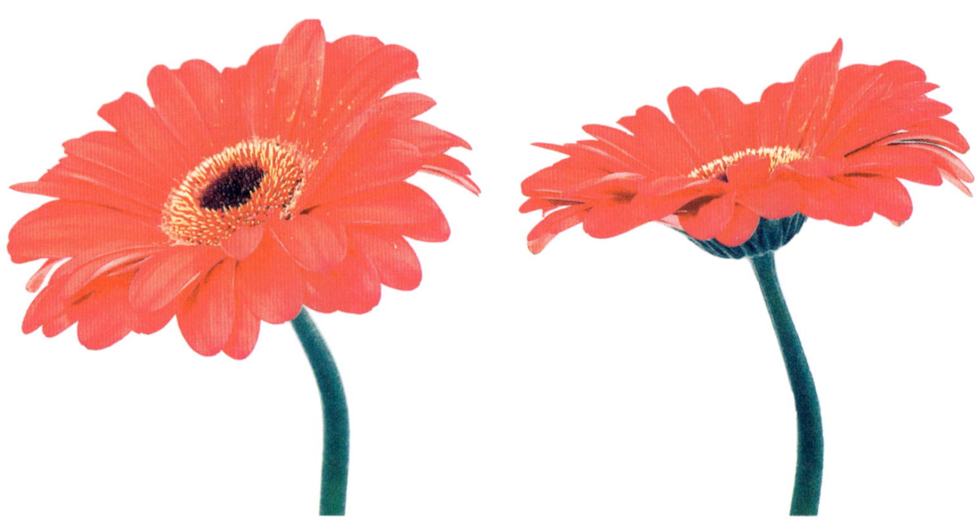

The key to drawing three-dimensional objects is learning how to see them. If you can visually flatten something, you'll be able to break it up into shapes instead of worrying about the three-dimensional reach.

For example, visually flattening a petal coming toward us lets us see it as an illustration; it's actually just shorter than the others, a rounder shape that sits at a base.

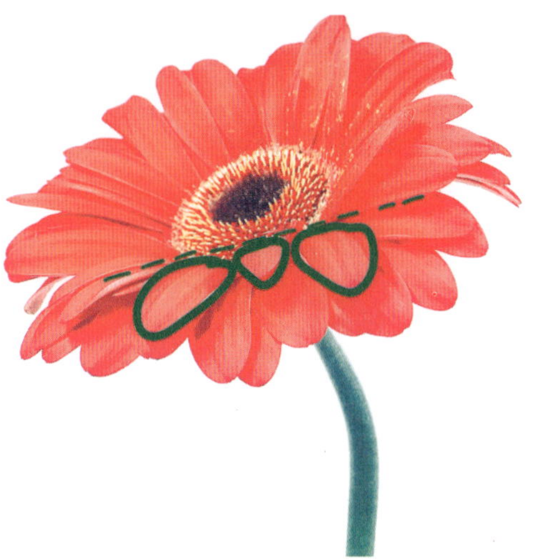

Petals will either be below the center line or they'll be above it. You can control this by tilting the daisy (except in this instance as I couldn't include a real pop-up Gerbera daisy in a book). If the bottom of the center is exposed, I'll start with that as the first step to my drawing. If the petals cover it, I'll start with the petals that are in front (meaning, when we visually flatten the flower, the ones toward the bottom).

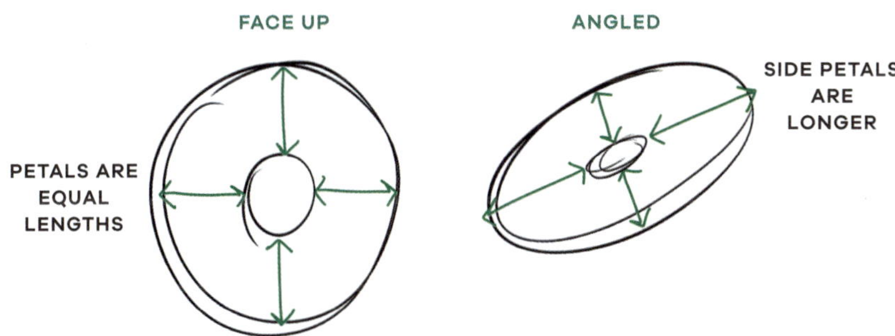

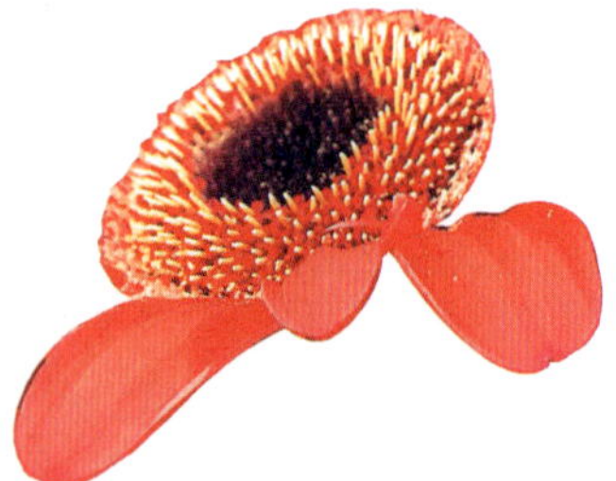

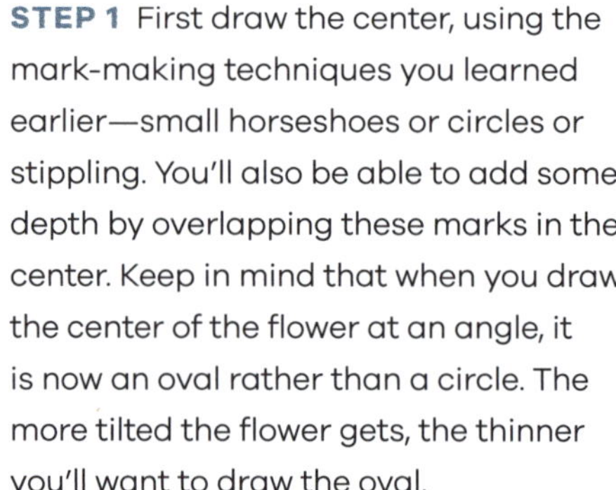

STEP 1 First draw the center, using the mark-making techniques you learned earlier—small horseshoes or circles or stippling. You'll also be able to add some depth by overlapping these marks in the center. Keep in mind that when you draw the center of the flower at an angle, it is now an oval rather than a circle. The more tilted the flower gets, the thinner you'll want to draw the oval.

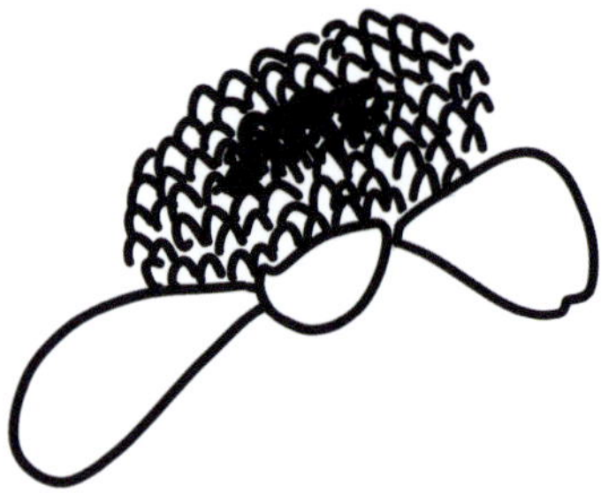

As you form the center, be sure to leave some space for these petals to overlap. Notice that they are much shorter and oddly shaped; the petal in the center, which points toward you, is the shortest. It arches at the top, covering a small part of the center, and follows through below with a C-curve.

The petals on each side of that one do the same, only they're each pointing to a different side a little longer than the petal in the center.

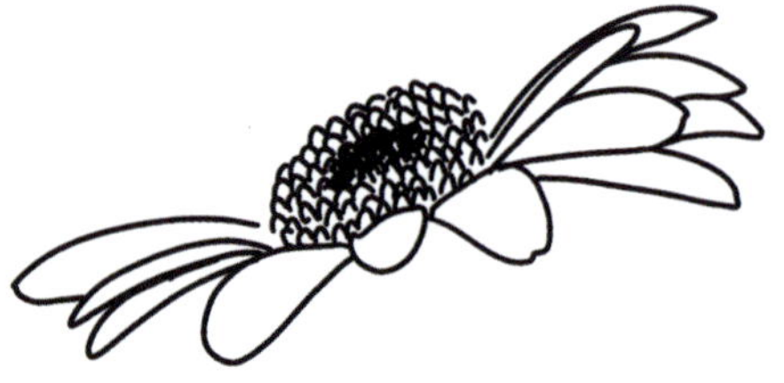

STEP 2 Draw the petals on the left and right sides of the center. These will be the most extended petals because their length isn't altered by our angled perspective. The only part about them that changes is that, just as with the center of the flower, they're going to appear thinner, as they're seen more from the side.

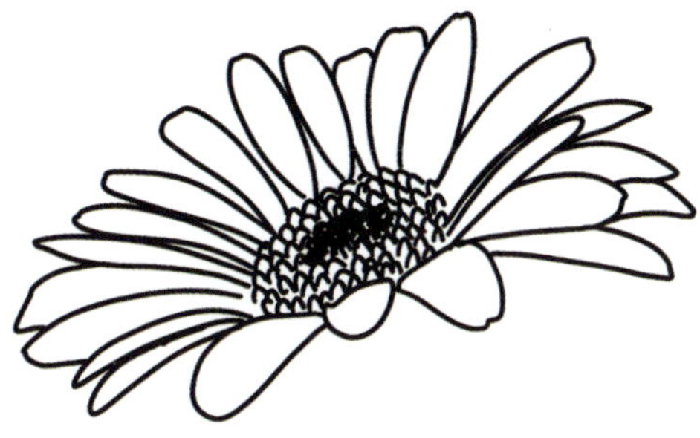

STEP 3 Now draw the petals in the back, or in this case on the top when the flower is "flattened." They are a little longer than the ones at the front. The indented tips won't be seen because they're usually on the other side of their curve and from this angle, we can't see them. That said, the petals should still have dimension. Remember that ripple effect I mentioned petals having? Create more of a small dip in some of the ends rather than a pointed indent.

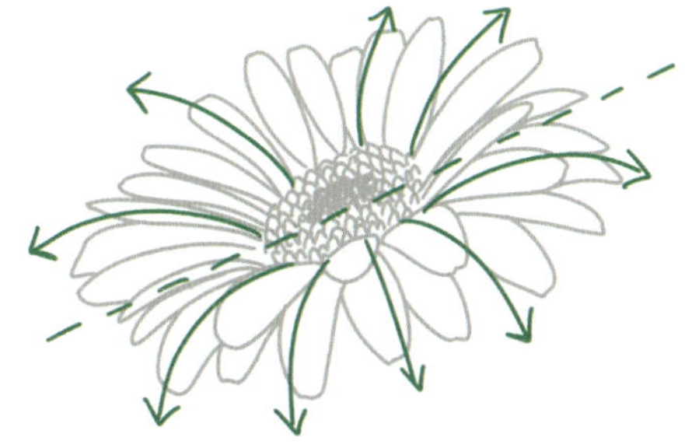

STEP 4 As you can see, additional petals that are closest to you will be a little longer, as they're a bit more visible to us. You'll want to guide your petals outward with rounder C-curves so they appear closer.

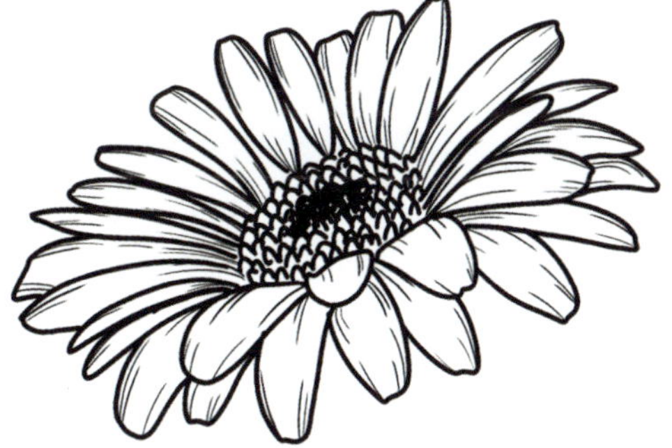

STEP 5 Use light hatching to add detail. Follow the curves of each of the petals to bring out the organic movement of the flower.

Petal Folds

When it comes to folds in petals, they occur at the tips or the sides and they can be on one side or both sides. You don't want to add a fold where it doesn't belong, so before you go for it, make sure that it makes sense with the petal.

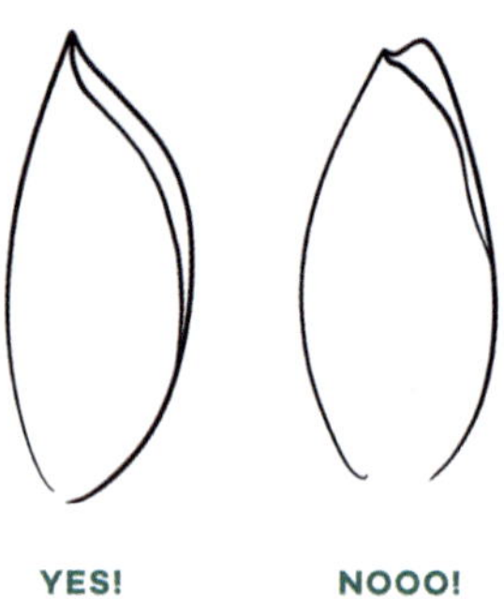

For example, if you have a slope near the tip and into the side, adding a fold here makes perfect sense. If you have a perfectly formed petal, however, it will look misplaced.

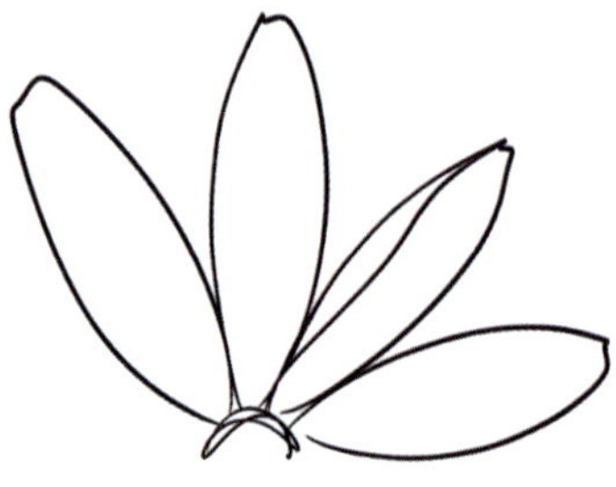

Pay attention to width when you add folds on the sides of petals. Try to stick to the petals that are a little skinnier than others.

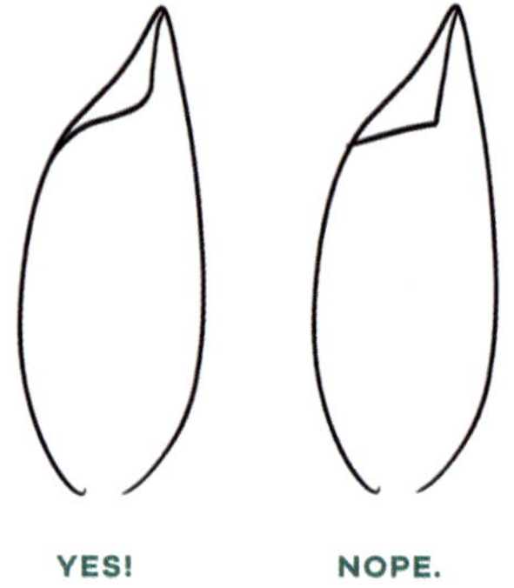

In addition to these rules, the other main thing you'll want to remember is that you don't want your fold to have a sharp connection. It won't look natural. Be sure to follow the lines of the petals so that they end up blending together rather than having sharp angles.

Part Two

LET'S GET COLORFUL! LEARN BASIC WATER-COLOR TECHNIQUES

Watercolor is one of those mediums that you can't ever go wrong with. It lets you keep your objects loose and playful, or you can get some incredible detail. The biggest advantage, I'd say, is the ability to transform an object's depth depending on the water-to-paint ratio. Watercolor invites us to play with transparency and many hues.

You can add pops of color anytime you want! Whether you're creating while out and about or you're doing it at home, in a studio, or at the corner coffee shop, always allow yourself to be inspired by the colors around you. And when I say "inspired," hold on to that word. You might feel moved by pops of pink, but the colors begging to come out of you might be oranges and reds. Inspiration is everywhere and your artwork is yours, so own it!

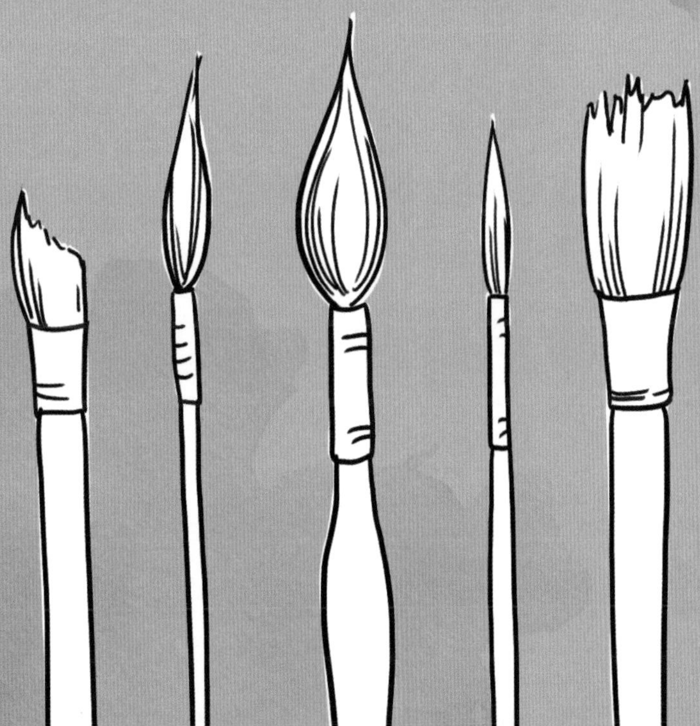

WET-ON-DRY TECHNIQUE

The **wet-on-dry** technique is the most straightforward—wet paint on dry paper. Watercolor paints need to be wet when they're applied, so if you wet your brush, load it up with paint, and slap it on dry paper, voilà! You've executed the wet-on-dry technique. This offers more control over your piece, and the colors will be more vibrant since they're not being diluted by water already on the paper (I'll explain this more as we get into wet-on-wet techniques in a moment).

Practice Wet-on-Dry

Let's get your brush onto paper, shall we? As mentioned, simply wet your brush, dip it into your paint, and place it on your paper. Creating a swatch by moving your brush back and forth is a great way to practice so you can see exactly how different techniques show up on paper. This is also a great exercise for trying new brushes and paints, as not all supplies are created equally! In the first swatch example shown below, my brush has a little more water on it than in the second swatch. You'll get to know your water-to-paint ratio more and more as you practice.

Next, try painting a shape. This could be a rectangle, square, or even a circle. Let that shape dry completely. Once dry, paint the same shape on top of it, overlapping it so you can see the new color it produces while both of the original colors still show. This exercise shows you what can be accomplished by layering paint. In my example opposite, I used a seafoam color and a royal blue, which when layered produced a lovely teal color.

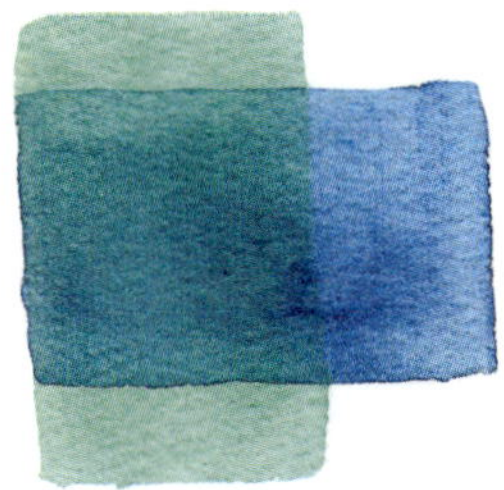

One of the most beneficial exercises that I recommend returning to often is playing with opacity in your swatches. To do this, start off with a good amount of both paint and water on your brush and create a swatch. Now, quickly flick your brush in water and then lightly drag your brush on the edge of your jar. Without adding more paint, create another swatch next to the first swatch. You will still have paint on your brush but it will be more transparent and appear lighter. Repeat this step. Dip in water and come back for another swatch. Repeat these steps until the paint is gone. This exercise helps you in determining exactly how much water versus paint you need in order to get the translucency you want.

WET-ON-WET TECHNIQUE

The **wet-on-wet** technique creates beautiful effects that better represent all that watercolor can do. Applying paint to a wet surface gives us less control but, in return, it challenges us to release the need for perfection and embrace the literal flow of our work. This is where we can enhance blends, create movement, and experiment!

The first exercise I'd like you to try is to wet your paper with water only. This means no paint should be on your brush. Get a generous amount of water on your brush and apply it to your paper with an overlapping zigzag stroke to create a swatch. Now, get some paint on your brush and first try simply setting your brush down onto the wet surface. You'll see the watercolor dance on the water as it disperses. It's oddly satisfying.

We'll do this again, only this time, paint a shape with paint and water, making sure that you have a good amount of water on your brush. Instead of waiting for this shape to dry like we did with our wet-on-dry practice, we're going to take advantage of the moisture. Rinse your brush off and pick up a different color paint. Touch the tip of your brush throughout your moist shape. You will see that satisfying dance of the new color bleeding into the first. I recommend trying this a few times, each time allowing the first layer to dry a little more before applying the new color. You'll generate different bleeds on each shape depending on how wet it is. I encourage you to practice different placements of your top color as well. In my first example, the second color was applied randomly, while in the second example the color begins in the bottom left corner and bleeds inward.

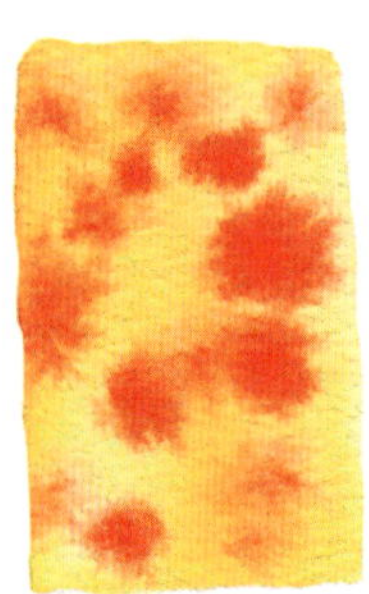
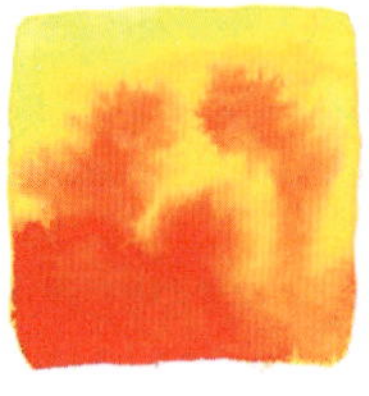

WATERCOLOR WASHES

Now that you've played a bit with paint-to-water ratio, let's dive into watercolor washes. A **wash** is a thin coat of paint that covers a large area of your paper. Washes are used frequently in watercolor painting, and you'll most likely incorporate them in nearly every piece you create.

Practice Watercolor Wash

There are three different types of washes: the flat wash, the graded wash, and the variegated wash.

FLAT WASH

A **flat wash** refers to an even color dispersement, with no change in opacity or value. I find that I get my best flat wash results on dry paper. Load your brush with water and paint, then paint a simple shape. If you need to grab more water or paint, do it! You don't have to execute the perfect wash in only one stroke.

GRADED WASH

A **graded wash** shows a gradual change in the transparency of paint on paper. The intensity and value decrease in the progression of this wash. This is the same idea as the opacity swatches we created on page 75, only instead of being separate swatches, the strokes are connected. After you lay down your first stroke, rinse your brush quickly and return to where you left off. You'll notice that the first stroke will bleed into the second stroke, and as you progress, you'll produce a lovely natural ombré effect. First try this by connecting swatches. Then use a rectangle shape for a more seamless transition.

VARIEGATED WASH

A **variegated wash** is a wash consisting of two or more colors that bleed together. This is a fun practice for your new wet-on-wet skills! Although you can use both wet-on-wet and wet-on-dry techniques to execute this wash, I like to do so using a wet start. Paint a rectangle with water only. Then, with plenty of paint on your brush, apply a full-pressure stroke of one color at one edge. Then repeat with a different color on the other edge. These colors will naturally travel inward on the wet paper, blending together to create a colored ombré. You can also do this by painting a section of the rectangle with each color, then thoroughly rinsing your brush and using only water to connect the two colors in the middle.

Creating Washes with Water-Based Brush Pens

Grab a plastic page protector or other slick plastic surface, and color directly onto the plastic with the brush pen. Use a spray bottle to spritz water over the plastic, then flip it over onto a piece of paper. Press down to transfer the color. As you remove the plastic, drag it slightly so the colors blend. Now, you have an instant watercolor background, perfect for nature-scapes!

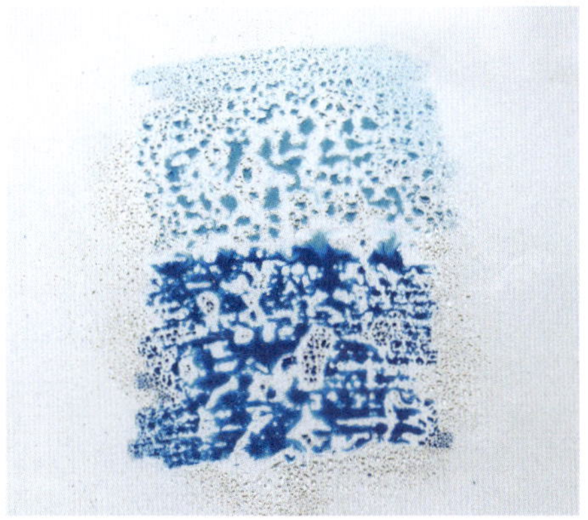
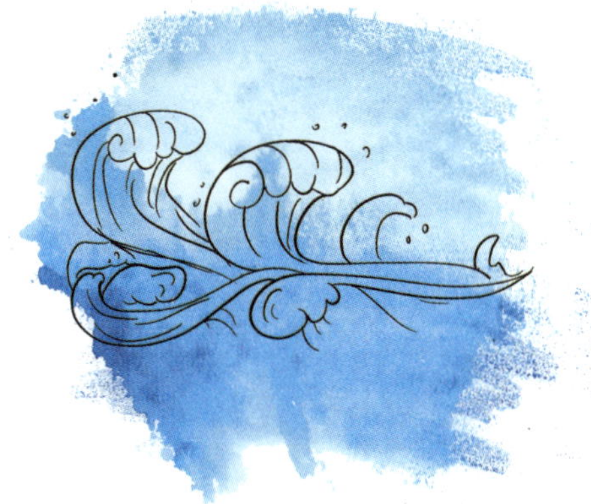

Use a nonporous surface—a Tombow Blending Palette or even a Tupperware lid—and color on the surface. Dip a paintbrush in water, then rub the brush through the color you just laid down. Just like that, you have watercolors from markers.

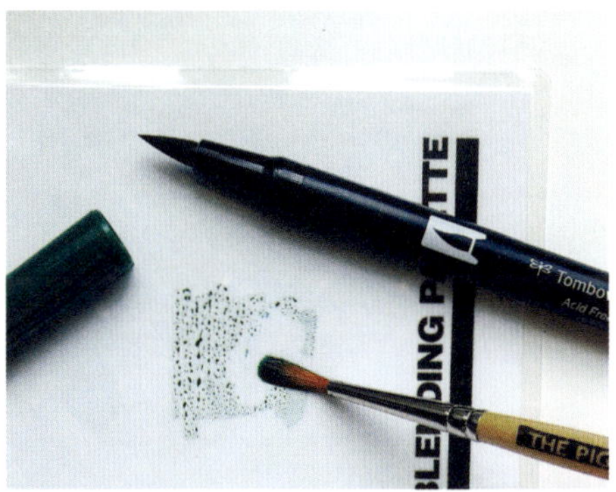
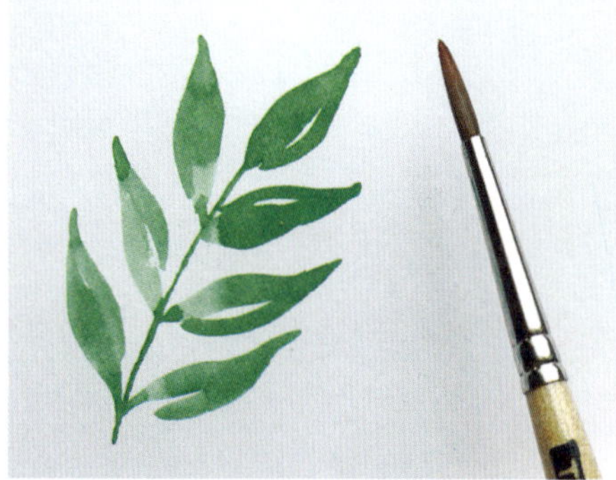

Create a quick ombré effect by laying down two (or more) colors, then use a wet paintbrush or the Tombow Blender (a clear brush pen) to blend the colors together.

You can also use brush pens for simple embellishments like leaves and flowers. Do this by holding the brush tip on its side and setting it on the paper, then lifting back up. Direct the tip outward from a stem for a classic leaf shape or toward the stem for more of a playful illustration. The same effect can be used for simple flowers.

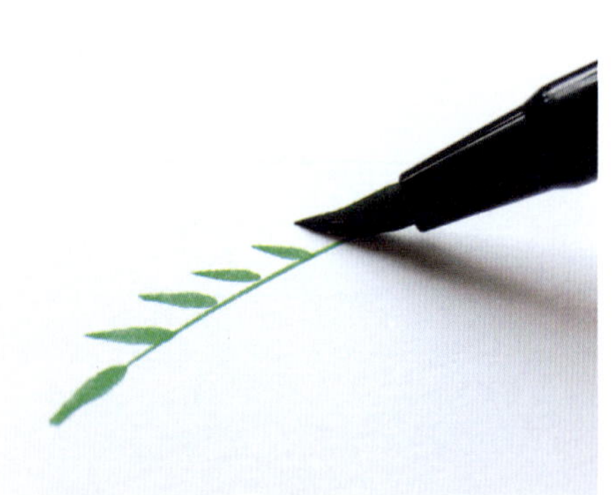

BLENDING WATERCOLOR

Blending color, particularly in swatches, is one of my favorite pastimes. I might love it a little too much. Watching colors bleed together and form a new color right in front of your eyes is so relaxing.

Practice Blending with Swatches

STEP 1 Ensure that your brush is saturated with water and paint and then lay down your first color.

STEP 2 Thoroughly rinse your brush and grab a new color.

STEP 3 Just as you experimented in trying the wet-on-wet technique, apply the next color while the first swatch is wet.

STEP 4 Now simply connect the two swatches with your brush so the water touches and the colors begin to blend.

Practice Blending with Circles

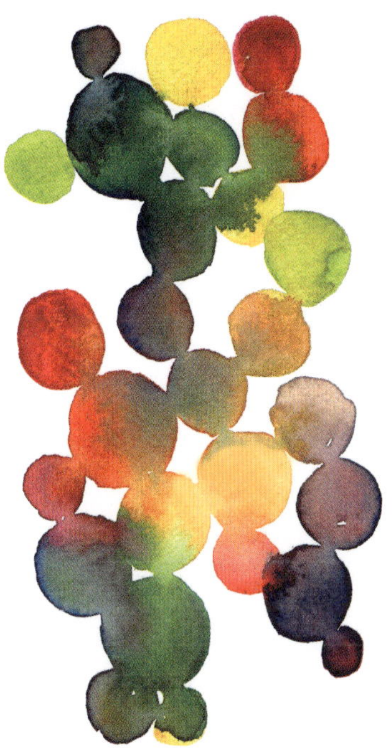

STEP 1 Ensure that your brush is saturated with water and paint and then lay down your first color, creating a circle.

STEP 2 Thoroughly rinse your brush and grab a new color.

STEP 3 Paint a circle with the new color right next to the first circle. Just as you finish, allow the two circles to touch while both are wet.

STEP 4 Repeat until you fill a page with this eye candy! Try different color schemes and sizes.

LAYERING COLORS

Layering colors is a fun way to play with how the light reaches through watercolors and bounces off the white of the paper. A lighter color or line will show that the background is separated from the foreground. I like to layer color because it covers a lot of ground with a very simple technique.

Practice Layering Colors

STEP 1 Apply a watercolor wash in the color of your choice.

STEP 2 Add another color on top and notice how the first color shows through to create a new hue where the colors overlap.

STEP 3 Practice doing this with several color combinations or try it with the same color and vary the amount of water you have on your brush each time.

BASIC BRUSH STROKES

The first thing we'll do to get you comfortable with controlling your brush as you paint is cover a few basic brush strokes. In all of the following practices, you'll want your brush to be completely submerged in water before you pick up paint with it. You may find it best to practice this a couple times depending on the pigment of your watercolors. Some are more pigmented, while others take a little more priming with more water. You'll know what I mean as you get into it. Don't overthink it, though. This is just practice!

Full-Pressure Stroke

Once you have your brush nice and wet and loaded up with paint, set the side of your brush onto your watercolor paper with full pressure, using the entire belly of your brush to create its thickest stroke. If you return to a light pressure before lifting your brush off the paper, it will form the shape of a leaf. This is the stroke you will use to create most of your leaves. You can do this as one stroke, or add another stroke beside it for a fuller leaf. Try leaving a thin white space in the center to act as a vein.

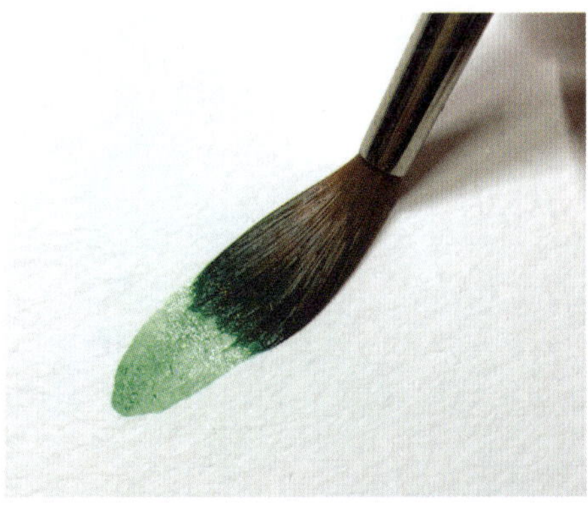
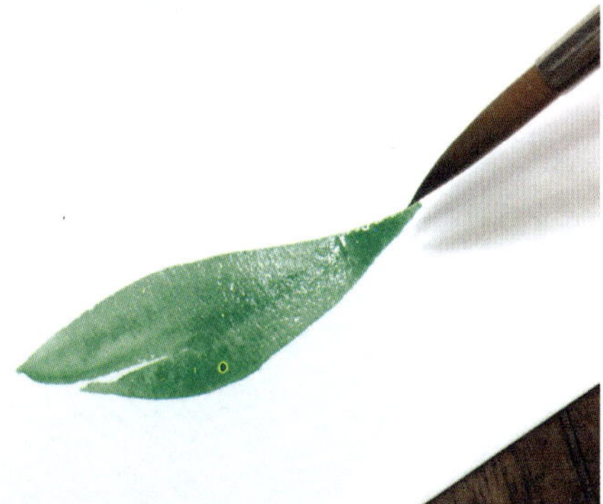

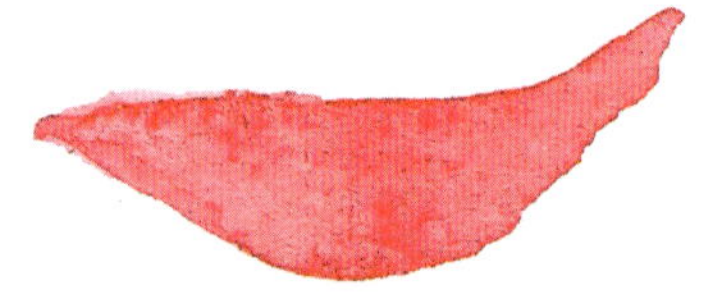

C-CURVE STROKE Curving your stroke creates a base for petals. Remember the C-curve we practiced drawing? This is the same slightly curved motion, only you're also applying and lifting pressure as you learned to do when practicing the leaf.

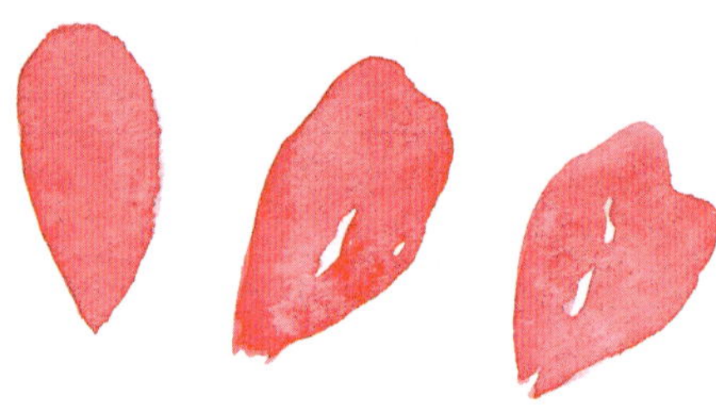

BUNNY-EAR STROKE The next stroke is what I like to refer to as a bunny-ear stroke, because it looks like a bunny ear. Just darling. Starting with the tip of your brush at the base of the shape, pull your brush away from you, and loop up and over using more pressure, then return with light pressure again at the base. As you get comfortable with this stroke, try loosening it up more with bends and irregular lines. Also take advantage of white space, as this can add to your designs.

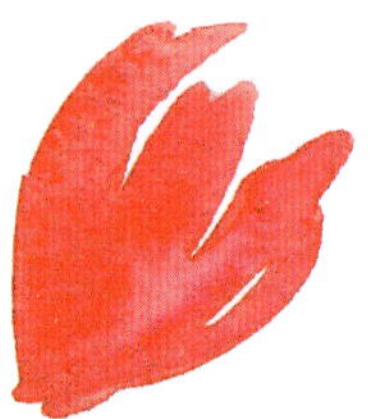

ZIGZAG STROKE Last, play with the tip of your brush by gliding it lightly in a zig-zag motion with one side concentrated together, allowing some lines to overlap and some to keep their texture. This will act as the base of a petal or even a quick flower.

Now let's apply these brush strokes to some flowers!

 Brush Strokes: Tulip
Practice Brush Strokes: Tulip

The tulip might be one of the easiest flowers to paint loosely. Create three full-pressure C-curve strokes that taper toward the top and curve inward to create rounded sides.

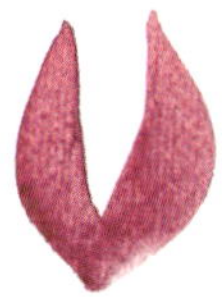

STEP 1 Start with the outer strokes, which curve inward.

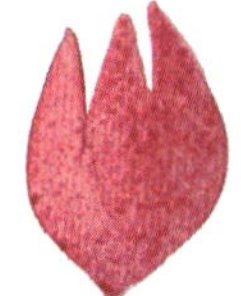

STEP 2 Add a middle stroke.

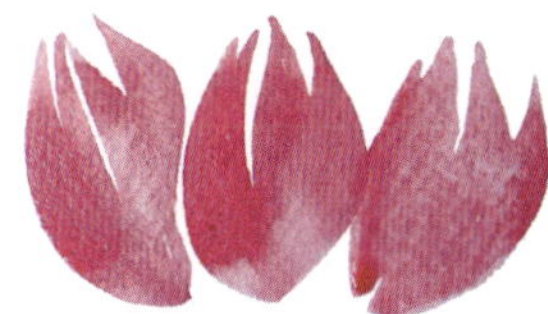

STEP 3 Repeat this step a couple of times on each side to create several more flowers to accompany the first. You can also use the tip of your brush to add one or two more points at the top for texture.

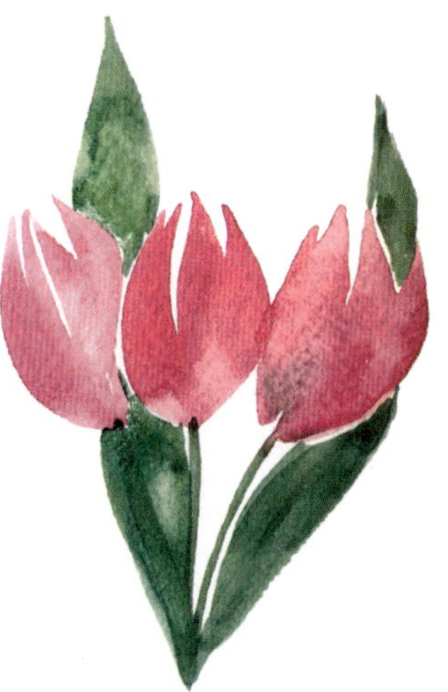

STEP 4 Then, just add the stems and a couple of long leaves! The stems should be painted with light pressure, using only the tip of your brush will help maintain thin lines. Paint the leaves using the full-pressure technique, but be careful not to run into your petals. That said, I intentionally run my stem into my flowers at times because I like the way wet-on-wet looks and how it can add a little depth to the base. If you want to avoid this bleed, however, wait for the first color to dry completely.

Would you believe me if I told you that's all you needed to do? It is. Loose florals are the best, aren't they?

 # Brush Strokes: Peony

Could this be the most desirable flower of all time? It's no wonder; I adore the layers and layers of soft blush petals loosely ruffled together. It's actually a very easy flower to paint considering how complex it looks.

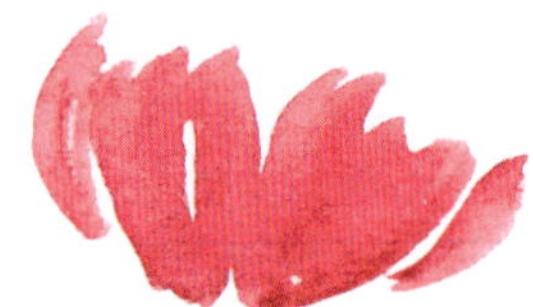

STEP 1 Using the wet-on-dry technique, start by painting two petals with the zigzag stroke, starting from the bottom and flicking upward, then meeting at the bottom in the same place you started, then go upward again to a new point, etc., which creates texture at the tips of the petals.

Add a C-curve on each side, as if they are about to hug the inner petals. Be sure to keep some white space between the petals so it's obvious that they're individual petals.

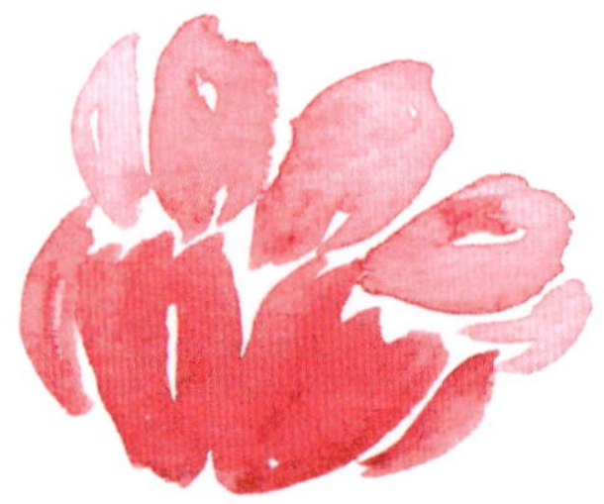

STEP 2 Create some smaller, slightly lighter petals on top of what you just painted. You can achieve lighter petals by using more water on your brush than paint. I recommend three centered petals, then two C-curves on the outsides.

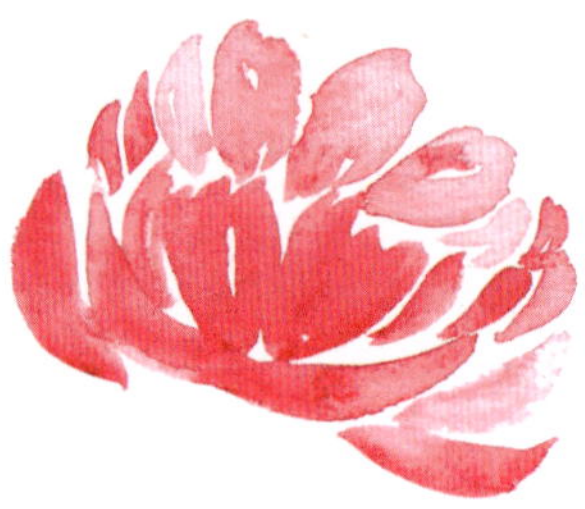

STEP 3 Next, paint two thin curved lines at the bottom, one from right to left and the other left to right, so as to cradle the bottom petals.

Add some more C-curves on each side, which will appear as layered petals.

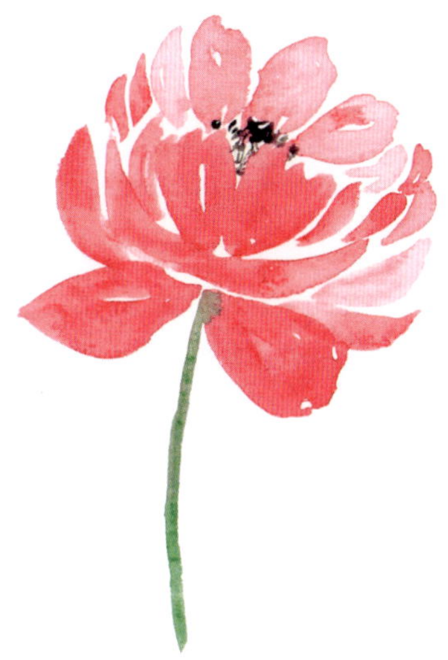

STEP 4 Now, add two petals directed downward from the bottom center. You can use full-pressure strokes that connect or bunny-ear strokes.

Allow your petals to dry. Then, starting at the base, drag a light, thin stem that extends down from the center, and add dark stamens poking up from the top of the very first petals you painted.

Practice Brush Strokes: Anemone

Let's play with creating a white flower using shadows.

STEP 1 Use a very watered-down gray or black hue to paint round petals around an imaginary circle. You can use the bunny-ear stroke to fill in any leftover white space, if needed. If your petals are too dark, dab them with a paper towel to pick up excess color.

While the petals are still wet, add some more watered-down gray or black to the petals closest to the center. Then use the tip of your brush to lightly drag a few strokes through the petals (just as you would when adding drawn details to petals).

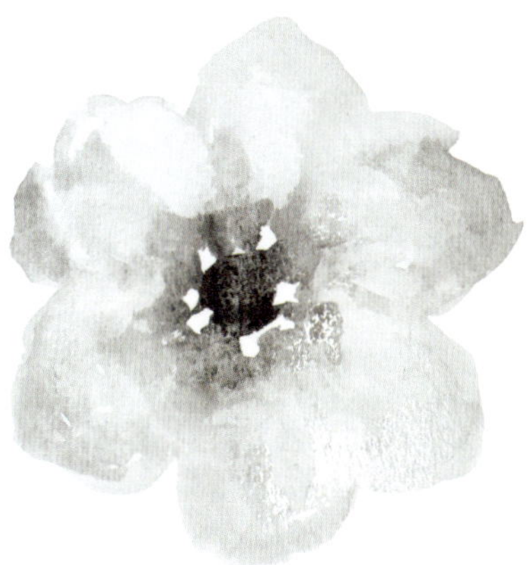

STEP 2 Let the petals dry, then use a very dark color, preferably with a cool hue like blue or violet, to create a dark center. Wet your brush and connect the center to the petals by setting the wet brush in between them in a few select spots so the center will bleed and blend into the petals.

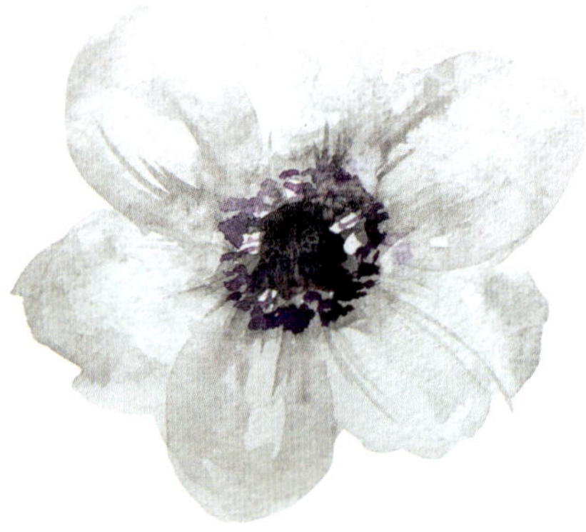

STEP 3 Once the center is dry, layer on some small dots around the center with a dark violet. These are the dark stamens that give anemones their bold character.

Practice Brush Strokes: Rose

The rose is easy-peasy. It's just a bunch of C-curves. The main rule in painting roses is to stay away from dipping into your paint again. The center will be accentuated with your darkest value, and the fuller the flower gets, the more opacity the petals will have. You'll notice that in the beginning the lines are very small. You can achieve all of the following strokes with one brush by using the tip of the brush and full-pressure C-curves.

STEP 1 To begin, fully saturate your brush with water and paint. Use the tip of your brush to create several C-curve strokes as the center of your rose. Keep them very close together.

STEP 2 Create two or three more C-curves around the center with the tip of the brush. Keep them very close together. Some may overlap, but be sure to leave a thin white space in between strokes to keep the petals separate.

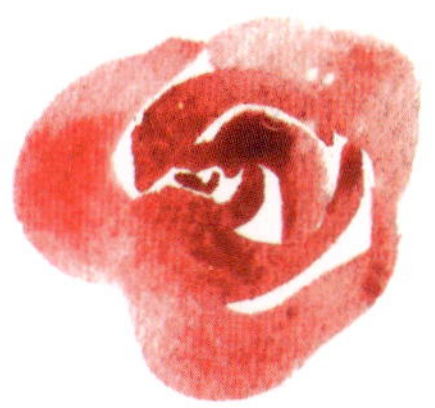

STEP 3 Dip your brush in water only once and return without dipping in paint to create three more C-curves around the center. This time, apply a little more pressure to your brush to get fuller petals. At this point, you should see the color lighten, as you're using a little less pigment.

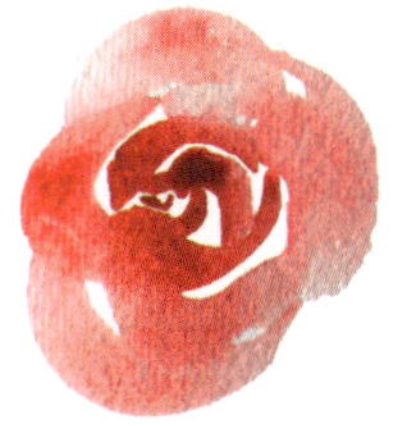

STEP 4 Dip your brush in water again quickly and paint another layer around the center with full-pressure strokes.

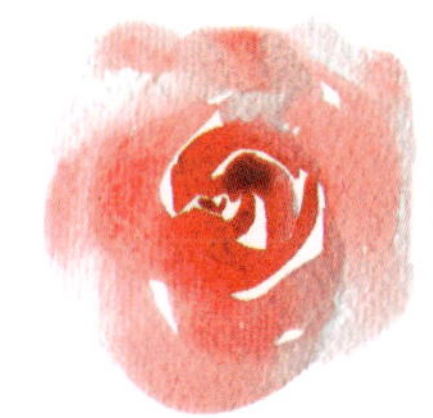

STEP 5 Create one last layer of petals after dipping your brush again. Your petals should be almost transparent now. You may want to drag some of your C-curves from the previous layer so a little paint bleeds into the new petals.

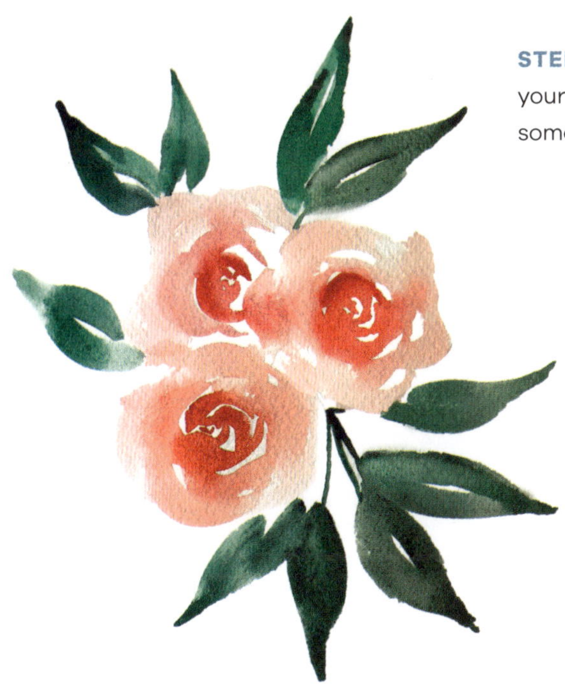

STEP 6 After this step, you're done with your rose. Create a few more and add some leaves for a lovely rose bouquet.

SAME OBJECT, THREE WAYS

Now that we've touched on both painting flowers and drawing flowers, let's combine the two. First, I'll go a step further and introduce the idea of experimentation before you dive into your project. There are a lot of different ways to accomplish one thing. This applies to a lot of areas of our lives. This creative freedom makes us thrive. In the following images, you'll find a watercolor painting of a flower next to an illustration of the same exact flower. Notice the different vibes each one gives off. They are the same exact object, just executed in a completely different way. The first flower is created with watercolor only, while the second is with only ink. My personal favorite is when it comes time to combine these two elements, putting a modern spin on classic watercolor by adding a little botanical line drawing with ink to the mix.

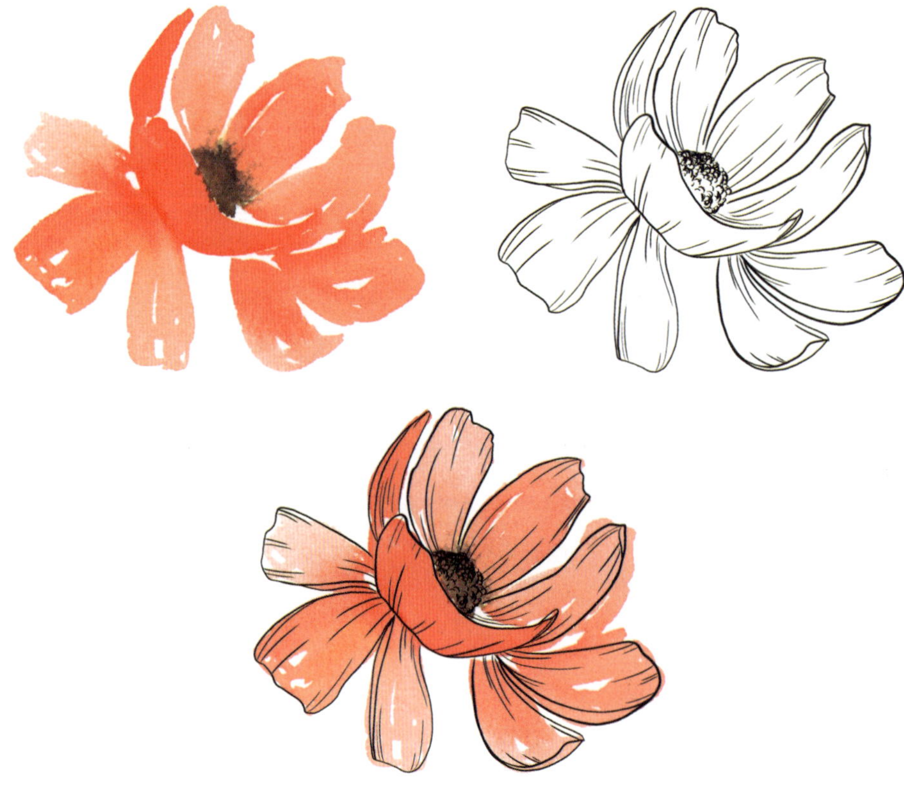

Let's practice these varying looks using a black-eyed Susan. We'll start with a simple loose watercolor.

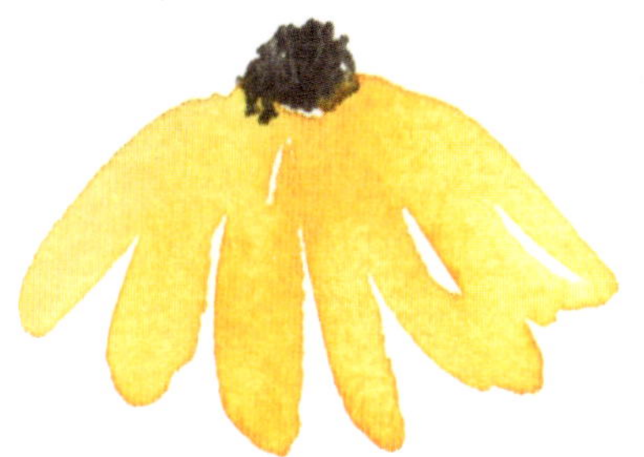

STEP 1 First, paint six or seven yellow petals moving downward from the center. Use a full-pressure stroke that curves at the bottom.

STEP 2 With a dark brown or black, create the center with small dots of paint, using only the tip of your brush. Make sure you create a nice arch at the top to show that the center protrudes upward rather than lies flat in the center of the flower.

Now let's approach the same flower with only line drawing. Opposite of the loose watercolor painting, this style focuses on movement, bends, depth, and detail. We can add more detail on the top left of the center than on its right side, creating the illusion of a light source on the right. You'll also see some bends in the petals, which assumes they're a little more on their side in our perspective. Let's break it down.

STEP 1 Instead of starting with the petals, this time we'll start with the center of the flower. Do this by drawing tiny horseshoes spaced out from one another. Add more to the areas where you want to create depth. As you continue, concentrate on one area and overlap the horseshoe shapes to create more density.

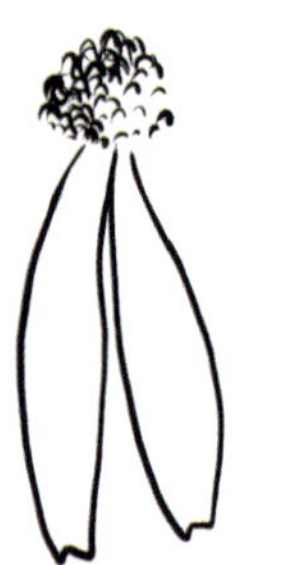

STEP 2 Create the first couple of petals coming downward from the center you just drew. Starting on the left side, draw a C-curve about three times as long as the center. When you get to the tip of the petal, draw a tiny upside-down *V*. This creates the illusion of texture at the end of the petal. Draw the right side of the petal coming from the other side of the *V* you just drew. This line should be imperfect. Notice that it's a little shaky and more of an S-curve than a C-curve.

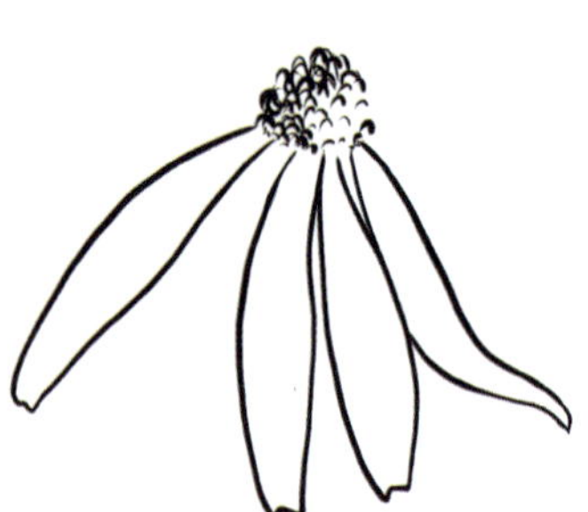

STEP 3 The creative part really kicks in as we add the additional petals. Because some of the petals are curving upward before they curve down, one side of a petal is a C-curve, while the other side of the petal is an S-curve. To show a bit of movement in this flower, one or two of the petals could be bent. Add a petal to the right side, touching the middle petals you first drew. Notice I've left a gap where it connects to the center as I start my C-curve. Then, I'll stop the line where it touches the petal next to it and continue it a little below to give the illusion of an overlap. This creates a point in the tip of the petal rather than a *V*, to show that this petal sits more on its side toward the end.

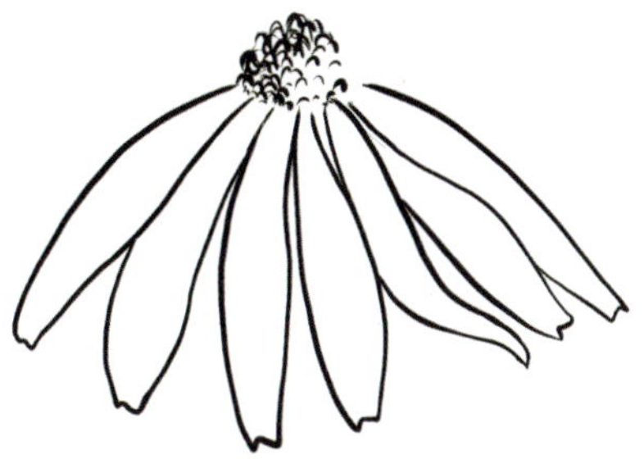

STEP 4 Add the rest of the petals now. Fill in the gap on the left side with a petal like the one that sits to its right. Because I intentionally left a gap, I assumed an overlap and started this petal with a C-curve coming from the middle of the petal on the left rather than from the top. After adding its textured tip, it then travels back up with an S-curve. Complete the last two petals on the right side, overlapping them. Remember to mirror the outer right petal in the outer left petal if you want to form a cohesive shape.

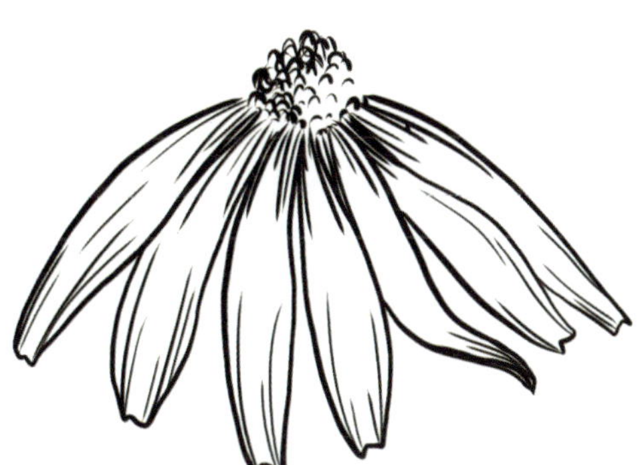

STEP 5 Complete the flower by adding petal details with hatching marks. These lines should be quick flicks coming from each end. If you want to make the petals look like they're more tucked into the center, draw additional short lines to create depth.

While both of these styles are great as standalone pieces, merging the two together really brings them to life (see page 94). To complete this look, I like to begin with watercolor. I like this method because if I start with watercolor, I'm less concerned with filling in the lines of my drawing and more focused on adding the effect I want with ink afterward.

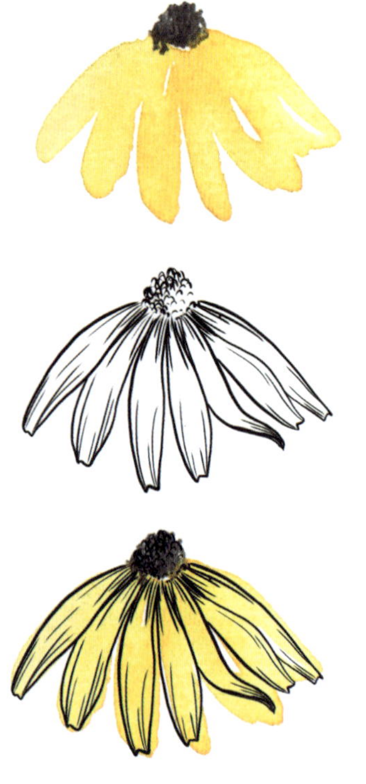

STEP 1 Create the first part of the flower with watercolor, as in the steps on pages 91–93.

STEP 2 Allow the watercolor to dry completely before adding ink.

STEP 3 Just as you drew your flower on its own without color, do the same thing now, only draw directly on top of the dried watercolor. Don't worry about staying along the watercolor outline. This is your chance to let the color be an enhancement, to be a literal splash of oomph that's added to your illustration. Your final result will add a playful tone to an otherwise more sophisticated illustration.

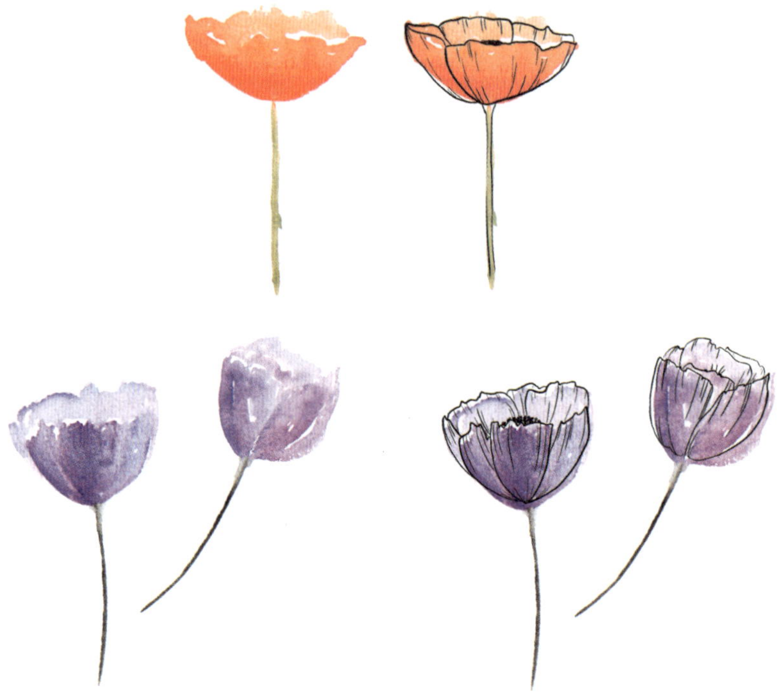

COMBINING ELEMENTS

One of my absolute favorite things to do is combine botanicals with unexpected objects. I started drawing this way when I discovered the curious nature of surreal photography. I really felt inspired by a particular photo by brilliant photographer and artist Luisa Azevedo. It was an eye-catching image of a cactus hot-air balloon. After diving deeper into this unimaginable world that we have the power to make imaginable, I fell in love with hybrid elements and added a little nature in some unusual places.

I encourage you to choose an object to add a bit of nature to. Notice that the flowers added to each of the illustrations on the following pages are extremely simple. There's not a whole lot to them, and the simplicity is a big factor in what makes the illustrations special.

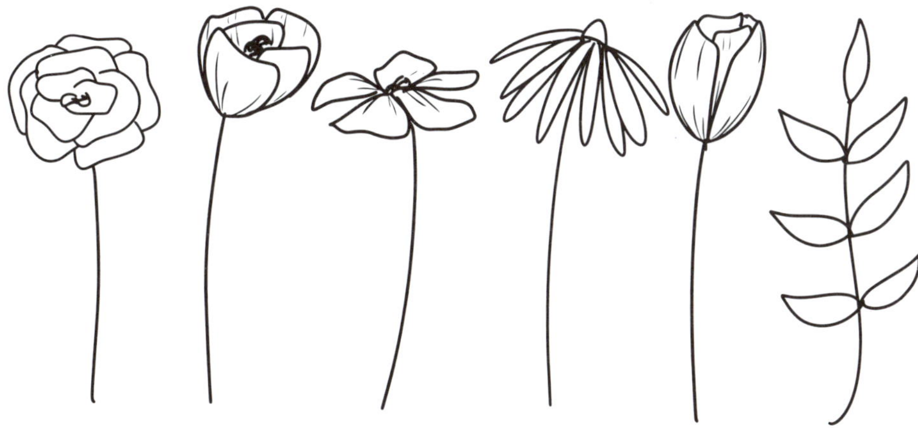

Try adding floral elements to unexpected objects, like an astronaut suit, or replacing something like a candle flame with botanicals. Maybe explore inserting flowers and leaves into part of a silhouette, like the tail of a squirrel!

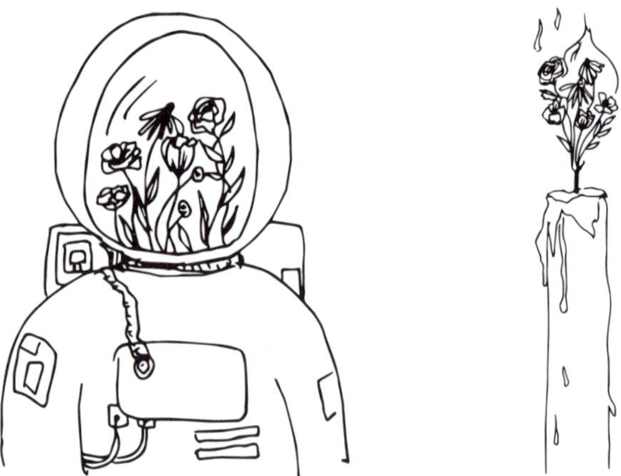

Practice Combining Elements: Antlers

I think the coolest thing I've found out in nature was a single antler. Being an animal lover who thinks a great deal about their well-being, I was mulling it over and needed to know how the antler could have ended up in the grass the way it did. You know how lizards and snakes shed their skin? Well, a deer sheds its antlers every single year and grows new ones. Every year! My mind was blown. I had no idea. Where are all these shed antlers? Why haven't I found more? I live in the Pacific Northwest, dang it! There are deer everywhere!

Deer are found in a variety of habitats, as they're highly adaptable and can thrive just about anywhere. We're going to hone in for a moment and focus on antlers and how we can adorn them in an illustration.

Antlers are easier to draw when you have a guide, and in this case, a circle will define the outer edges of our antlers. Begin by using a cylindrical object to trace a circle. Plates, mugs, and fat candles are great for this; trace lightly around the circumference. My circle was drawn freehand, and you can definitely go that route too. You really only need the bottom half.

Once you have your circle down, draw two lines at the bottom, sandwiching what would be six o'clock. These lines will mark the space between your antlers. Draw two lines just outside the first two; these will be the first points of the antlers. Now draw two lines on each side of the circle at four o'clock and eight o'clock. So far, these lines have all been drawn going into the circle. Draw the next two lines just above the last two you drew, but this time come off the circle toward the outside. Then draw two more lines that begin outward but travel inside the circle at three o'clock and nine o'clock.

Now we'll make our first mark to follow this guide. Return to the base and draw loose lines with slight arches that reach outward, then turn inward at the bottom of the higher three lines. That was a lot, I know. It's why having visuals makes it so much easier.

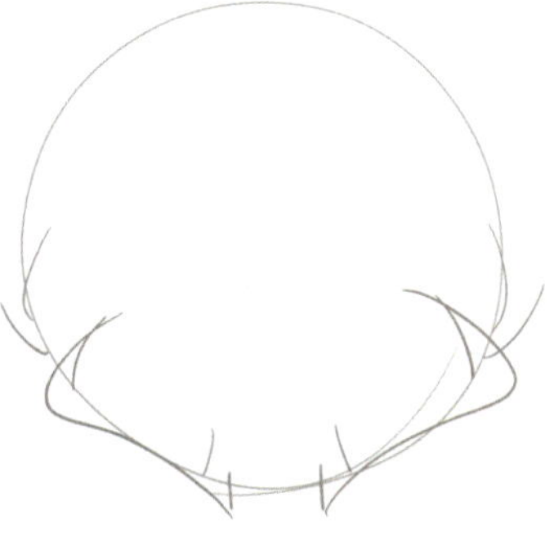

STEP 1 To begin drawing the antlers, draw a line from the base mark and up into the first point. The points will be thinner than the main trunk of the antler. Draw another line on the bottom that reaches all the way to the line that reaches outward from the circle.

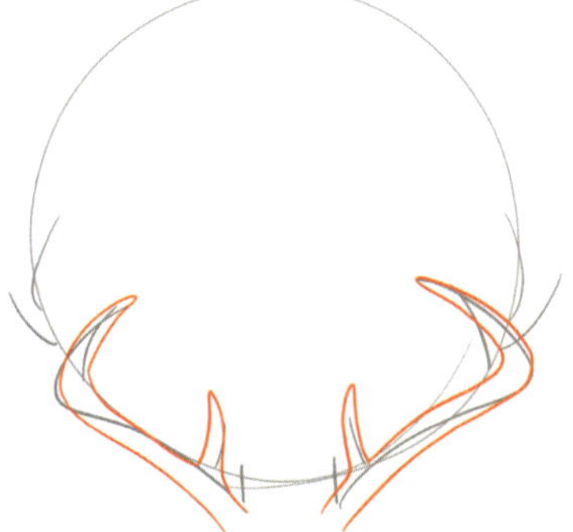

STEP 2 Create another point using the guide. Bring that line down to complete the point and curve it inward to connect to the first point.

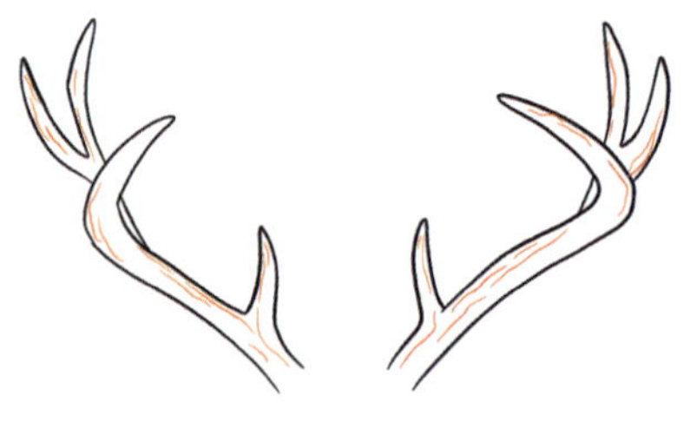

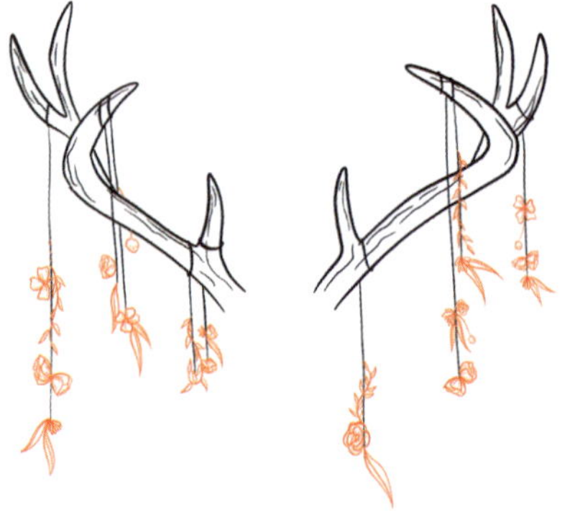

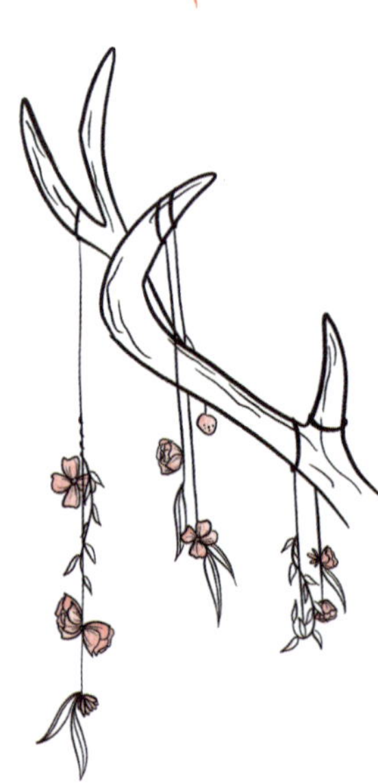
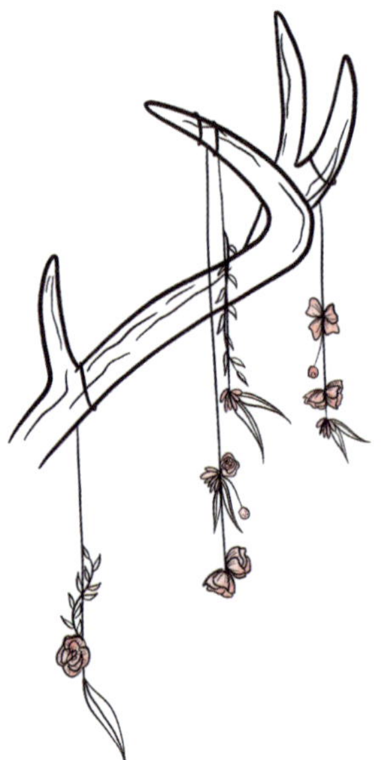

TO ADD COLOR Use any medium you want! If you use watercolor, make sure that the ink you use is not water-based, or the ink will bleed and your details will be lost (unless you want to be very careful not to touch the lines with water as you paint). For small detail like this, markers are always a great option (especially the smaller end of the Tombow Dual Brush Pens). Just set the tip of your marker onto the area to color and usually a dab'll do ya!

Part Three

STUDY OBJECTS FOUND IN NATURE

There are so many amazing living creatures out there! When we start to apply our observations to artwork, we think about recording what we see. There aren't rules here, though. For example, we see fish from above unless we're diving or snorkeling (my favorite activity). You can work from photographs or angles you've seen from your own experiences. We see birds from all angles all the time. We see them from beneath while they're in flight, perched on a tree branch, and rinsing off in a puddle on a rainy day. As we move through this section, you'll learn how to create objects using shapes as references. When you can draw these, you can draw anything you find in nature!

My hope is that through this journey, you are able to notice the life around us more and embrace how unique these beings are. I love discovering random facts about plants and animals, especially the ones that are weird or funny, so there are some little details sprinkled throughout this section for your enjoyment.

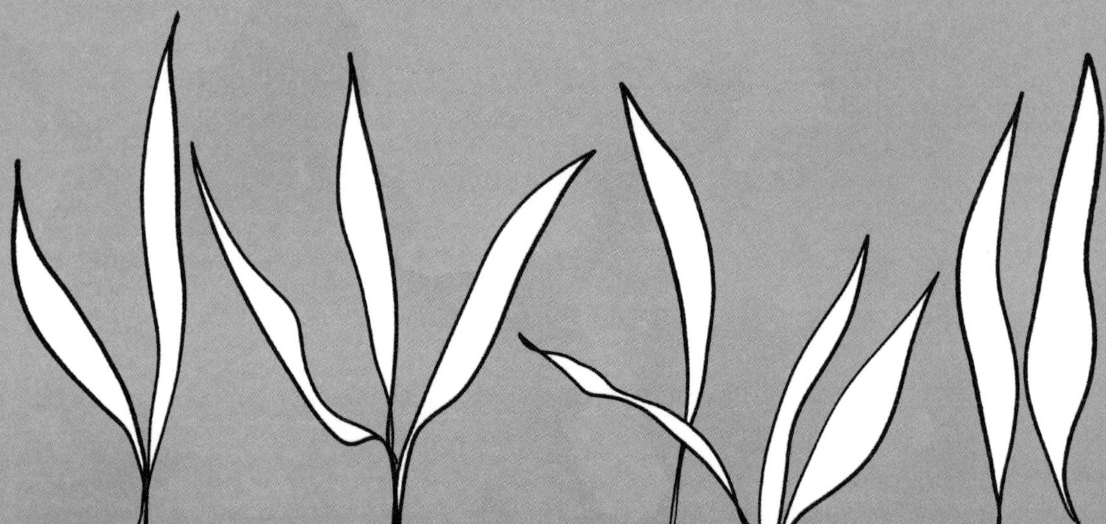

THE FLOWER STUDY

Let's continue our flower drawing adventure with a few more recognizable flowers. Each flower has its own unique characteristics. After illustrating each of these, you'll have a solid knowledge of different shapes that you can build on to continue drawing even more beautiful flowers.

One of the most common outbursts from attendees in my botanical line drawing workshops is, "I drew that?!" and then toward the end, "I still can't believe I drew that." Remember: We're looking at shapes. We're breaking the image up, looking at bits and pieces, then building upon them and combining them. After that, we go in and add detail. When finished, we look at what we drew and can't believe that it came from our own hands. So remember the rules. Remember the steps. If you follow them, you just might surprise yourself by drawing an exquisite flower out of what you thought was an oopsie that looked like a weird chicken leg. (I've seen things.)

Cherry Blossom

Cherry blossoms are most recognizable as they sprinkle long, reaching branches with small, delicate flowers in pink or white. They are seen in clusters rather than as standalone flowers, and we naturally interpret them almost like leaves in the form of flowers. This means that they can be loosely illustrated on a tree as a whole, or the focus can be much closer, in a small grouping. Because of their delicacy, you'll want to draw a lot of movement in the petals. Most blossoms have five petals, although some species have more.

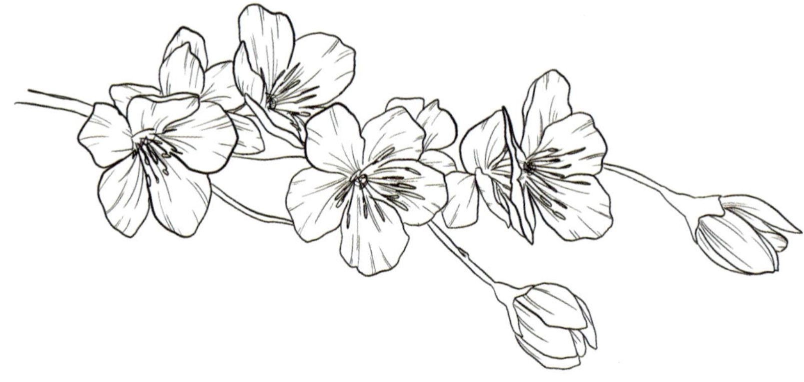

Let's take an even closer look. What do you notice? Break it down. Looking at only the petals, we see that they have a cup-like form, which will mean quite a few bends in our lines when we draw them. The stamens are reaching in all directions, and there are a lot of them. Since we see bends in these petals, we'll apply the same knowledge picked up previously.

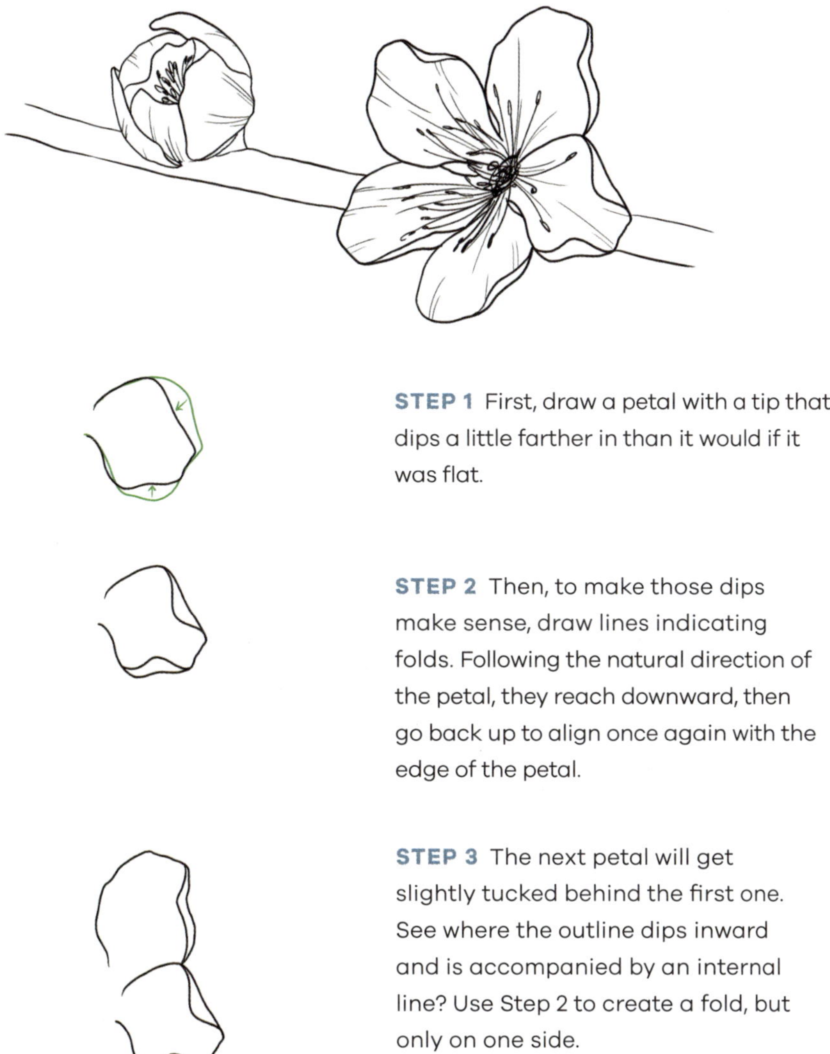

STEP 1 First, draw a petal with a tip that dips a little farther in than it would if it was flat.

STEP 2 Then, to make those dips make sense, draw lines indicating folds. Following the natural direction of the petal, they reach downward, then go back up to align once again with the edge of the petal.

STEP 3 The next petal will get slightly tucked behind the first one. See where the outline dips inward and is accompanied by an internal line? Use Step 2 to create a fold, but only on one side.

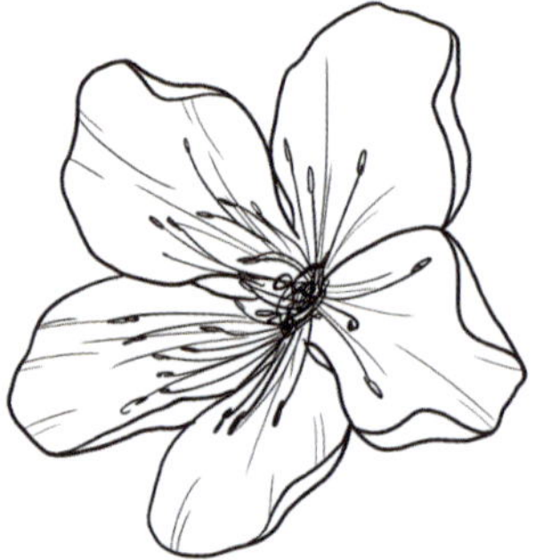

STEP 4 Complete the rest of the petals in the same fashion. Draw the center and light C-curves for the stamens and finish with light line detail.

When you begin illustrating on your own, remember that by no means do the petals need to look exactly like these. You can choose where you want bends and folds to go or whether to have them at all. Don't hold yourself back from experimenting with how you draw what you draw.

FUN NATURE FACT

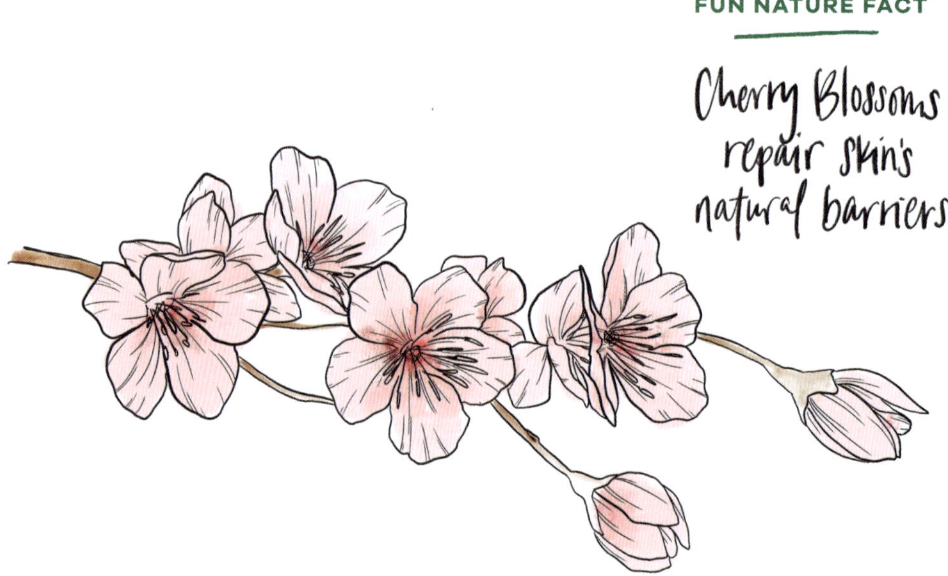

TO ADD COLOR I'm all about that loose, effortless look. Here, I've applied some very light washes of soft pink in my petals, plus brown on my branch. Once dry, you can add more detail, like the red pop I've added to the blossom center. If you decide to add color, sometimes less is more! Remember: If you're applying water media over ink, you must ensure that your ink is not water-based or your beautiful illustration will bleed!

Peony

There are upward of fifty different peony species, with thousands more cultivated species. But that double peony . . . I don't know a single person on Earth who doesn't swoon over a double peony. Illustrating nothing but a few peonies and greens can make for such an elegant piece, and these illustrations pair up beautifully with weddings, showers, and more.

The first thing to note about drawing the peony is that its petals have no need for uniformity or perfection. They come to life in illustrations when the tips are jagged and varied.

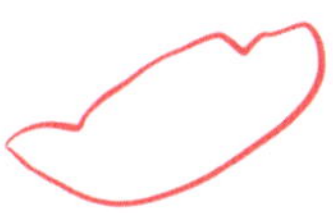

STEP 1 Tackle your first petal and embrace that it's imperfect. Create a smoother bottom by drawing a C-curve and then place indents on the top with a jagged line.

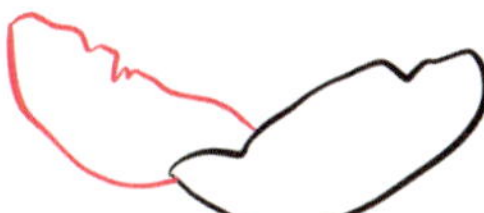

STEP 2 Do that again. To imitate overlapping petals, draw a wobbly C-curve from the left side of the previous petal to form the bottom of a new petal, followed by a jagged line with small indents that will connect to the petal on the right.

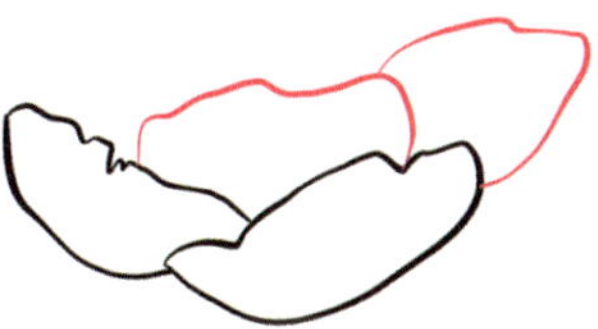

STEP 3 Build onto your first two petals by placing a few more on top as though they're slightly tucked behind. Remember to create movement and variation at the tips with jagged lines and slight S-curves.

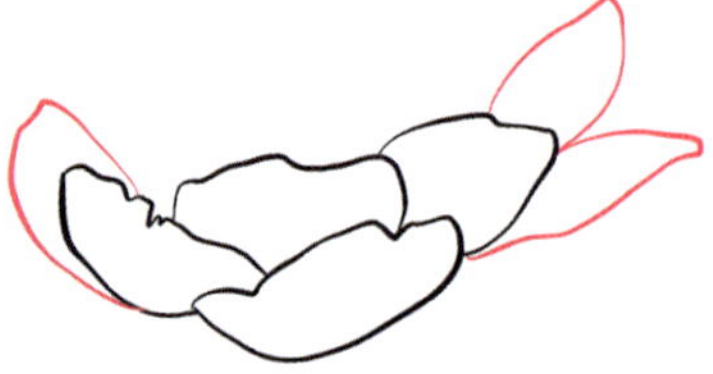

STEP 4 As peonies open up, their delicate petals stop hugging each other and start to fall outward. You can begin creating petals that change direction by drawing the bottom of the petal at a slighter arch instead of as a deep scoop. The top petals will look the same. This will then make it seem as if the tip of the petal is on the side rather than the top.

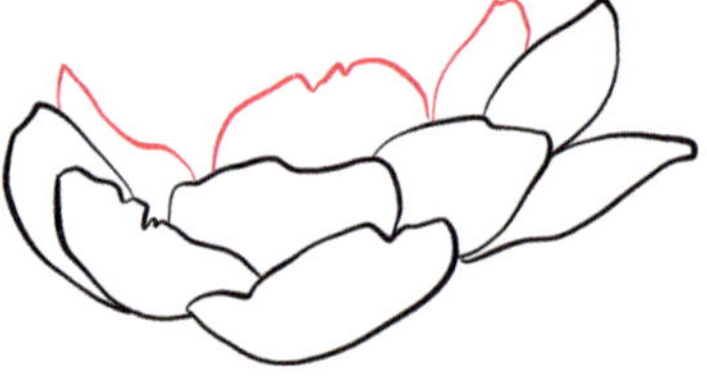

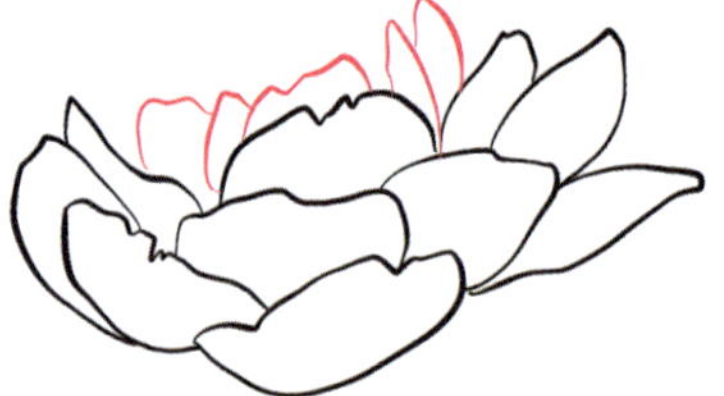

STEP 5 As you get closer to the middle of the peony, the petals get more tucked in. Notice that these petals are a bit shallower than the other rows, and the next row gets even skinnier. The curve of the side petals inward gives the illusion that the petals are showing us their sides. For the center petal, draw two C-curves to form the sides of the petal, then connect the lines with a small jagged line. The petals on the left and right of the middle can be executed using short C-curves on the outermost edges that are then brought back in with a long S-curve.

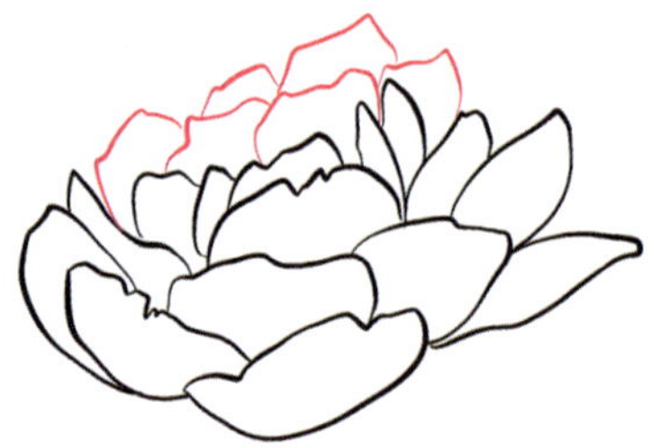

STEP 6 Now start drawing the petals on the far side of the peony's center. Draw your petals wide again as in Step 1. You want to make sure that these petals stay condensed and shallow by drawing the outer lines of each petal much shorter than the petals closest to you. Doing this keeps the flower in an oblong shape, giving the appearance that the flower is slightly tilted. If the petals were longer, they would look disproportionate.

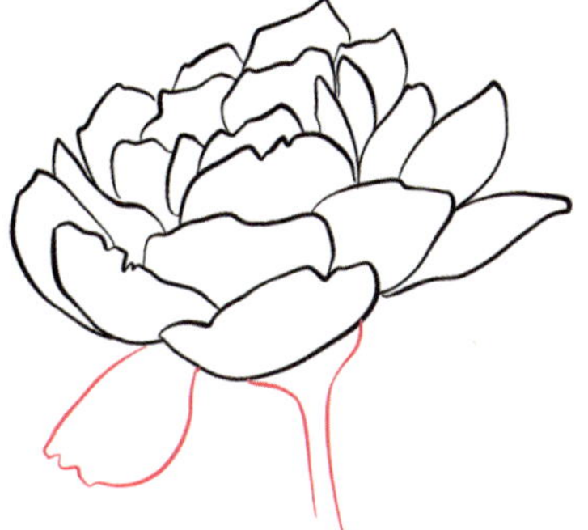

STEP 7 As peonies continue to open, many of their petals can droop downward. I've drawn one here as an example. Draw the line nearest the center as an S-curve, while keeping the line toward the side straighter. This creates specific movement in the petal to show that it's facing us more. If the lines swapped positions, it might look more like it's on its side. Neither choice is wrong. It's just good to know that these small choices make a difference in how our elements look.

The flower is only slightly tilted, so add the base that the petals are cradled within. If the flower was tilted even more, we would see it from above and it wouldn't make sense to show this part. From there, draw a simple stem descending from the base.

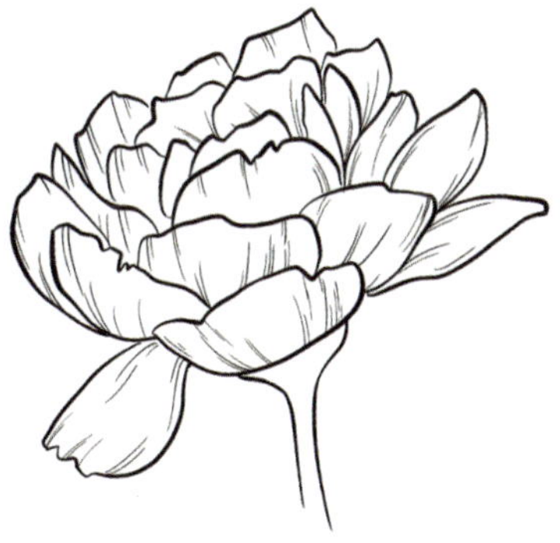

STEP 8 The final step in this peony is adding the detail. You know how to do this with hatching. To draw proper movement, keep in mind where the breaks are in the tips of the petals. Remember to keep lines on the sides of these inward dips.

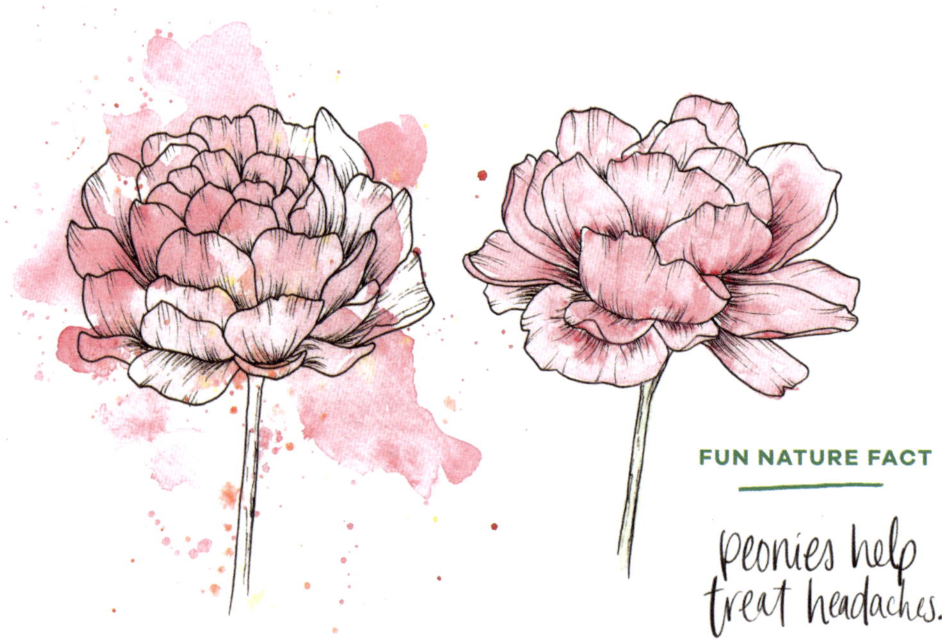

TO ADD COLOR Since we've already played with painting a peony in its actual shape (pages 86–87), I figure now is the perfect time to color outside the lines. I dare you to let go and allow the color to find itself on your page. Wet your brush fully and drag it along your paper. Then follow it up with some pigment and BAM! You've a got a beautiful watercolor bleed. Add some splatter: Hold your brush over your paper, parallel to the surface, and lightly tap the ferrule (or metal piece just above the bristles) of your brush against your finger.

If you opt for a more classic look, place the first layer of color on the petals, then return with a heavier layer of pigment or a different hue and tap it onto the areas that have the most depth, such as the bottom parts of the petals.

Sunflower

A bright and characteristic member of the daisy family, the sunflower is
a favorite of many. It's a happy, inviting flower that feels full of life, fueled
by the sun. Aesthetically, this giant yellow flower radiates energy with its
face to the sun. A single sunflower can have up to two thousand seeds. You
might say that it's made up of a bunch of other flowers. It's magical. Drawing a sunflower is very similar to drawing a daisy (pages 47–54). The petals
are short and layered with line details that create movement. Don't feel like
you need to get literal with your illustration. As you draw, always remember
that you are interpreting the information your eyes are receiving into art,
and the way you visualize and translate nature to paper is unique to you. Be
encouraged to explore other ways of layering patterns and mark making to
create effects such as depth and natural lines.

A sunflower has a large center, while a daisy's center is smaller. They are
both a part of the same flower family, but their differences make them
stand apart. Notice how the daisy's petals are straighter and have a small
indent at the tip, while the sunflower's petals appear to have more movement, are a bit wider, and have a pointed tip.

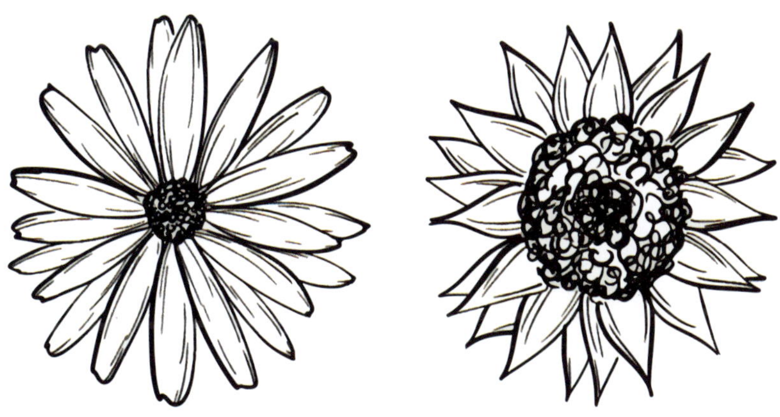

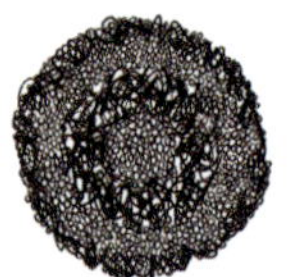

STEP 1 Begin drawing the center the same as you would for the daisy, but this time, use your marks to enhance the darker areas in the center more. Applying different mark-making techniques can give the illusion of variations in depth. I've drawn small circles in the inner center and created more sporadic lines in between. Adding more marks to the outermost part of the circle and again in a ring around the innermost part makes the center look like it has more definition.

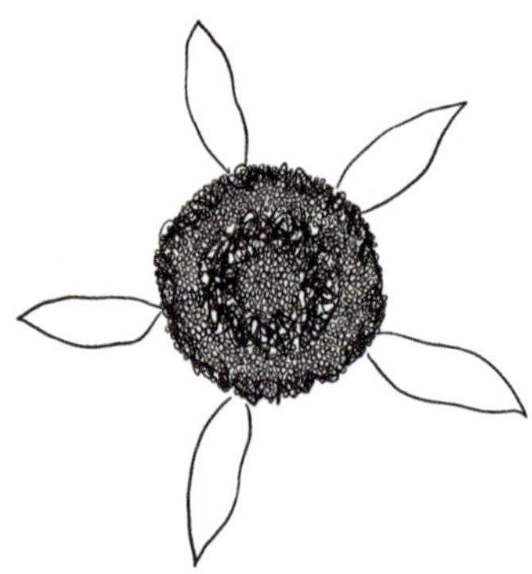

STEP 2 Next, draw five petals evenly spaced around your center. Just as we did with the previous flowers, make sure your petals are similar lengths. Because we're looking at this flower from the top, the petals should be even all the way around. To do this, start on one side and draw a petal. Jump to the other side a bit off center and draw another. Working around the flower like this will make it easier when it's time to fill in the rest of the petals.

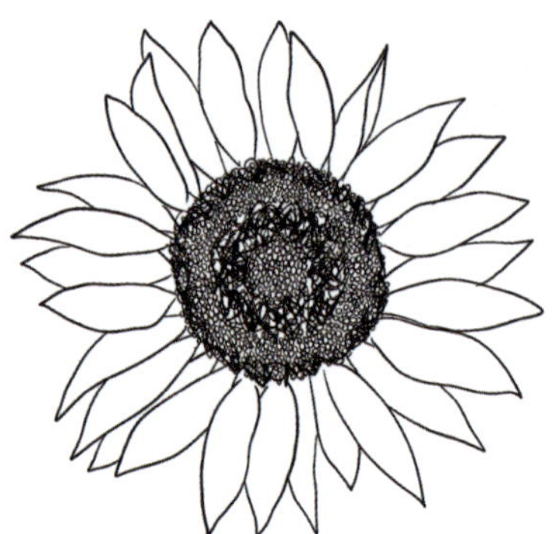

STEP 3 Fill in the rest of the petals. As you do, overlap them slightly. Remember that you have the freedom to play around with edges by making some lines C-curves, some lines S-curves, and even adding some jagged lines like a petal that's twisted or bent.

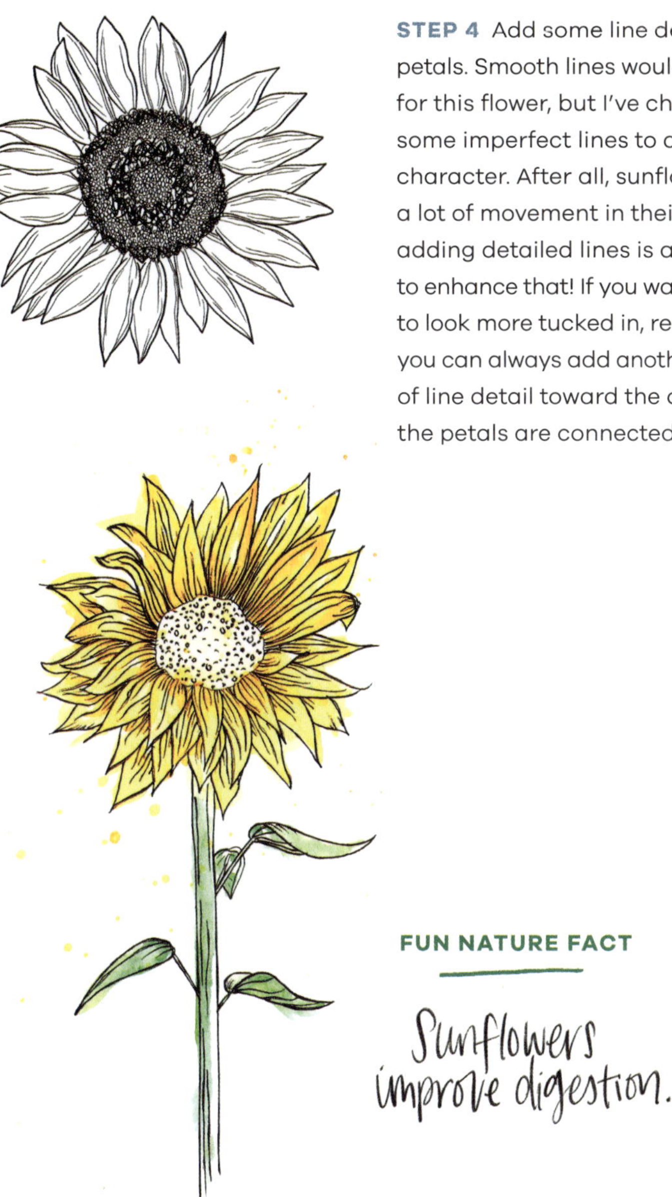

STEP 4 Add some line details to the petals. Smooth lines would work great for this flower, but I've chosen to use some imperfect lines to add more character. After all, sunflowers have a lot of movement in their petals, so adding detailed lines is a simple way to enhance that! If you want the petals to look more tucked in, remember that you can always add another short layer of line detail toward the center where the petals are connected.

FUN NATURE FACT

Sunflowers improve digestion.

TO ADD COLOR Sunflowers are so cheery, and color can bring that out in your illustration. While we're touching on the loose washes, it's a good time to also incorporate a little depth. After applying the main yellow throughout our petals, add a little dot of a deeper yellow or light orange at the base of each petal where it connects to the center. Want to really spruce it up? Add some splatter! Hold your brush over your paper, parallel to the surface, and lightly tap the ferrule of your brush against your finger. Your paint will kiss your paper in little dots of love.

Hydrangea

The hydrangea is a lavish and popular plant. There are more than seventy species of hydrangea, and they are the perfect adornment to a garden. They're quite simple to draw when broken down. Look at only one floret on a bundle; notice that it's made up of four petals that are essentially rounded square or diamond shapes.

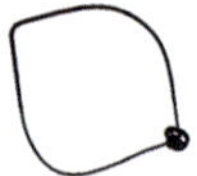

STEP 1 Start by drawing a small dot for a center. Since these petals are more square in their shape, be sure that you really get the petals to reach wide as you draw them.

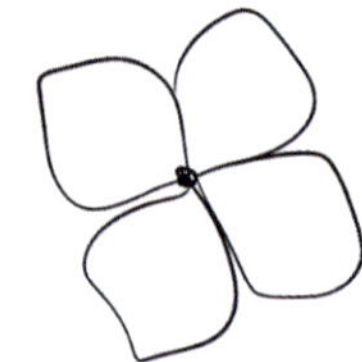

STEP 2 There are only four petals on a hydrangea floret. In this case, you don't need to worry about staggering petal placement. The easiest way to ensure they are in the correct spot is to think of each of the four petals as a square sitting in one of four quadrants of a larger square.

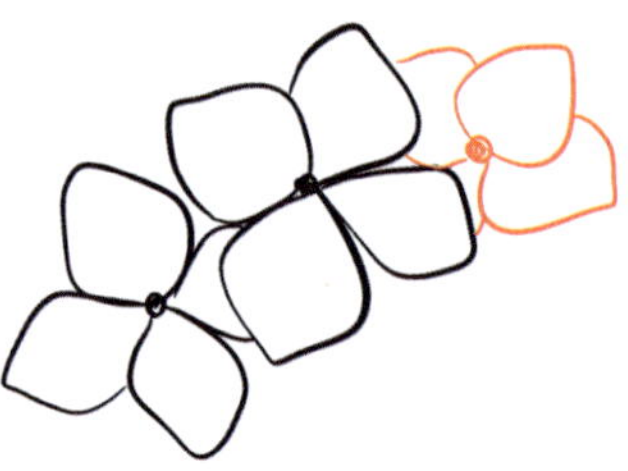

STEP 3 Just as we have built up and overlapped petals, we'll build the round ball that is a hydrangea by drawing overlapping florets. Draw one to the left and one to the right of the first.

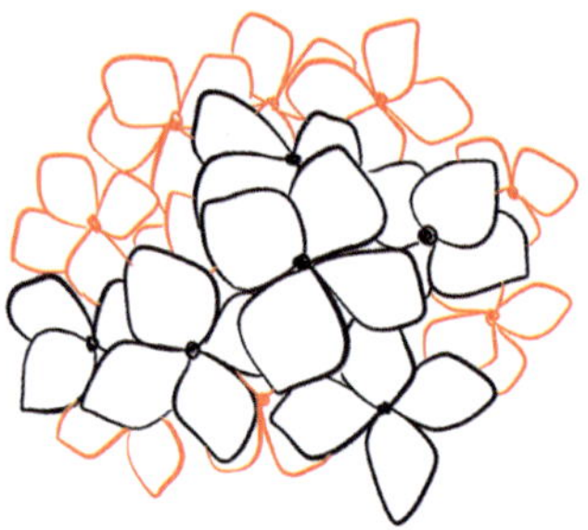

STEP 4 Continue adding florets and, as you draw more, begin to tuck them behind others more and more. Some petals are hiding, and some can even be drawn as narrower shapes, as if they are being seen from the side.

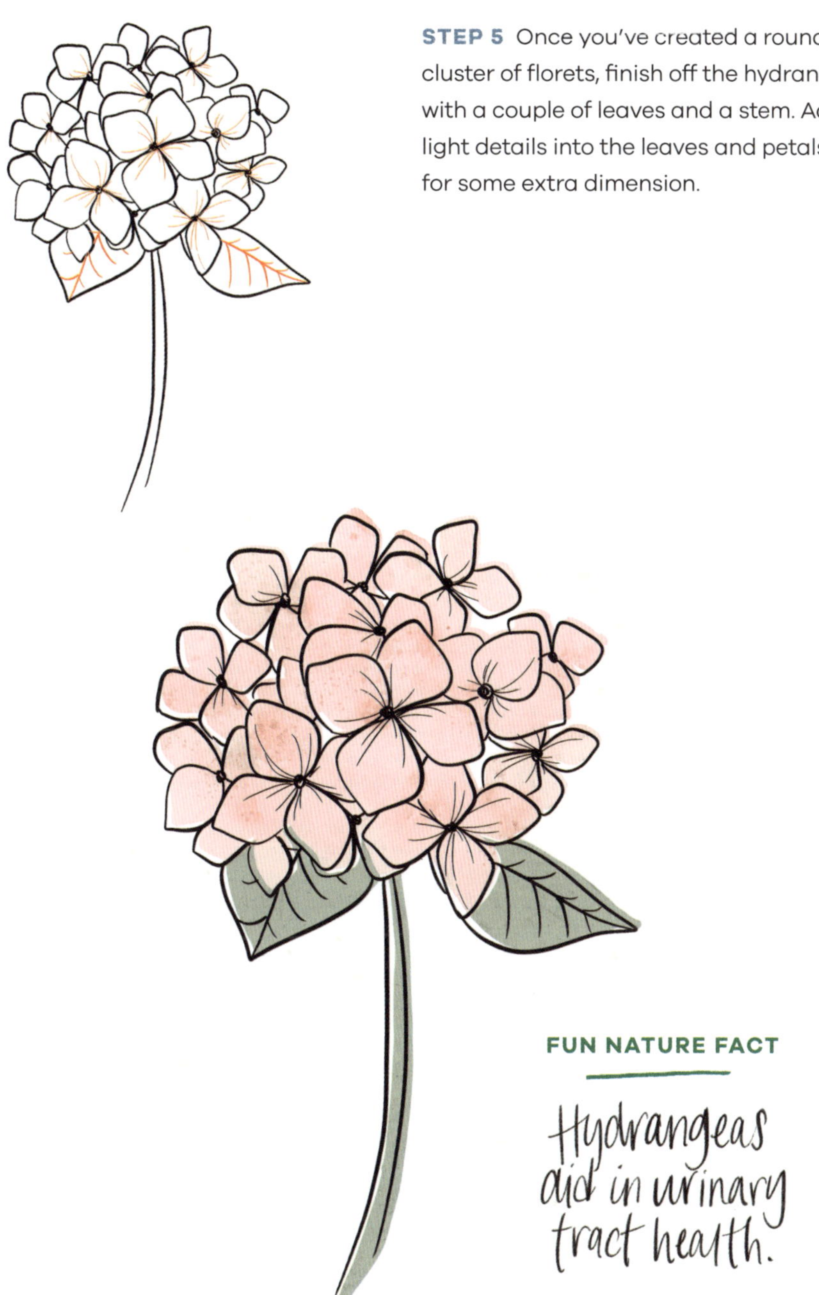

STEP 5 Once you've created a round cluster of florets, finish off the hydrangea with a couple of leaves and a stem. Add light details into the leaves and petals for some extra dimension.

FUN NATURE FACT

TO ADD COLOR Hydrangeas sport soft shades of purples, pinks, blues, and pale greens. Choose a favorite shade and layer on your color!

Orchid

Orchids are, no doubt, loved by so many people. The orchid is an elegant, unique flower that doesn't need accompaniment to enhance its refined beauty.

STEP 1 Begin by drawing two coffee bean shapes with the flat sides touching to make the center of the flower.

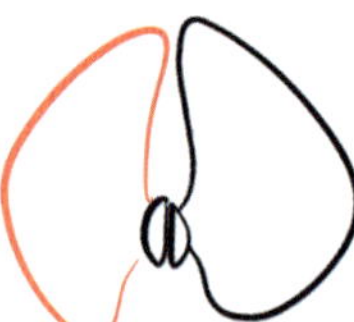

STEP 2 To create the basic shape of the flower, draw two large petals placed on each side of the center. The base of the petal is very skinny. It loops up and creates a rounded edge, reaches outward with a sharp C-curve for another rounded edge, then does the same at the bottom. Do the same thing on the other side. The petals just barely touch at the top.

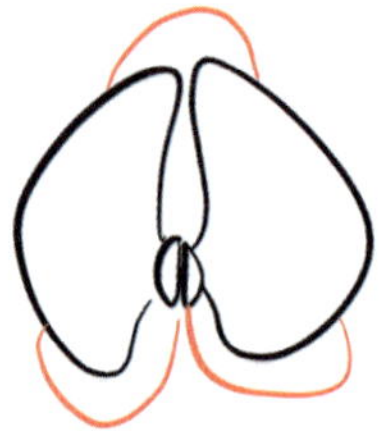

STEP 3 The orchid has three extra petals tucked behind the main two. Draw a C-curve over the peek-a-boo at the top. Then draw two more C-curves at the bottom.

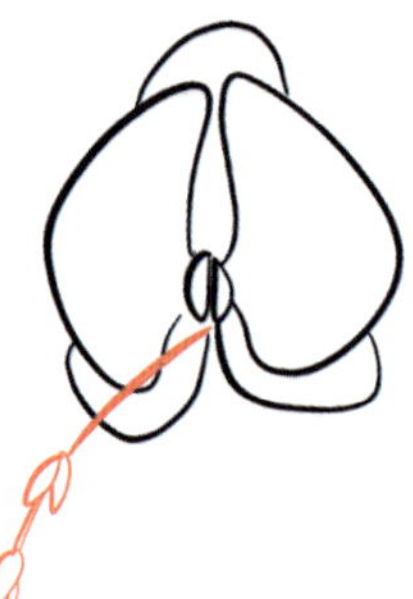

STEP 4 Next, add the stem that reaches outward from the flower for additional blooms. The stem travels through the flower and almost looks as though it's floating. Draw a C-curve from the bottom of the center. Add additional oblong buds on this stem.

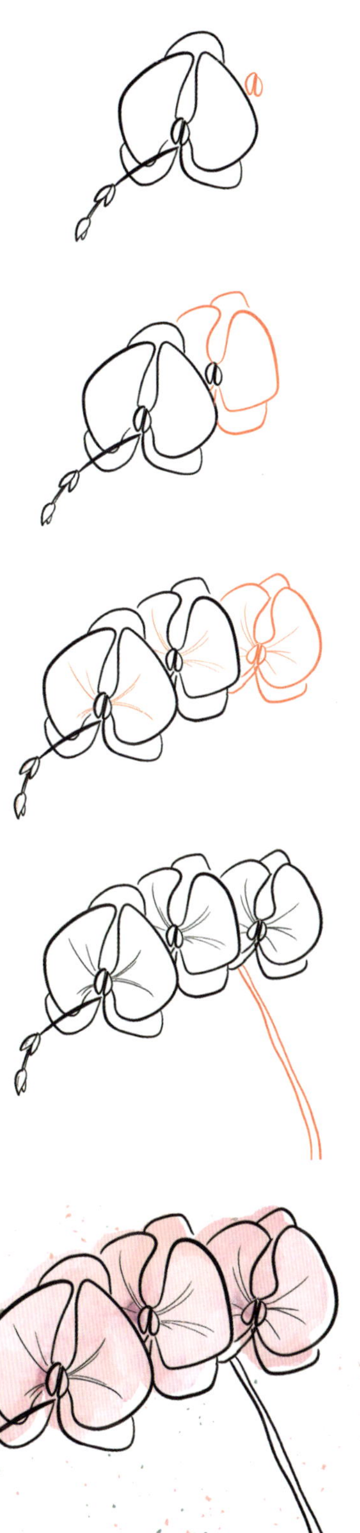

STEP 5 Now we're at the easy part. All you need to do is repeat the same steps that we just did, but do so behind the first flower. Draw two small coffee-bean shapes near the top right.

STEP 6 Create the same petals as in Steps 2 and 3. Remember that you can hover your pen in the areas that are tucked behind as you work. This helps you maintain the shape.

STEP 7 Create one more of these flowers, but lower it a bit so it's to the right of the second flower. Think of the stem as an invisible line that travels through all three flowers.

STEP 8 The last step is to add the base of the stem. Offset this stem to connect in between the second and third flowers, to reinforce the look of flowers branching off of the stem.

TO ADD COLOR One of my favorite techniques when it comes to adding color is to offset it by leaving some white space on one side of the illustration and going outside the lines on the other side, like a misaligned color print. It really makes the drawing come alive!

Wildflowers

When I think of wildflowers, I think of a thick carpet of color patches attached to long stems. I'm particularly drawn to fields of reds and blue-violets. Have you ever seen fields of Indian paintbrush (or prairie-fire) and bluebonnets? It's a sight for the dreamer at heart.

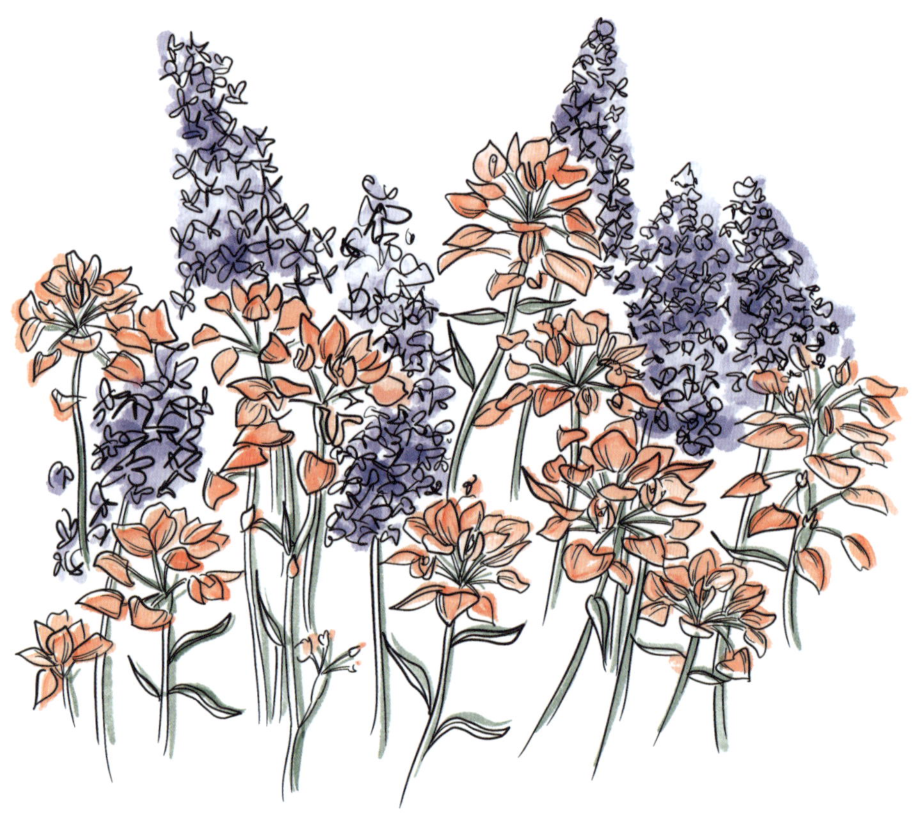

Wildflower illustrations should show flowers in their natural state, ungroomed and perfectly imperfect. Once you've got them down as standalone drawings, blending them together and overlapping them a bit can showcase a beautiful mix of color.

Indian Paintbrush

Indian paintbrush is a wildflower named for its spiky clusters that resemble the tips of paintbrushes dipped in red paint. These blooms have blossoms all along the stem, with more saturated color toward the tops. If we hold one of these stems out at eye level, some of the petals will be closer to us, some on the sides, and some in back. Whenever you feel stumped, especially by blooms that look more complicated than a single rose or daisy, remember that the idea is to see the object as if it were flattened.

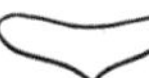

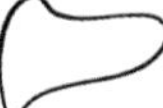

STEP 1 Let's start with the petals closest to us. Drawing a petal growing outward "toward us" is simple. First, draw a line that dips down in the middle, then connect the sides below in a point. When a petal is growing straight out, not drooping or growing upward, it will look flatter to our view. Now we'll draw another petal below the first one and slightly angled to the left. Draw the same line you began the previous petal with, but this time, make the center dip on the left side. You'll still connect the sides with a point, but the left side of the petal will arc downward, while the right side mimics the first petal. Do you see how that changes the form?

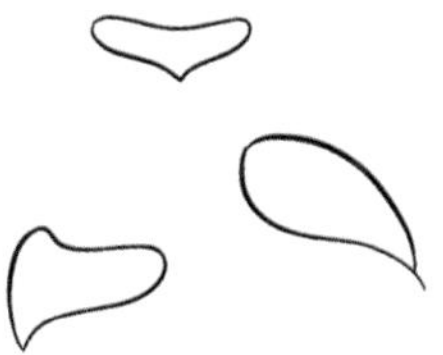

STEP 2 Do the same thing with a petal that is angled downward, but see how, instead of appearing to be growing outward, it looks as though it's growing downward more? You can also add petals, similarly to leaves, on their sides by drawing a C-curve on top and an S-curve on the bottom.

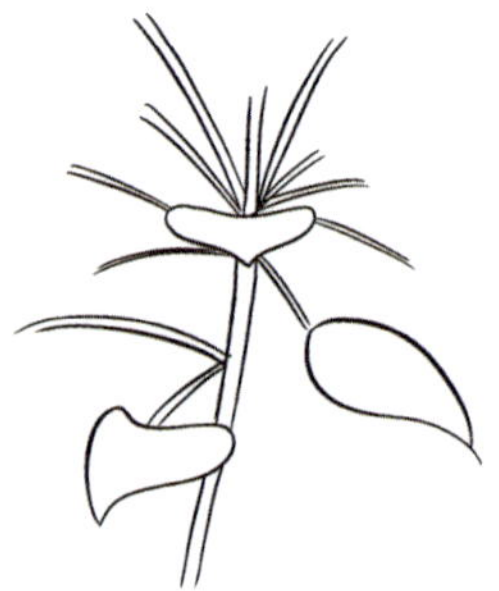

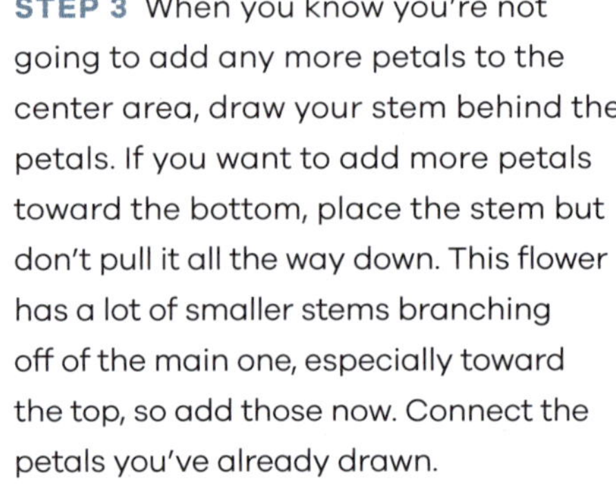

STEP 3 When you know you're not going to add any more petals to the center area, draw your stem behind the petals. If you want to add more petals toward the bottom, place the stem but don't pull it all the way down. This flower has a lot of smaller stems branching off of the main one, especially toward the top, so add those now. Connect the petals you've already drawn.

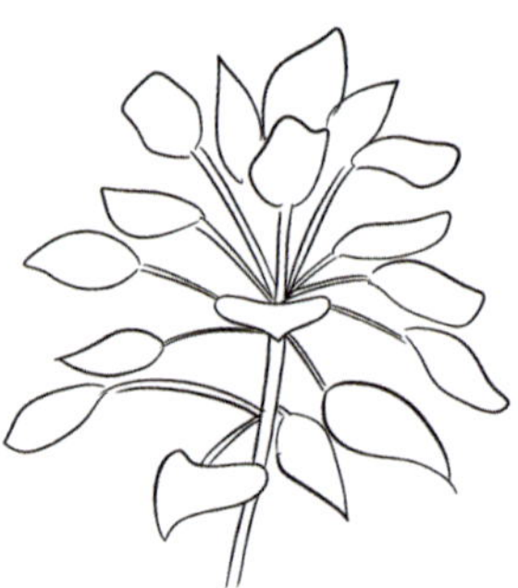

STEP 4 Once the smaller stems are in place, attach more petals. This flower has unique petals that are pointed at the tips, but from the side, they vary, looking pointed, rounded, and even sometimes flat. I always like to tuck a few petals behind the top, adding depth. Add additional petals lower on the stem. These won't be as concentrated as at the top, as they get sparser toward the bottom of the stem.

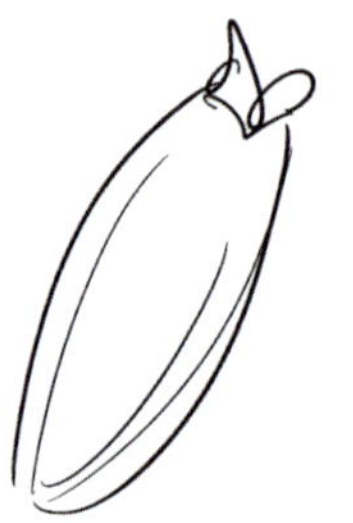

STEP 5 You may even find a few unopened blooms on this plant. To draw them, just create two outer C-curves as you would on a petal, but don't connect the top. Instead, add some quick mark making, which will complete the bloom.

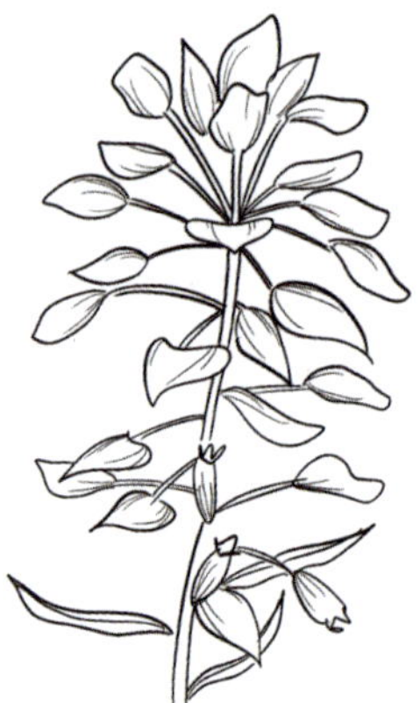

STEP 6 Last, add some leaves and a little detail using C-curve flicks that follow the outer edges of the petals.

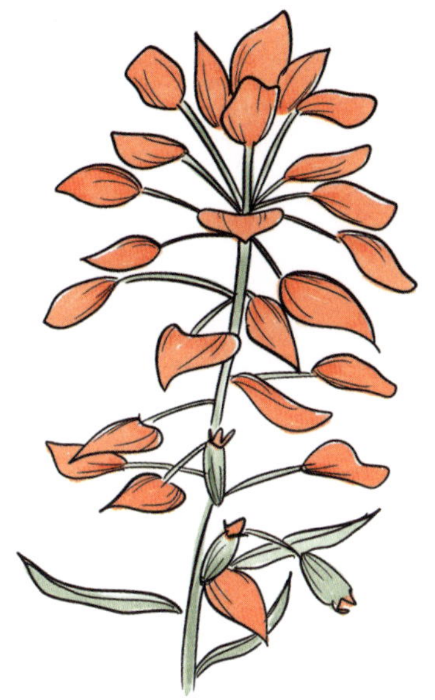

TO ADD COLOR You can simplify your illustrations with flat washes. Watercolor can do a lot of things, but don't be afraid to go back to basics with some even, flat color.

Bluebonnets

This hardy perennial plant, a member of the legume family, has dozens of tiny blooms forming a thick cluster around its stem. I'm going to take a different approach to breaking this one down because, once open, the bluebonnet's tiny florets can be a bit intimidating. The first thing I'll say is that there is no reason to put all of this detail into the illustration if it's going to be small.

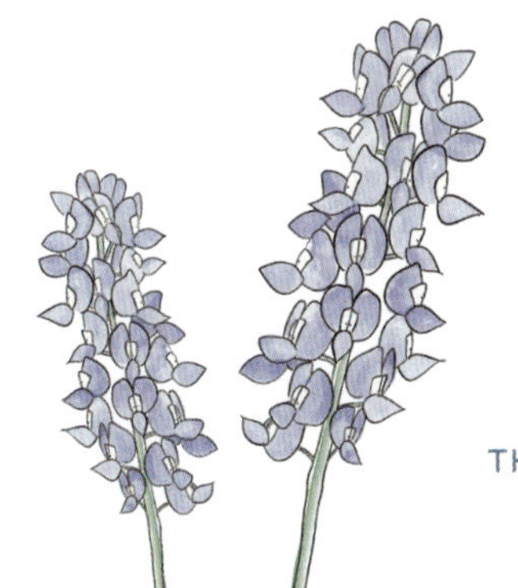

Oh yeah. We're making a face. Look at this silly thing. It's like the beginnings of a cartoon character with a thick, bird-like nose and giant eyes.

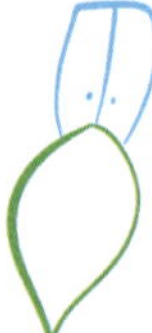

STEP 1 Start with the nose by drawing two S-curves that start at the top and meet at a point at the bottom.

Add eyes, which are a rectangular shape drawn at the top of the nose, and add a line down the center of the rectangle. Then add two small dots toward the bottom inside part of each smaller rectangle.

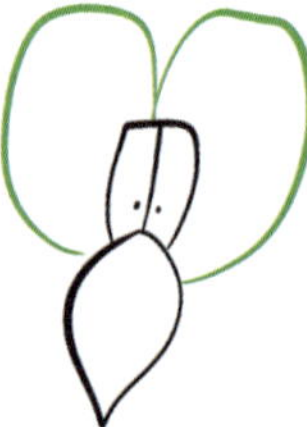

STEP 2 From there, draw two round C-curves that reach up and around to meet at the top of the nose on each side of the eyes.

Now, here's what that same bloom looks like from the side: the "nose" points outward, showing one eye, and the side profile in all its glory.

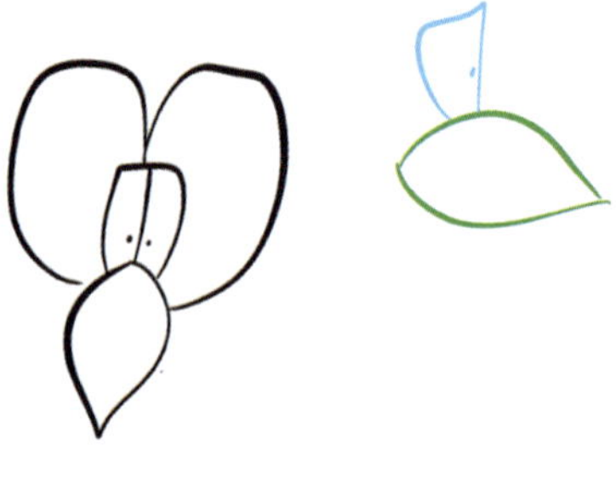

STEP 3 Draw two S-curves that begin on the left and meet in a point on the right side to form the nose profile.

Draw a tall rectangle on the top of the nose, slightly to the left, and add a dot inside and close to the right side of the rectangle.

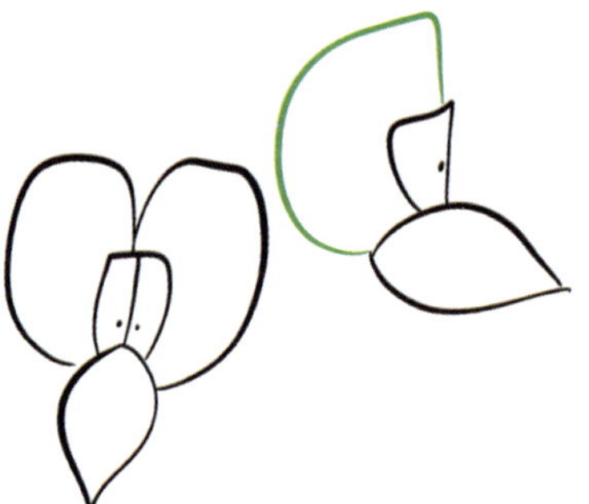

STEP 4 Last, from the top of the rectangle (the eye), draw a straight line that then curves to the left, turns into a large C-curve, and connects to the left side of the nose. Not too difficult, right?

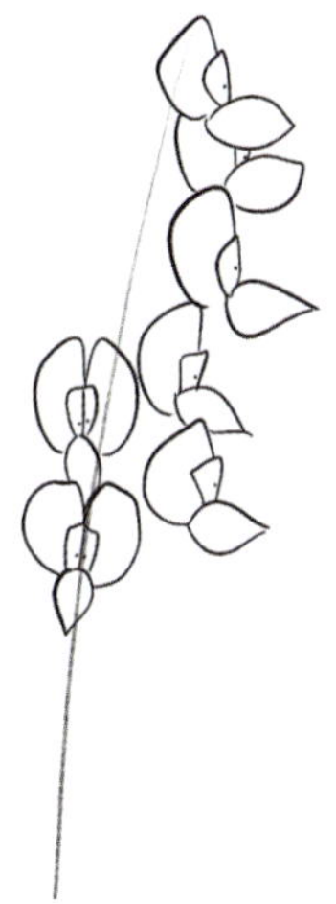

STEP 5 Now it's time to group your blooms together. You can picture a stem or, if it helps, draw with a pencil a light line to act as a stem. We're going to stack faces on top of each other. (You'll never be able to look at bluebonnets the same way now that you've seen their little cartoon faces!)

STEP 6 Finish by tucking in the stem. When you take a step back, you can really see the flower forming with details you never knew you could create.

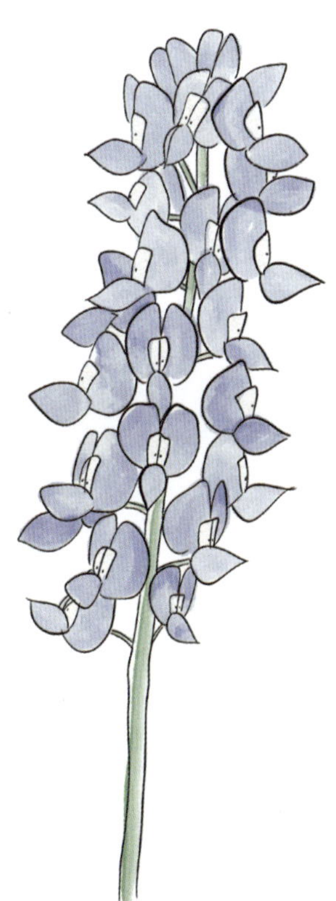

FUN NATURE FACT

Bluebonnets are toxic.

TO ADD COLOR Flat washes can be varied separately. Some flat washes have more pigment than others, and using the wet-on-dry method you can simply vary each bloom with a different opacity. Fun!

Lavender

The nice thing about this flower is that it has a ton of little buds that can be drawn with less detail without losing the look of lavender. My preferred way to draw lavender is with small loops.

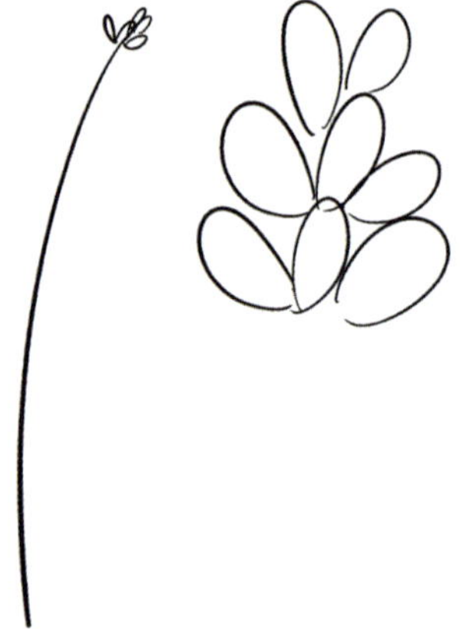

STEP 1 Draw a C-curve to form the stem.

To create the buds, start at the top and draw a fat loop up and around, ending back where you started. This is essentially a fat bunny-ear stroke.

Layer these a few times. I like to stagger the number of buds throughout the stalks. For example, draw two on the top, then three in the middle and three on the bottom. Try drawing the loops in a pattern like so: 2, 3, 4, 4, 2, 4, etc.

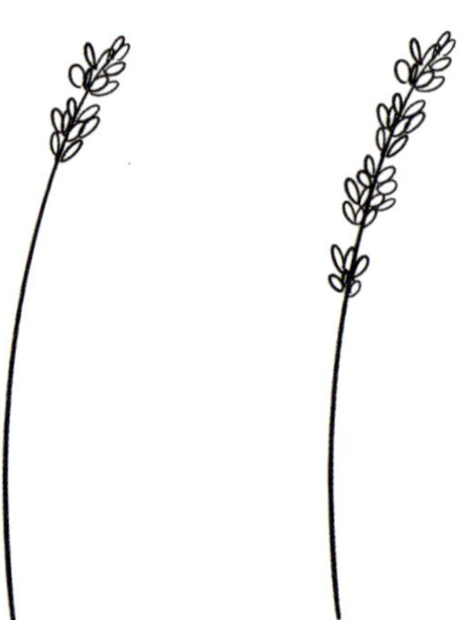

STEP 2 Create some separation on the stem by leaving a skip in the flowers. Continue adding bundles of buds until you're about halfway down the stem.

 Group a bunch of these stalks together for a lavender bouquet!

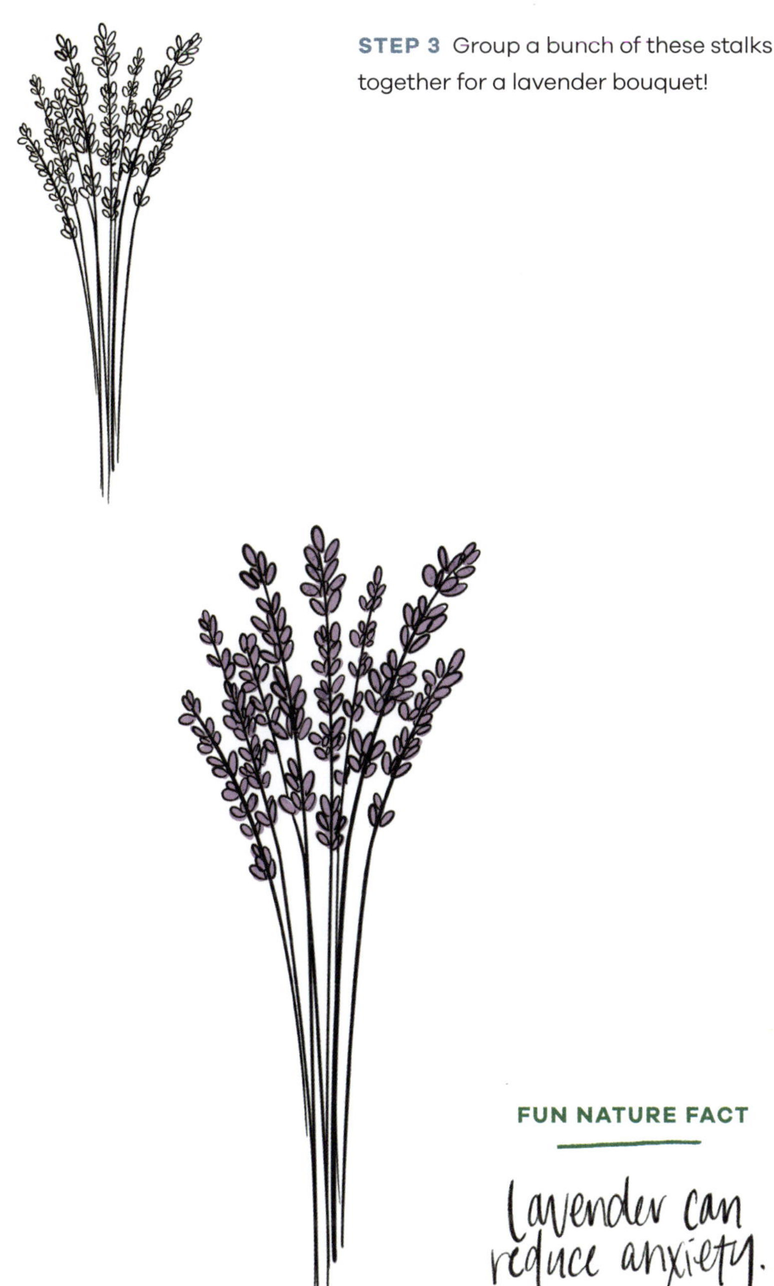

FUN NATURE FACT

Lavender can reduce anxiety.

TO ADD COLOR Try using two different shades of purple to create a little depth!

Lily of the Valley

There are a few legends about the Lily of the Valley that are tied to religious themes. You may have heard that they sprang from the tears of Eve when she was banished from the Garden of Eden, or that they sprang from the tears of Mary when Jesus was crucified on the cross (which is why the flower is also called Mary's Tears or Our Lady's Tears). Because this flower famously blooms in May, it's also known as "May bells." It's a reasonably simple flower to draw.

The leaves of this flower are really unique. They're very long and simple. They also have vertical lines, which I use to enhance my illustrations. Doing so puts more attention on the leaves rather than the florets, but that's a creative choice. There are so many choices to make along this journey.

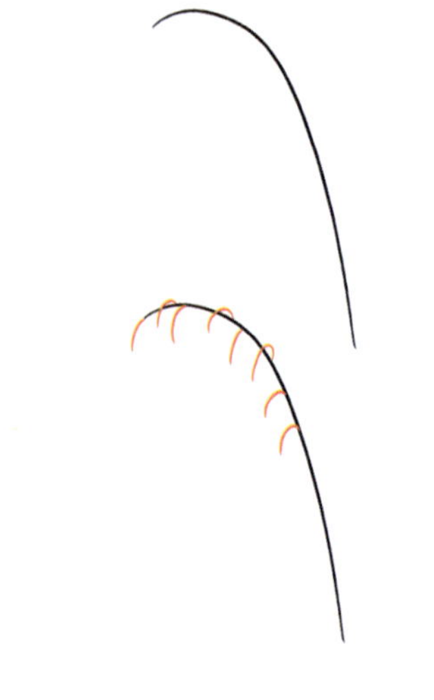

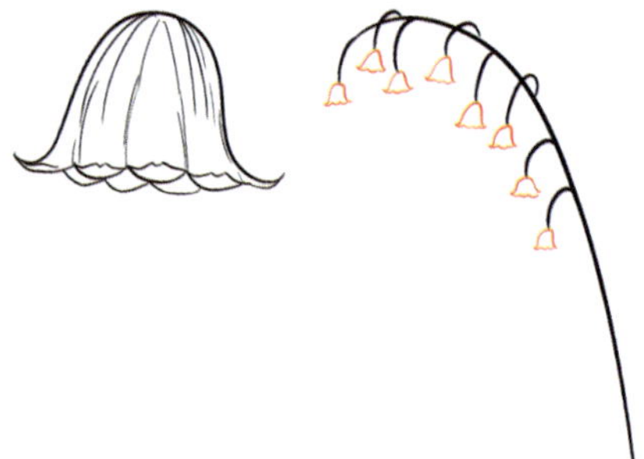

STEP 1 Start by drawing the stem, long and curved at the top.

STEP 2 From there, small stems branch off of and below the main one. Draw these extensions in the natural growth direction of the stem and allow them to hang down. Draw some lifting up and off the stem before turning downward.

STEP 3 To draw the florets, keep their general shape in mind. They look like shallow bells with tips that curl outward and upward. (When we draw them so small, we don't need to worry about all of this extra detail, but it's helpful to see beforehand so you have a general idea of the shape you want to draw.) Create an arch that flares out at the bottom of both sides of the bloom. Connect the bottom edges with small C-curve strokes.

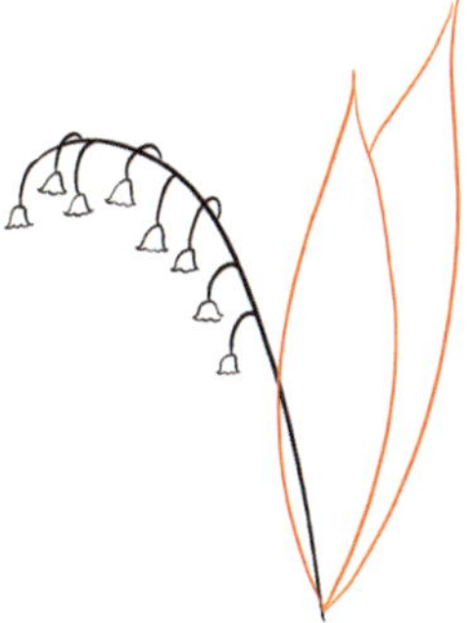

STEP 4 Draw two S-curves to form the outer edges of the leaf. They should start at the base of the stem and reach about the same height as the top of the stem, curving in to meet at a point. Add another leaf just behind the first.

STEP 5 Let's add detail to these leaves. First, try drawing a central stem down the middle with a straight line. If you crave more, have fun with adding many more vertical lines! Using a small amount of detail to the florets will also give them a little more interest.

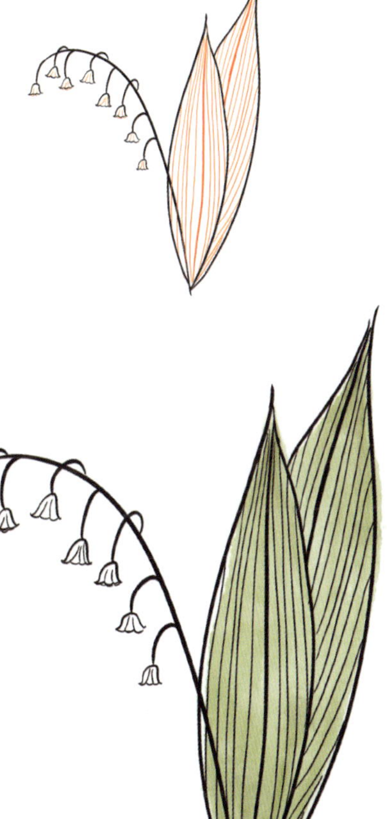

FUN NATURE FACT

Lilies of the valley assist in treating paralysis.

TO ADD COLOR Try isolating color to only one element of your piece, like the muted green leaves here. Then, if you want to get really crazy, splash a couple splatter marks over the top!

THE PLANT STUDY

I know I've talked a lot about my favorites, but if I have a favorite of favorites, it's greenery. The unique shapes, textures, and many shades of green sing to my heart when I see them. I'm going to go over a few plants with you that are easily recognizable and, most important, so fun to draw!

Bamboo

Ever since I can remember, I've been attracted to bamboo. It makes me feel immersed in a captivating rain forest. Drawing bamboo is exciting because you can play with its jointed stems.

BAMBOO STALK AND LEAVES

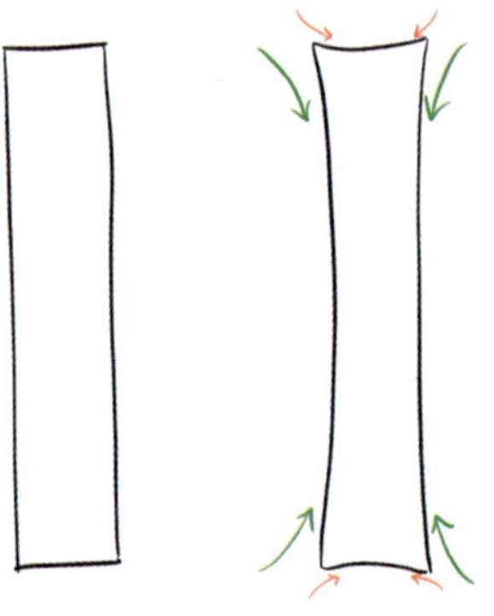

STEP 1 Let's look at bamboo in sections. We want to exaggerate its shape to enhance its appearance. As we visualize only one piece of the stem, the joints are on the top and bottom, and we know that it's long and narrow. We'll capture this in a long rectangle. Draw the rectangle, but instead of using straight lines, we'll indent them, so all of the sides are concave.

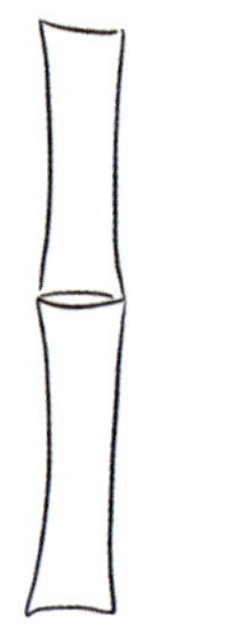

STEP 2 Repeat this shape, one stacked on top of another. You'll now notice that the distinct inward direction of the tops and bottoms will act as the joints of the stem.

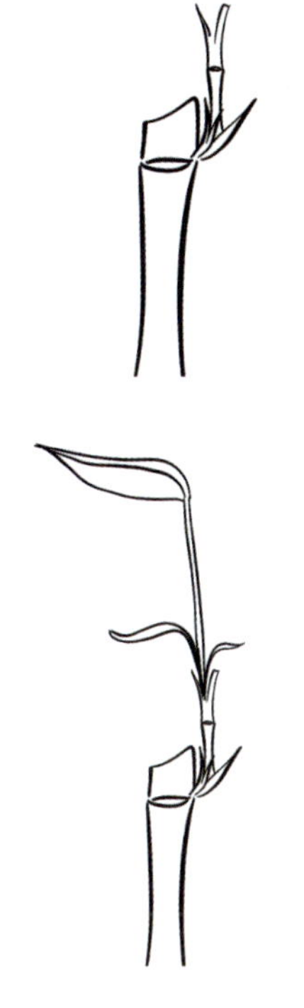

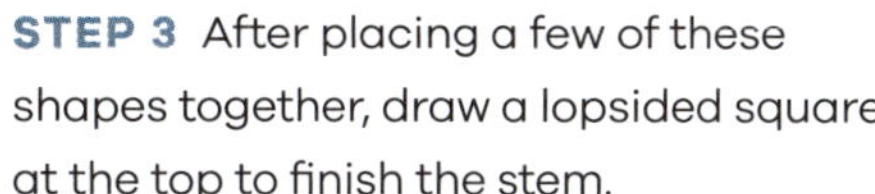

STEP 3 After placing a few of these shapes together, draw a lopsided square at the top to finish the stem.

Next, add a thin leaf coming off of the stalk and a tiny stem sprouting out of the main leaf that splits off at the top.

STEP 4 The stem you just drew will hold three leaves. First draw two tiny sprouting leaves at the top of the stem, one facing to the left and one to the right. They dip down and back up to a point in an S-curve.

Now, add a larger leaf in the center of the two leaves. I drew mine in the same way as the first, focusing on the leaf's angle. It curves around, dipping down then back up to its tip. To make the angle look more realistic, add its center line toward the top part of the leaf rather than the center. This makes it look like it's at more of an angle.

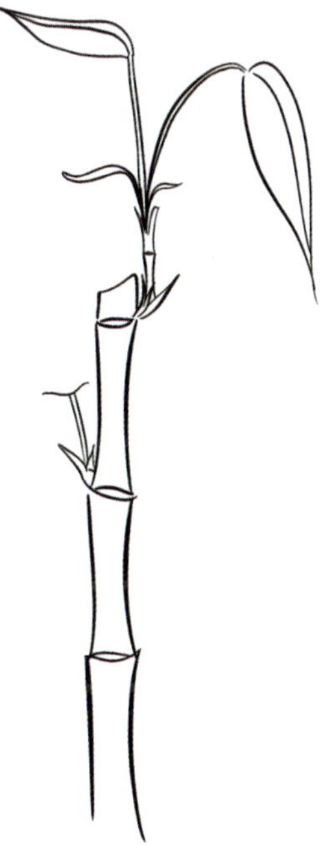

STEP 5 Add an additional downward-facing leaf sprouting off of the same area, and curve its stem to the right. I kept its middle vein-line more in the center on this one (although it would also work if it was more toward the right). Experiment with center line placement as you draw your leaves and you'll see what I mean.

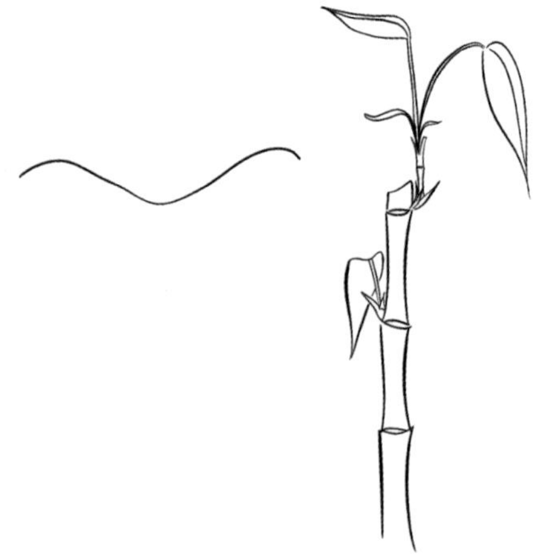

STEP 6 The last leaf I want to show you is facing away from us. Draw another small leaf on the left side toward the middle.

Create a couple of tiny leaves at the base of your new sprout, and place a small stem coming out of the center. Here's the part to pay attention to: Creating a leaf that is facing away from you starts much differently than the other leaves. First, draw a slight S-curve just on top of the stem. It will curve over, under, and over again.

DO THIS　　**NOT THIS**

STEP 7 To complete the leaf, draw each side coming down into a point! Not too difficult after all, right? Keep in mind that drawing the bulk of the leaf on one side of the stem will make it look more believable because it provides the illusion that there is some space in between the stem and the leaf itself, which is more realistic in nature.

BAMBOO ROOTS

If you're like me and you want to feature bamboo in all of its glory, it might interest you to add its roots. Although these aren't as apparent in nature, small bamboo stems are a popular houseplant choice, and in that context the roots are often exposed, accompanied by pretty rocks or marbles.

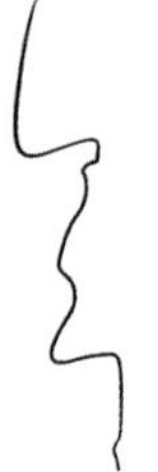

STEP 1 Think of an imperfect line. It's not just simply a wavy S-curve—it's squiggly and jagged. Put your type A perfectionism aside and draw this line. Add character by breaking the rules!

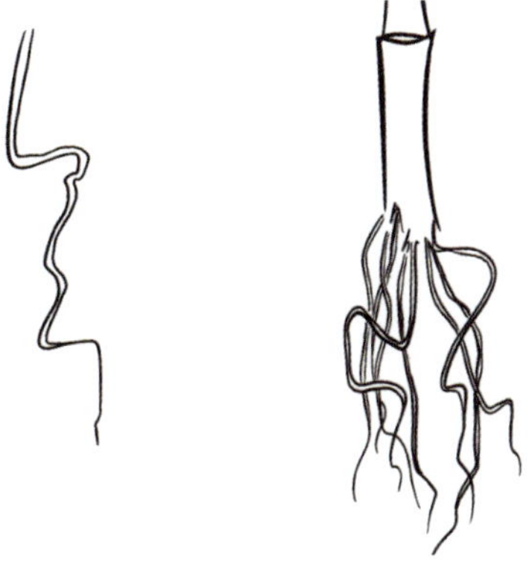

STEP 2 Once you've drawn your first line, draw another line mirroring it. Don't worry about it matching up perfectly. Variations in thickness only add uniqueness.

As you reach the bottom with the second line, join it with the first one, making the bottom of the root thin and stringy. That's it!

Now create a small cluster of these guys.

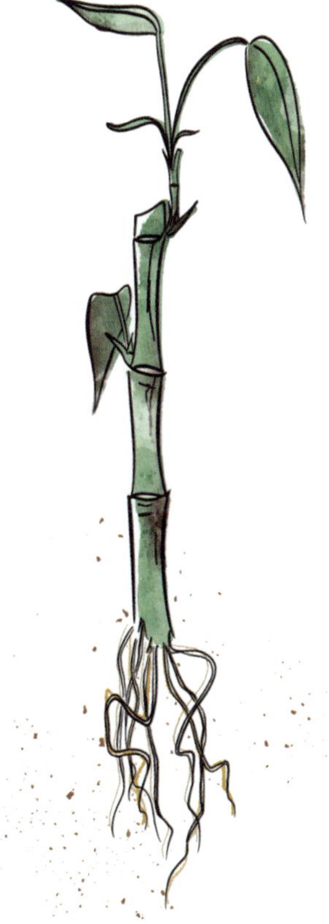

FUN NATURE FACT

Bamboo shoots are high in fiber.

DID YOU ALSO KNOW . . .

- Bamboo produces 35 percent more oxygen than trees.

- Bamboo is used in place of wood to make a variety of items, including furniture.

- Many bamboo stalks grow so tall they may look like trees, but bamboo is actually grass!

TO ADD COLOR Getting into the greens in nature is my favorite because when I add color, I can dirty it up. I love a good brown bleed in a stalk or a leaf. Try blending other colors on top of your greens to show depth and to give a more organic quality.

Vines

Plants such as pothos (devil's ivy) and philodendrons are great climbers and will grow up and around an entire tree. They also look absolutely lovely hanging, and their rapid growth makes them excellent houseplants. When these vines reach toward the ground, they create a column of greenery, adding the perfect pop of nature to your space.

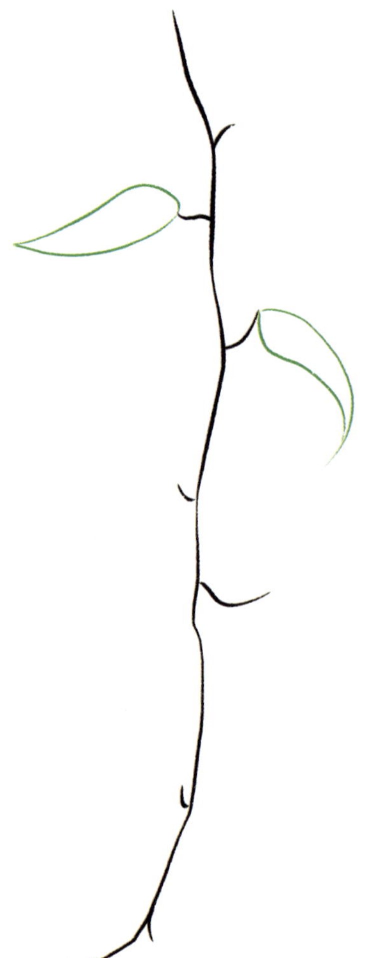

STEP 1 Draw a slightly wavy, jagged line.

STEP 2 Use short C-curves to add petioles along both sides of the line.

STEP 3 Draw a few leaves on their sides. To give the appearance of a leaf bending upward, draw an S-curve for the top line and a C-curve on the bottom, connecting at a point. To give the appearance of a leaf bending downward, draw a C-curve on the top and an S-curve on the bottom, also connecting at a point. Notice that the direction of each C-curve is the direction in which the leaf bends.

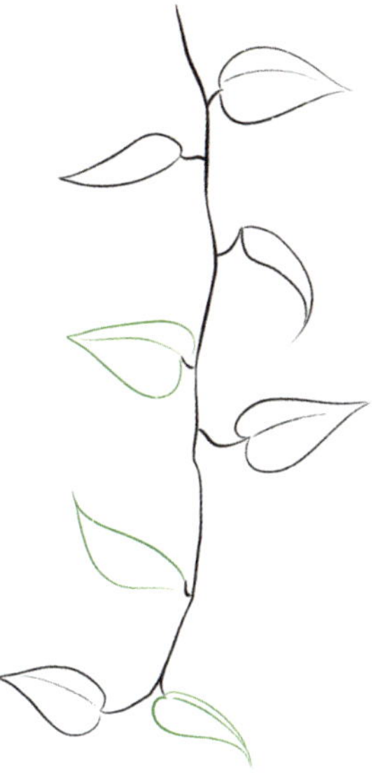

STEP 4 Draw a few fuller leaves. These can be a combination of S-curves and C-curves, or they can be the same type of curve, such as the leaf on the bottom right.

STEP 5 Keep until each petiole is connected to a leaf. Try creating a hanging vine or cluster illustration by drawing several strands together.

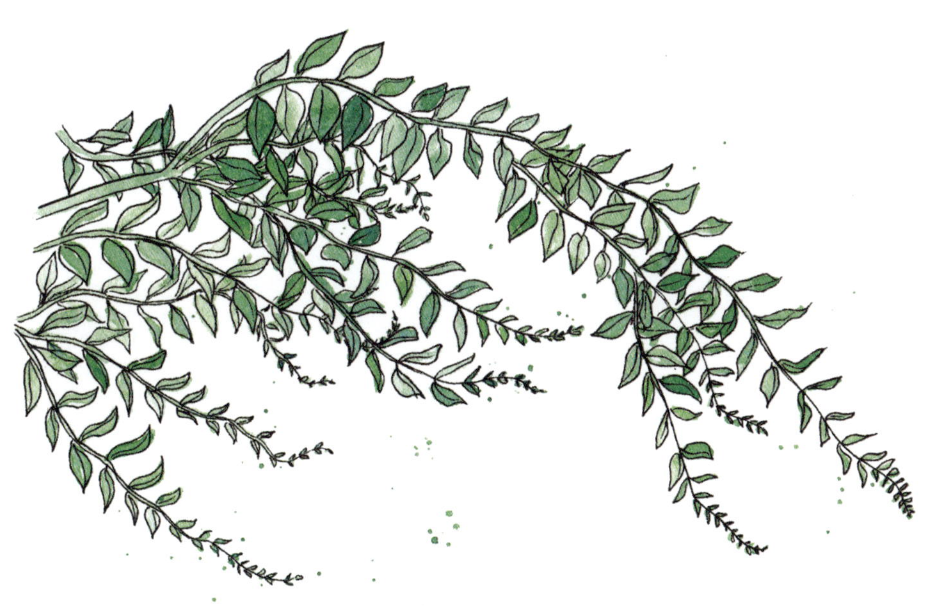

TO ADD COLOR Vary several shades of green for depth. Then, if you want to get really crazy, use your brush to splash a couple splatter marks over the top!

Eucalyptus

Eucalyptus is well-known not only for its beauty but also for its medicinal and aromatic purposes. When applied as an essential oil, it can relax the muscles and mind. Have you ever tried hanging fresh eucalyptus from your showerhead? It's a magical experience that I recommend you try. Like, now. There are more than seven hundred species of eucalyptus, but we're going to explore the silver dollar variety.

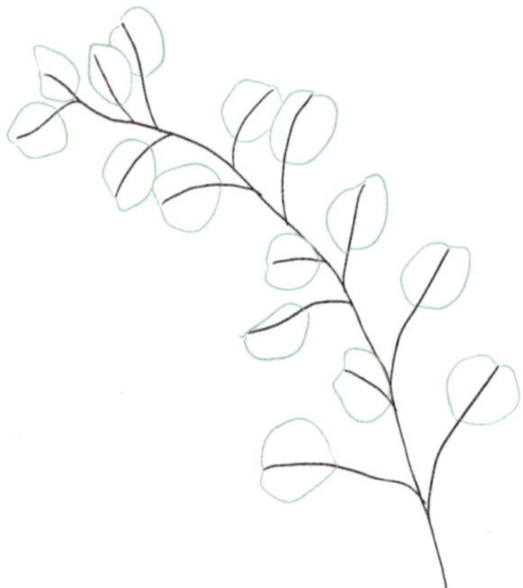

STEP 1 Draw a curved stem and add long jagged lines that branch off. Use different lengths and spacing.

STEP 2 Draw rounded leaves off of the stems that branch outward. You can choose either round or oblong, or a mix of both.

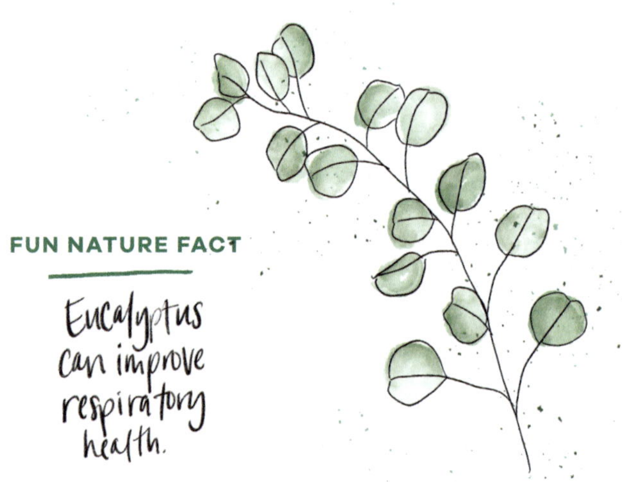

FUN NATURE FACT

Eucalyptus can improve respiratory health.

TO ADD COLOR Add a soft watercolor wash and you've got yourself a lovely eucalyptus branch.

Fern

There are more than twenty thousand species of ferns in the world. Let's draw each one! Kidding. (But let's be honest, that would make an incredible illustration. The creative in me is salivating at the idea.) Ferns are among my favorite plants, but if you're not on the same page, it's fine. We just won't be as good of friends anymore. Okay, enough jokes. Let's draw these beautiful forest blankets.

I've picked two ferns with different characteristics, so you'll have a couple to choose from when incorporating these guys. My hope is that you'll also reach beyond this book to explore others and use the techniques you've learned here to draw even more plants. For now, we'll explore the Boston fern and the maidenhair fern.

BOSTON FERN

Boston ferns are popular houseplants often seen growing in hanging baskets. From a distance, this fern looks almost like a puffy green ball. Its leaf edges are smooth and wavy.

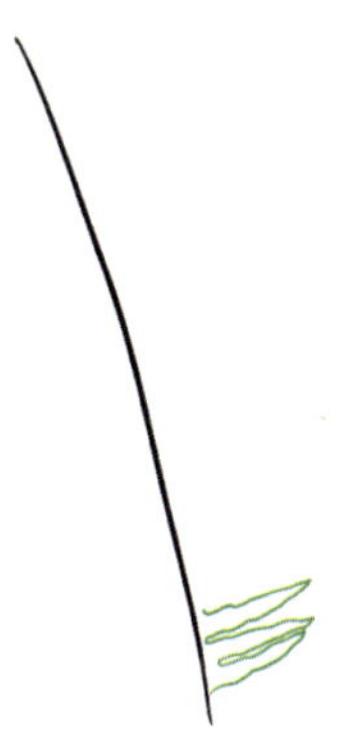

STEP 1 Start off with a curved stem. Begin adding leaves that are connected to each other and made with wavy lines. You can tuck a few leaves behind others.

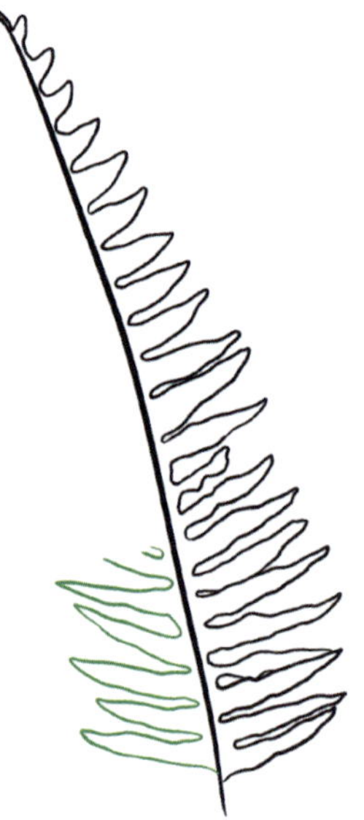

STEP 2 Gradually draw the leaves shorter and smaller as you move up the stem. Nature isn't perfect, so variations give each leaf more character. (Have I said that before?)

STEP 3 Let's say you want to overlap one of the higher leaves instead. Just create the beginning of it and stop short. When you draw the next leaf, cover the gap.

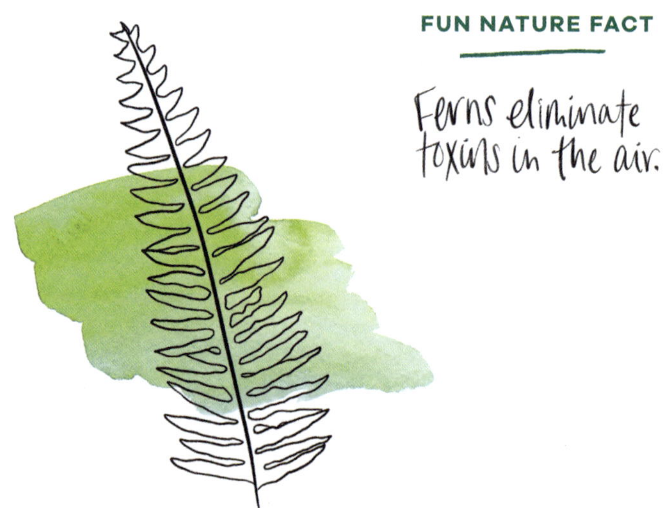

TO ADD COLOR Who says color needs to make sense? This is an especially exciting thought in watercolor because a splash on an illustration adds energy and life! I prefer to paint these swatches before I draw, but you can always do it over the top of your illustration. As long as you're not loading up with a ton of pigment, your lines will show through just fine. Create a swatch with zigzag strokes in any shade of green!

MAIDENHAIR FERN

The maidenhair fern is a distinctive plant with soft, lacy leaves. Because of its delicate appearance, it's perfect as a standalone plant or when accompanied by flowers.

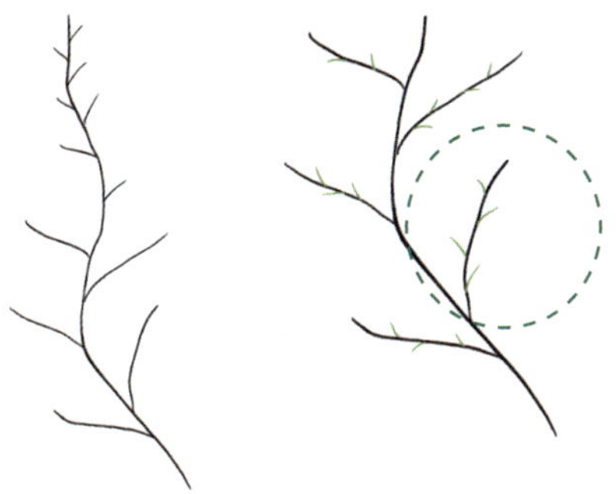

STEP 1 Begin by drawing a wavy line down the center of your paper. Don't get crazy and draw a ton of waves, just enough to show some movement.

Growing outward from the line you just drew are smaller, alternating stems that gradually get shorter toward the top. Even smaller stems are added to some of the longer lines toward the bottom.

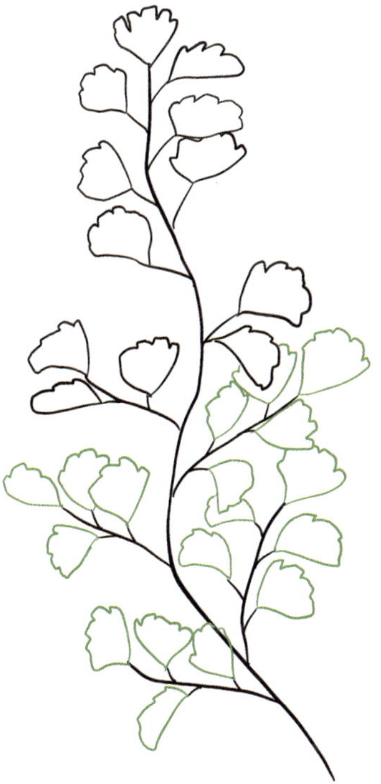

STEP 2 The leaves on maidenhair ferns are fan-shaped, with texture at the top. Draw the sides angling outward from the bottom, then connect the leaf at the top with little dips in the line.

You can also draw a few leaves as if they're being seen from the side. To do this, keep one side flat, which will sit horizontally, then loop up and around with a textured top.

STEP 3 As you work toward the bottom, where there are multiple leaves branching off of one stem, they will begin to overlap. Just as you have overlapped leaves in previous lessons, you'll apply the same techniques here. Simply tuck some leaves behind others.

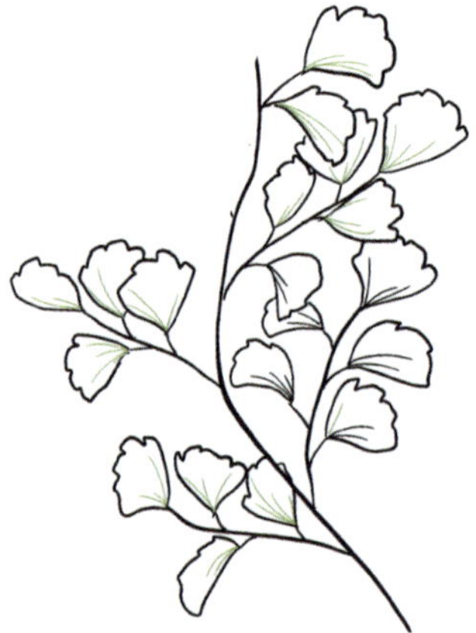

STEP 4 Add just a few thin lines coming from the center of each leaf to add some detail. Remember to create curved lines, which imitates movement. After that, you're done!

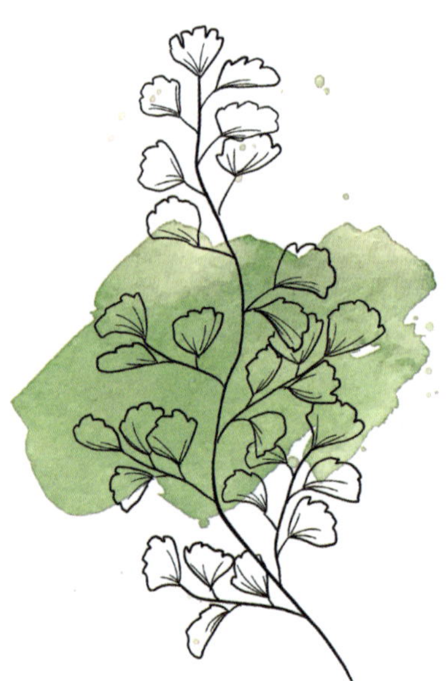

TO ADD COLOR Just as we added a simple splash of color to our Boston fern, we'll do the same with our maidenhair fern. This time, choose a new shade of green.

Cattail

I love a cattail. They're so interesting! Not only do they serve as a food source for wildlife in wetland habitats but they also have a wealth of medicinal and nutritional benefits for humans. That's right, you can eat every part of a cattail at different periods of its growth.

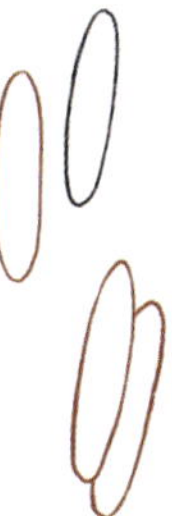

STEP 1 Draw a slender oval.

STEP 2 Draw a few more. Try over-lapping one or two. This will make them look like they're bundled together.

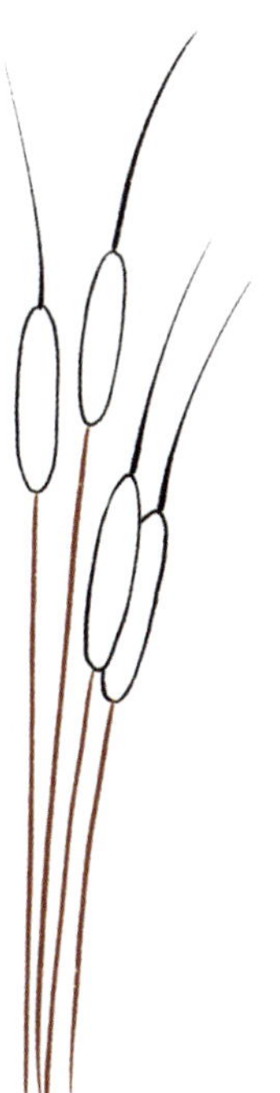

STEP 3 Create wispy lines at the top of each oval for the cattails' unique flowering spikes.

STEP 4 Draw the stems bunching together toward the bottom.

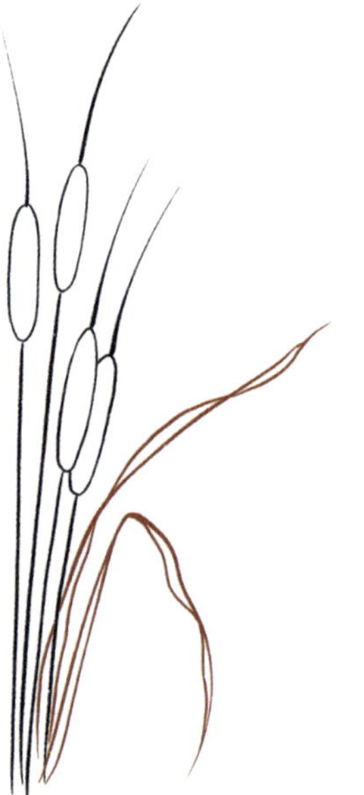

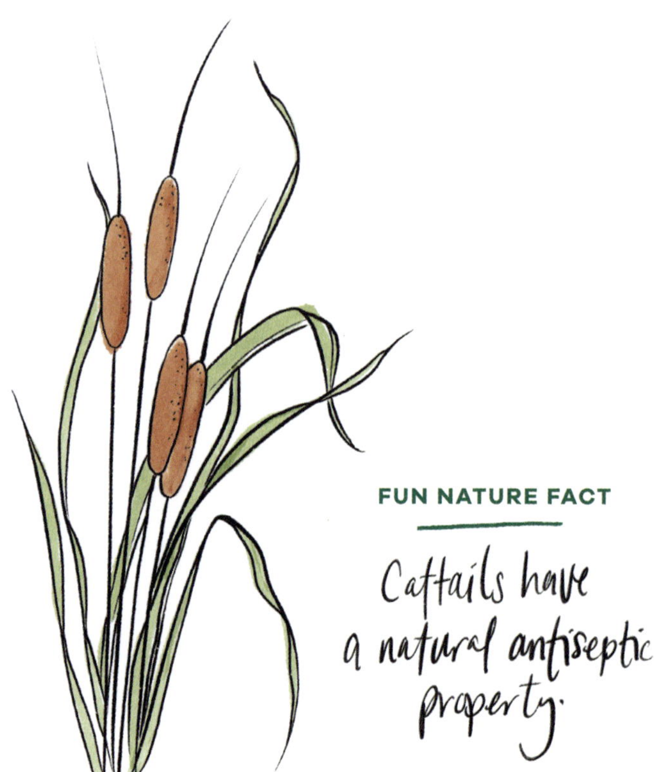

TO ADD COLOR If you decide you want to add color, cattails are a nice warm brown with light yellow-green leaves.

Saguaro Cactus

When we see drawings of cacti in the desert, most of the time they're of the saguaro. Did you know that saguaro is pronounced with a soft *G*? And it's not like a soft *G* that sounds like an *H*. It actually sounds like a *W*: suh-WAH-roh. When I found out, this blew my mind and I felt like everything I knew was a lie (ha)!

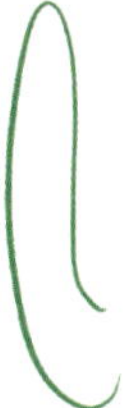

STEP 1 Draw an oval shape that will make up one of the arms of the cactus. Although you can start with the main part, starting with an arm will let it overlap just enough to give a little dimension. Draw the bottom part of this arm curled under.

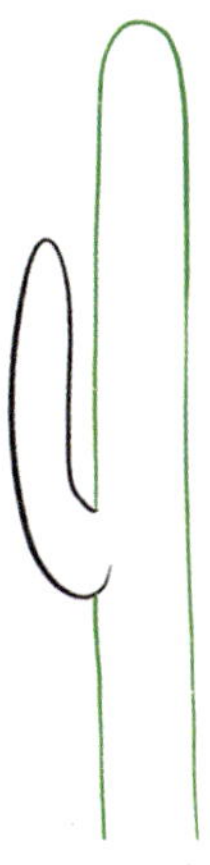

STEP 2 Add the main part now. Starting from the top open end of the first shape, draw a straight line upward, arch over in a C-curve, and draw a straight line down. For the base, instead of connecting to the edge of the bottom of the arm, move outward slightly and draw a line straight down from its curve. See? Now it looks like that arm is on the front.

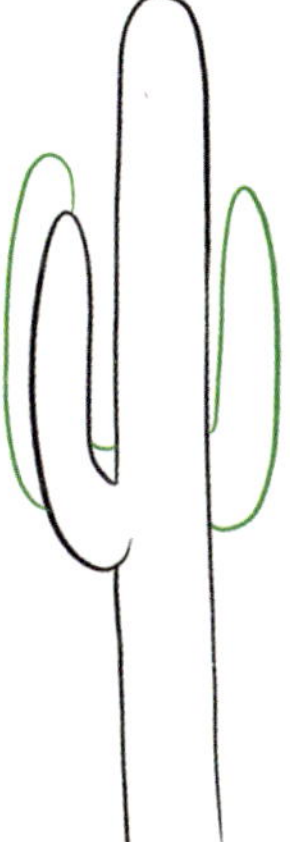

STEP 3 Adding to the dimensional aspect of our cactus, we'll now draw two more arms, one on the right side and one on the left, overlapped by the first arm we drew. Simply draw a line up a bit higher from the base of the first arm, hugged close to its side. Curve it around and then connect the downward line to the top of the first arm. Finish this arm by drawing another line in the gap between the first arm and the main stalk.

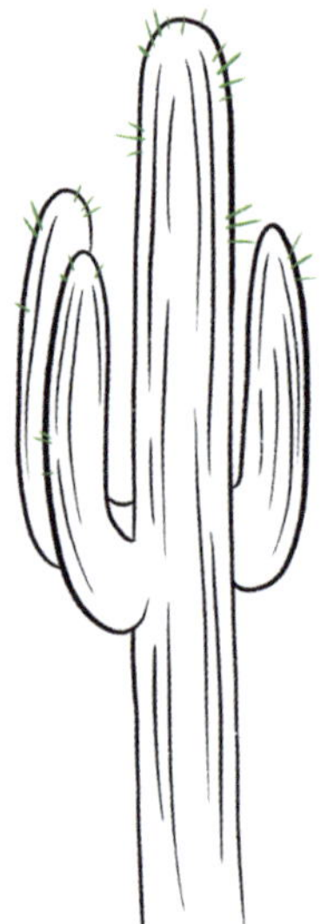

STEP 4 Add some thin lines inside each section for texture. Last, draw a few spines sprouting from the cactus.

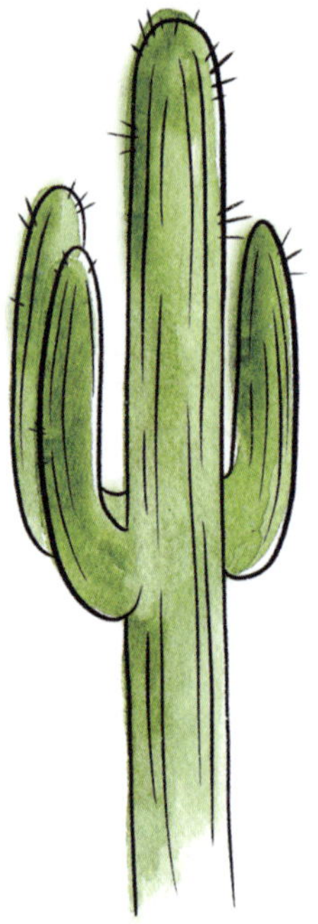

FUN NATURE FACT

Saguaros have antiaging properties.

TO ADD COLOR Lay your first color down and let it dry. Use the same color to add another layer along the edge on one side of each arm to create depth.

Lily Pad

Lily pads are often accompanied by frogs and fish in tranquil settings, such as ponds and water gardens. They're a natural habitat feature for frogs, protecting them from predators. Lily pads can be easily drawn from above in the shape of a pie with a slice removed.

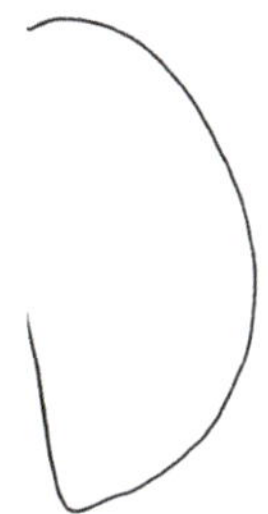

STEP 1 Begin with the first half of the lily pad by drawing an angled line downward from the middle. When you reach the bottom, draw a C-curve upward to form the first half of the circle.

STEP 2 Repeat the first step on the other side to complete the second half of the circle.

STEP 3 Draw a thin line from the middle of the circle upward toward the top. This line gives the illusion of a little crease in the pad. Then draw a few light lines directed from the center outward. These lines won't reach the edges of the circle.

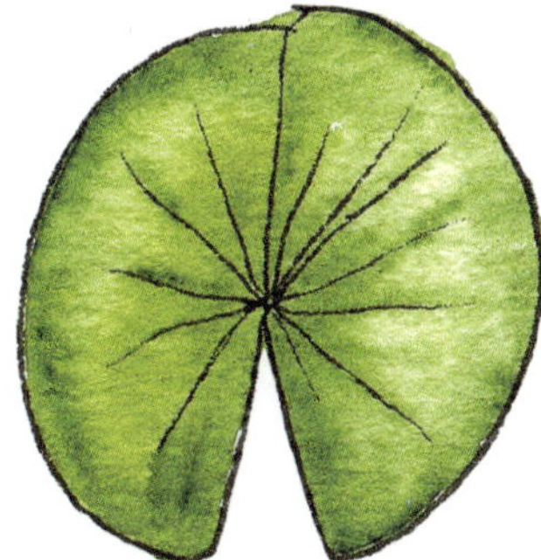

FUN NATURE FACT

TO ADD COLOR Using the wet-on-wet technique, apply a layer of water, then a layer of green, then another layer of slightly darker green along the edges. Dab some darker color in the center as well. Adding a deeper color to the edges and center will accentuate the lighter areas, making the lily pad look like it has a little lift.

THE FISH STUDY

Let's look at drawing fish for funsies. You might be thinking you'll never bother drawing fish. I challenge you to give it a try. They're magical little guys, and if nothing else, you'll learn how to draw half of a mermaid (and you can't deny that you love that idea).

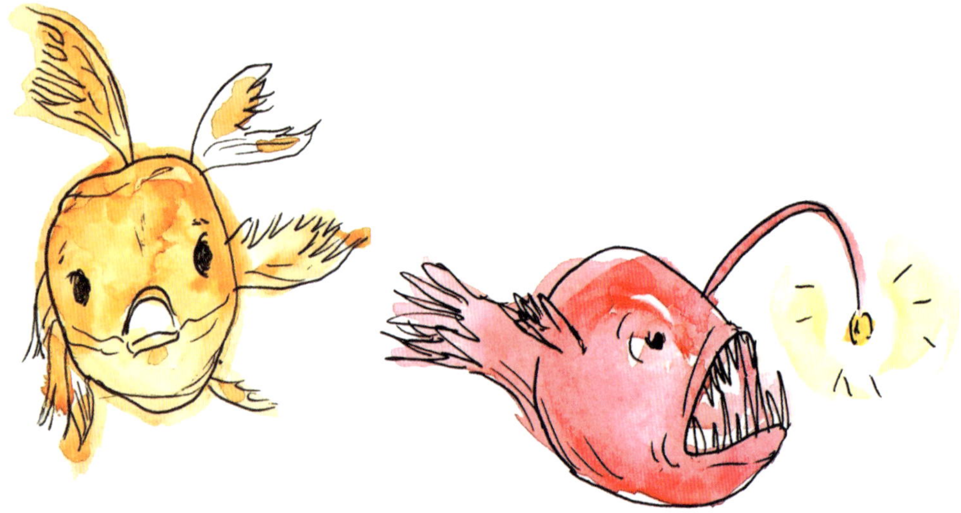

Before we start, I have to share some random facts about fish. #themoreyouknow, right? Here are some bizarre things that you'll probably never actually need to know.

- The ocellated icefish has transparent blood. Like, it's clear.

- Sheepshead fish have teeth shaped like human teeth. Look it up. You're about to either get freaked out or have a real good laugh.

- A school of herring can have upward of three billion fish. Not thousands, not millions . . . billions.

- Most fishes have tastebuds all over their bodies and can taste things without opening their mouths.

- There's a city in Honduras where locals believe it rains fish! The *New York Times* published an article on it in 2017.

- Some species of fish are able to change their sex.

- The lungfish, as its name implies, has gills but also a lung. Because of this, it can live without water for years.

- The plural "fish" refers to only one species, while the plural "fishes" refers to multiple species.

The fish we'll draw are all based on the same shapes; we'll just stretch, shorten, widen, and alter them in other ways to represent different species. If you can still draw that fish you drew as a kid, you can draw a fish. You know the one, that loop with a tail that only takes one pen stroke? And there's nothing wrong with still using that little fish now in doodles! It's like using the two connected arches for birds. It has just enough detail to show what it is, and doodles are all about staying fun.

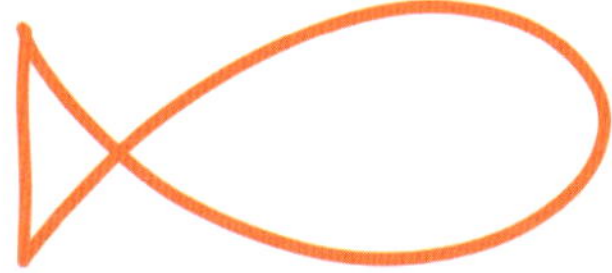

Fish From the Side

If you decide to take it a step further, the beginning of all your mermaid-drawing desires starts here. Let's look at the main shape and lines we'll be using to draw fish. We'll start by identifying a fish's parts. Its body is an oblong shape with different sides. One end is its little mouth. (For some reason, anytime I call something its name with the word "little" in front of it, it's automatically adorable. That's how I picture the mouths of fish . . . adorable.) The other side of the oblong shape is the most recognizable: the tail. I say that because of those doodles I mentioned before. We didn't bother drawing all of a fish's fins when we first started drawing that one-stroke fish; we just knew the fin was a tail and that's all that mattered. Well, we're building on that idea. The shape of this fin varies depending on the type of fish. We're going to start with a flowing tail with a middle split. Then, we've got four other fins: the dorsal fin, the pectoral fin, the ventral fin, and the anal fin. After that, we'll add the eye, scales, and fin details! I'll take you through it step by step.

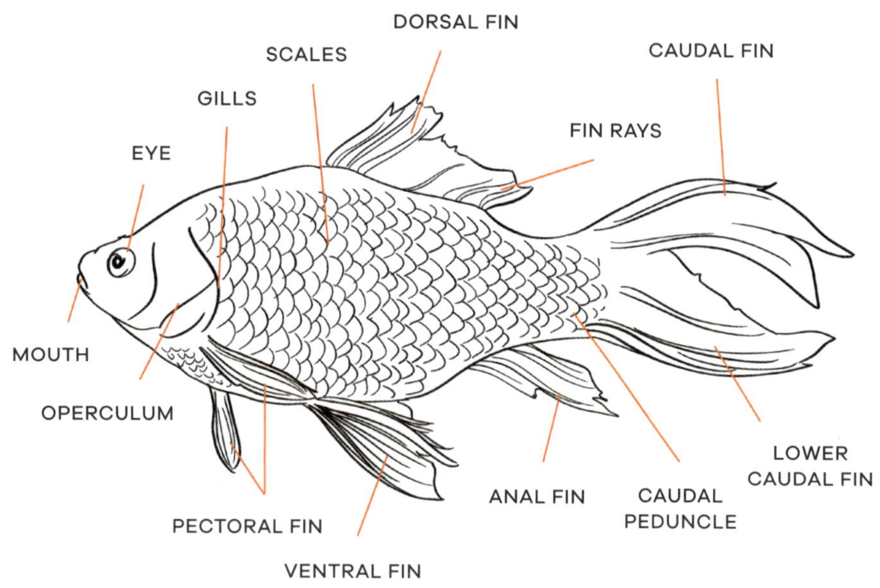

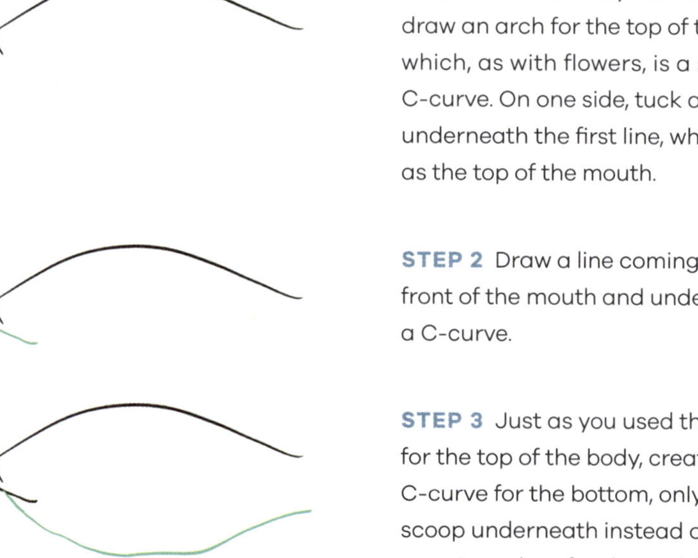

STEP 1 For the body's oblong shape, draw an arch for the top of the body, which, as with flowers, is a simple C-curve. On one side, tuck a short line underneath the first line, which will act as the top of the mouth.

STEP 2 Draw a line coming from the front of the mouth and under again in a C-curve.

STEP 3 Just as you used the C-curve for the top of the body, create another C-curve for the bottom, only this time scoop underneath instead of arching over. Don't be afraid to wobble your lines a bit. It'll make the fish look a little more realistic.

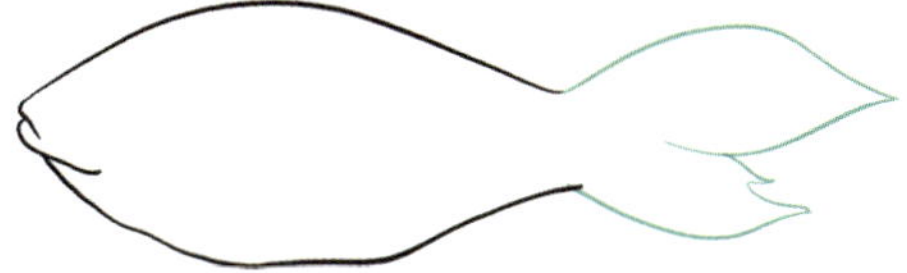

STEP 4 The other side, opposite the mouth, is going to feature that beautiful tail, which is actually called the caudal fin. First, draw a soft S-curve, followed with another underneath. Leave a gap for the second part of the fin, which will mimic the first part. Try adding a small second point to the tip of the lower caudal fin for a little more character.

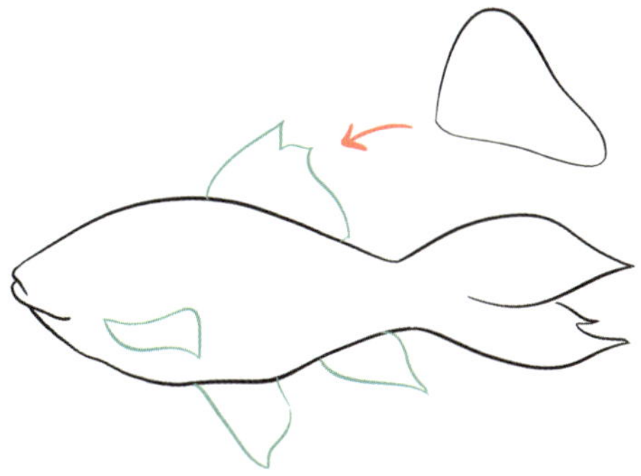

STEP 5 The rest of the fins take the shape of a triangle. If you can visual-ize this shape as you draw them with C-curves and S-curves, the added details come easy. You're no longer looking at a complicated object to capture. Instead, you have a base to work from.

Notice that the top (dorsal) fin takes on the triangle shape almost perfectly. See where it dips down on the top? That's all you need to do to create the outer line details. The other fins mimic the same shape. You can create them slightly wider or shallower. Remember: The base shapes are there as a reference. They shouldn't be taken literally or you'll have a bunch of triangles all over your fish.

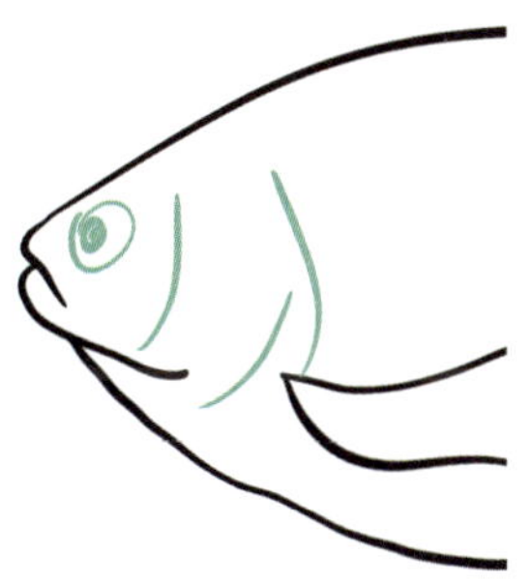

STEP 6 Draw the eye of the fish, which is found very close to the front of the body. Depending on the fish, the eye could be very small or quite large. Some fish even have eyes that bulge out from their bodies, resembling little bubbles. I happen to love those. Next, use C-curves to add gills.

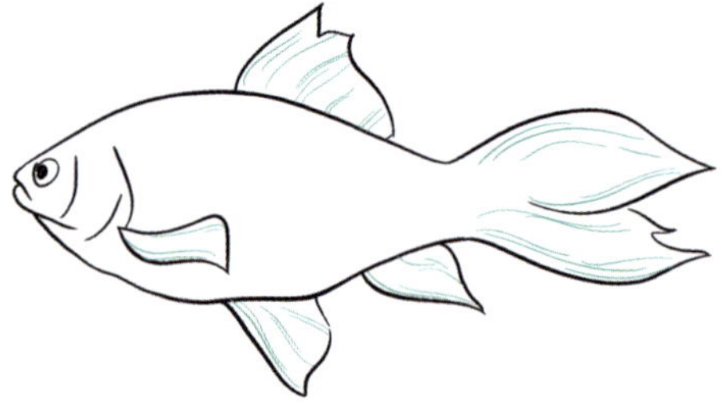

STEP 7 We need to get some details on this guy. These fins aren't heavily structured, instead, they give more of a flowing appearance. When this is the case, we want soft, curved lines that follow the natural direction of the fin. Remind you of anything? If you thought flower petals—bingo. Isn't it great when art comes full circle?

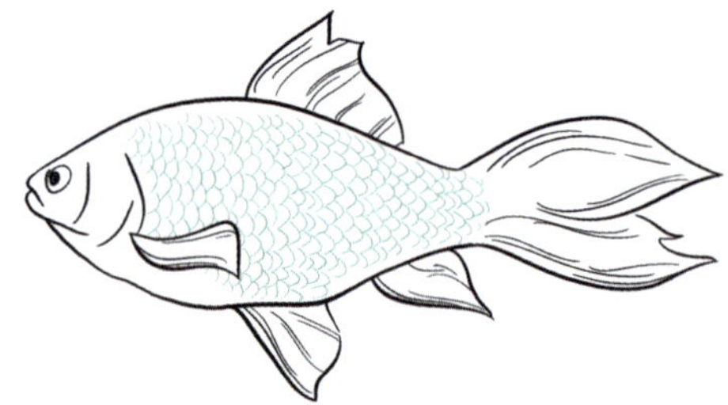

STEP 8 Add some small C-curve scales to the body and you're done!

Fish from Above

Unless we're diving or viewing a majestic aquarium setup, we mostly see fish from above. One of the most elegant, graceful fish is the regal koi. They can be found in peaceful water gardens and ponds all over the world. There's actually not a natural habitat for koi, as they were originally bred from the common carp in the 1800s for domestication in Japan and used for decorative purposes and food. Today, they're not often eaten but rather kept for their beautiful color varieties and as companions. Yep—companions! It turns out they're quite friendly.

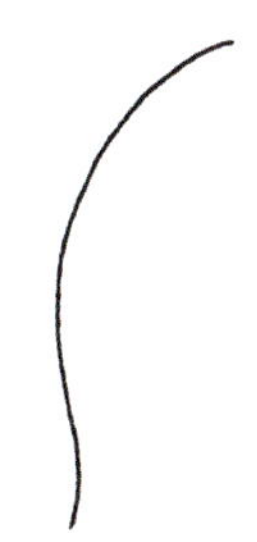

STEP 1 Begin with an S-curve, focusing on a large curve at the top.

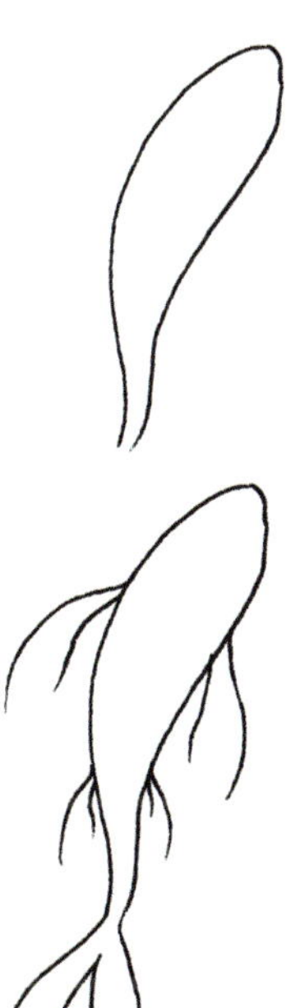

STEP 2 From the top, curve outward in the opposite direction, creating another S-curve. This line will taper inward so the bottom is very narrow.

STEP 3 There are three areas to focus on when drawing fins on koi from above. Just under the widest area toward the top, draw two C-curves on each side.

Do this again just under the middle of the fish. The top C-curves in each set should be a bit longer than the bottom ones. At the bottom, draw two long C-curves that arch outward. Now, instead of another set of C-curves, create a small V-shape just inside the bottom two C-curves.

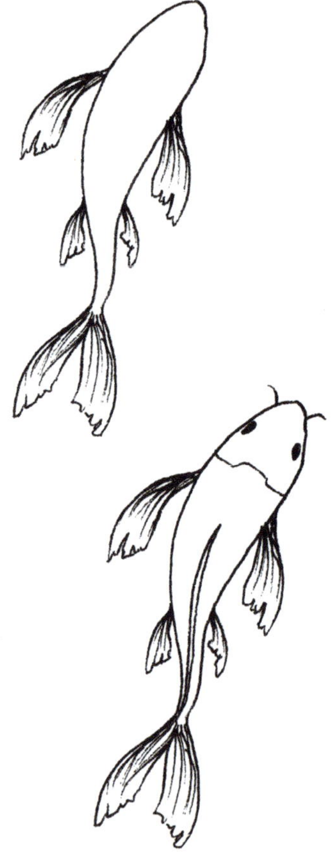

STEP 4 Connect the two C-curves in each section with a jagged line.

Now, use your mark-making skills to create some texture in the fins. Starting from the body, flick your pen downward in the same angle that the fin is traveling. Think of this as guided hatching. Add more depth near the body and get wispier toward the end of each fin.

STEP 5 It's time to make this fish come to life!

Add two oval-shaped eyes toward the top of the body.

Add two whiskers coming from the top of the fish with two small C-curves. These little whiskers are actually called barbels (and barbels have tastebuds, so koi can taste things without even opening their mouths!).

Draw a very light curved line across the widest point of the fish, accentuating where the head meets the body.

Now draw a center line that follows the S-curve of the body. Draw another line right next to it, connecting to two points at the top and bottom.

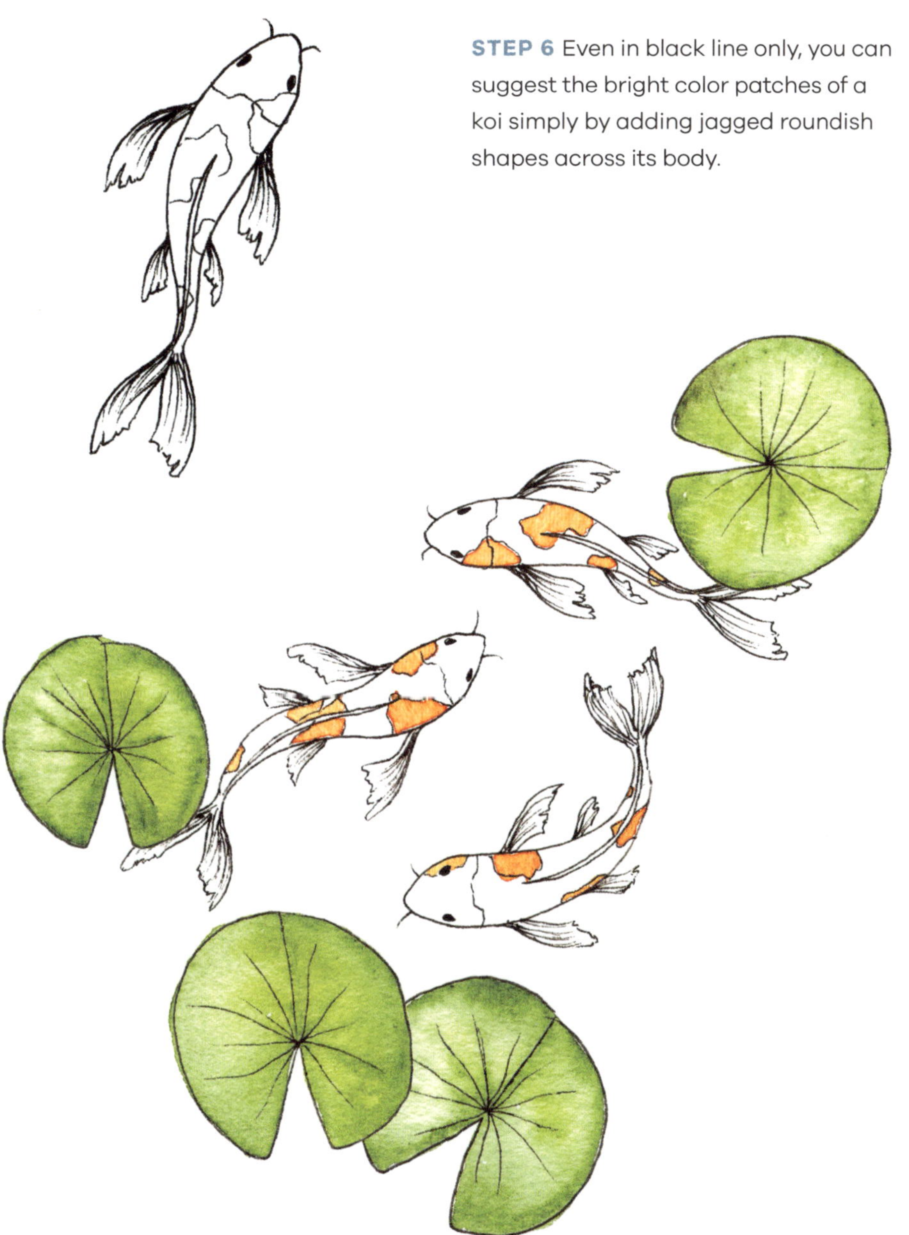

TO ADD COLOR Try using spot color. Some koi fish have lovely orange and sometimes black markings, so let's apply orange only to enhance them.

Watch, now you're going to be drawing fish all the time. Forget the mermaid idea. You're welcome.

THE BIRD STUDY

When I think of birds, I feel relaxed and energized all at once. Their spring energy and sweet chirps in the morning sun pair perfectly with a glass of lemonade and the daily crossword. I'm pretty certain that if you were to start listening to a relaxation soundtrack you'd hear some birdsongs.

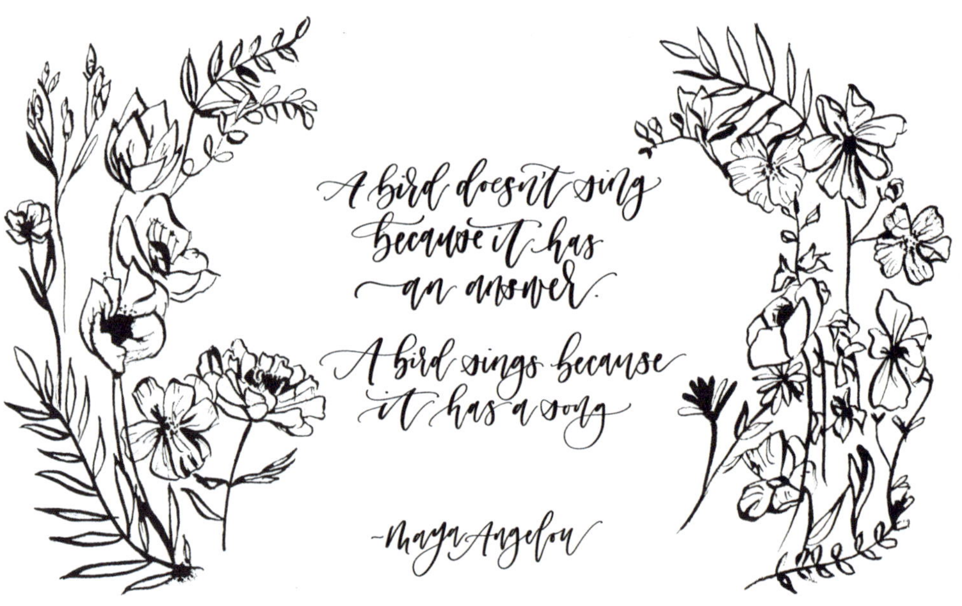

Here are some weird bird facts I bet you didn't know.

- I once heard on NPR that there are certain bird species, including blue jays and cardinals, that engage in an activity called anting, in which they rub ants, crushed or alive, all over their bodies. There are theories about why they do it, but we have yet to solve the mystery.

- Bassian thrushes find food by repeatedly farting. You didn't misread that. This worm eater's flatulence disturbs the earthworms and reveals their location.

- Turkey vultures use vomit as a defense mechanism against predators. They can blast it up to ten feet, and it's effective. I worry about their throats.

- Bearded vultures are like that aunt who has a new hair color every time she comes over. We all know the character I'm talking about. The *National Geographic* website mentions that this vulture soaks its feathers in natural substances to add beautiful highlights to its plumage.

- The California condor is mistaken for a small airplane more often than it is for another bird due to its massive wingspan. This bird unfortunately became extinct in the wild in 1987, but with much effort after purposeful breeding, it was reintroduced into the wild in 1991.

- Pigeons have been used as message carriers as early as the time of the ancient Persians. Homing pigeons were also used by the US military in World War I and World War II.

Okay, enough weird. Let's draw a simple bird.

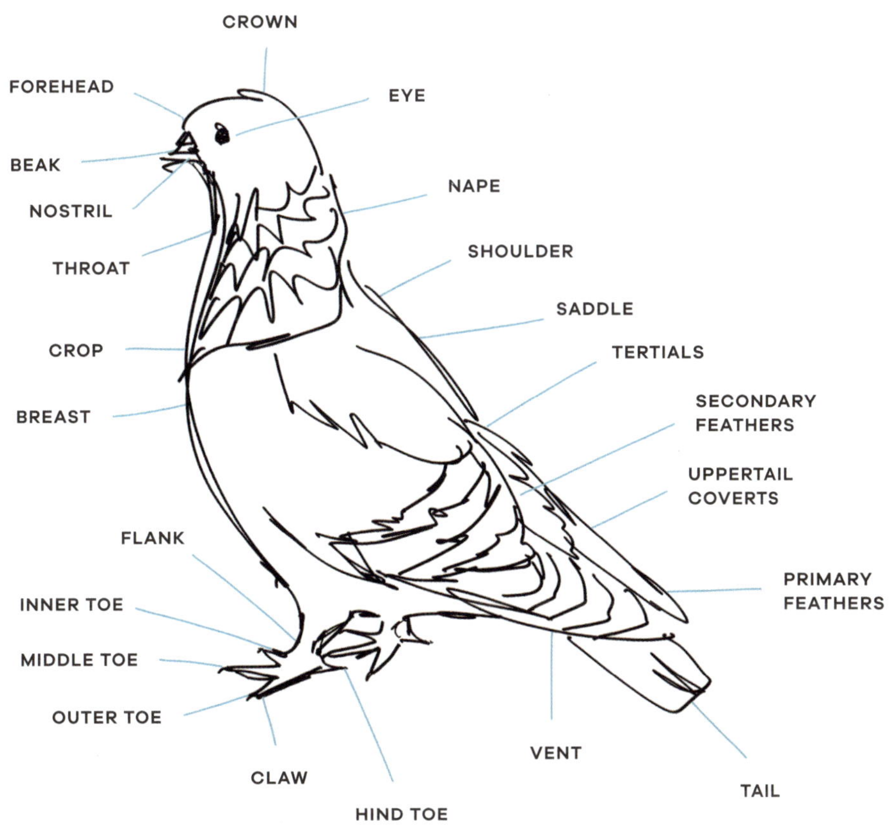

Birds from the Side

Just as we did with the fish, we're going to build a bird with shapes. For some, drawing a bird can be a little trickier, so it might help to use a pencil to create some preliminary shapes.

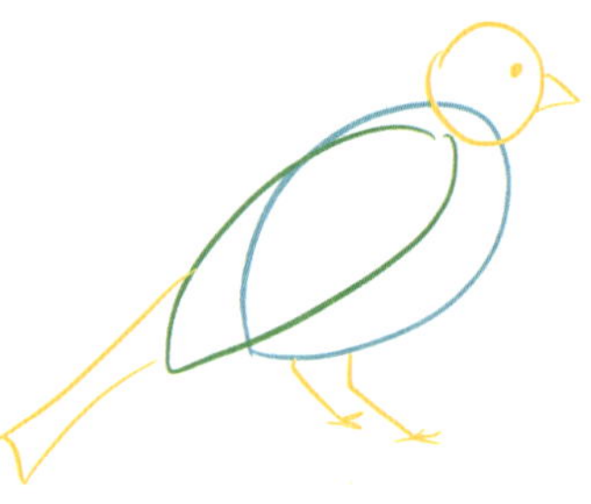

STEP 1 Notice that our bird is made up of a slanted oval shape (blue) for the body, a narrower oblong shape (green) that sits toward the top half of the first oval for the wing, a circle and triangle (yellow) that sits on top of the oval body for the head and beak, a long rectangle (yellow) for the tail, and two legs coming off of the oval body. It's pretty simple when it's broken down this way. When you start to draw the bird itself, use these shapes as reference, but smooth out the transitions.

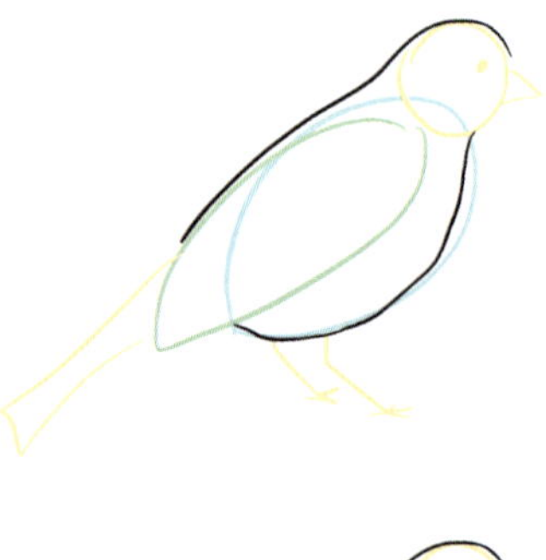

STEP 2 Look at the black lines. Add a wobbly C-curve on the bottom and a lesser curved line on the top. The top line has more of an arch for the top of the head, then softly slopes downward with a slight arch over the top of the body.

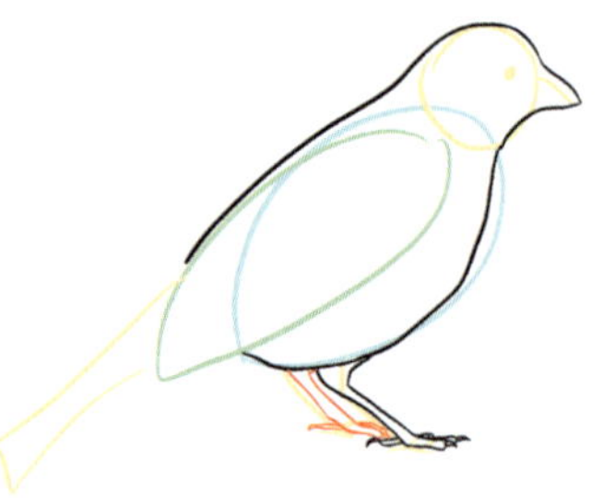

STEP 3 Next, add the beak. The head is rounded down and then out for the top of the beak, followed by a C-curve that tucks underneath to create the neck. I've also started drawing its legs, but whoa . . . what's the deal with that foot?! It looks intimidating, but it doesn't have to be.

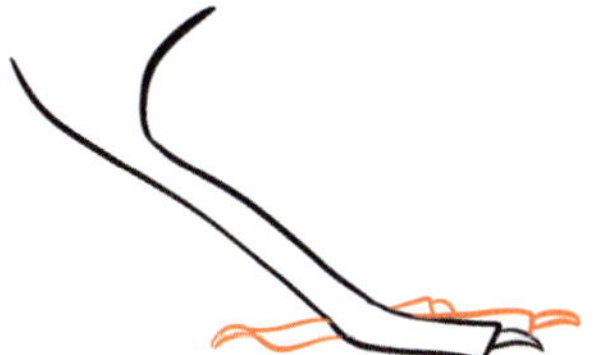

STEP 4 Let's zoom in. We know the leg needs to attach to the body, so the top of the leg is in a shape like a funnel. Instead of traveling downward in a straight line, birds' legs are angled forward, and then the angled lines flatten at the bottom. It's like a long, bent rectangle. Add a small C-curved point for a claw. Then just tuck some of those tiny rectangles with claws behind the first one and finally add one more going in the other direction. That's not so bad, right?

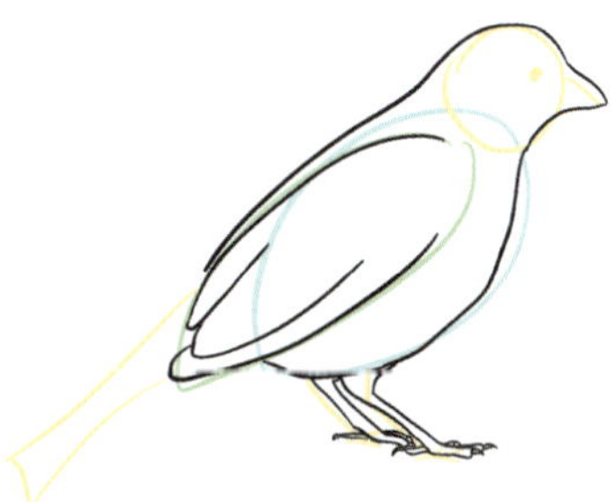

STEP 5 Onto the wing. I'm not going to overcomplicate this. The top of the wing is curved downward from the shoulder in a C-curve, then tucked under to give the appearance of a feather. The bottom line does the same. Next, a middle feather is drawn in a soft U-shape that pulls the two lines together.

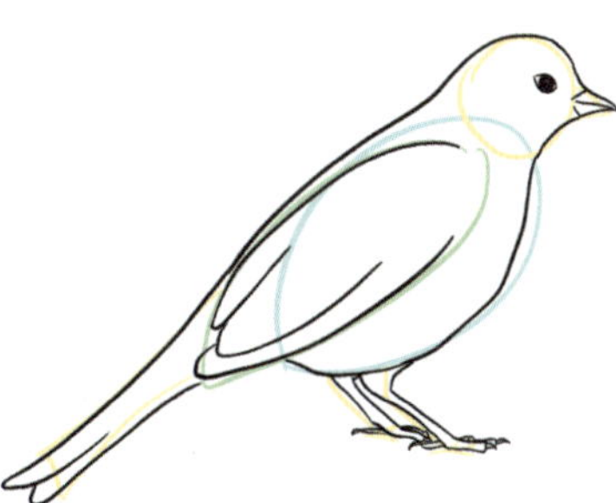

STEP 6 Time for those tail feathers. Just as we drew the wings with a slight curve to give the appearance of feathers, we'll slightly curve the ends of two lines to create the tail. From there, add an eye and a line in the center of the beak, and you're done!

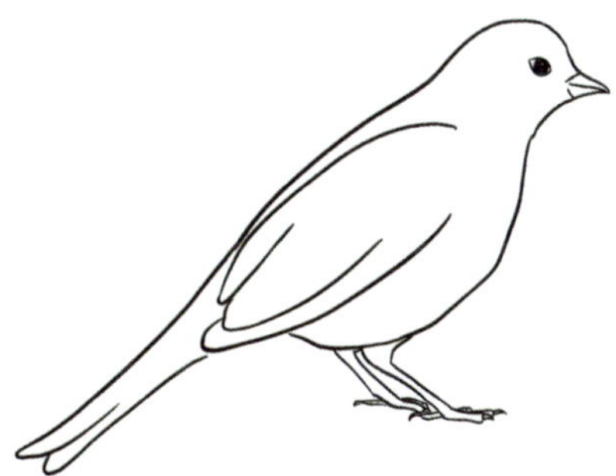

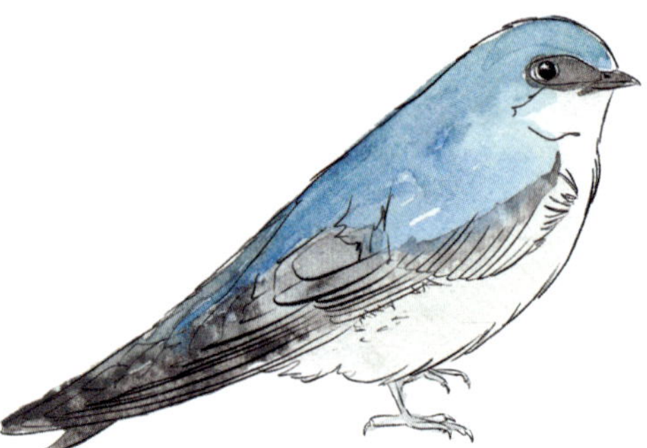

TO ADD COLOR Splash some color along the top of your bird, a darker color along the wings and tail, and a lighter color for its chest.

Birds from Below

Go outside and look up. It might take a second, but if you stand out there for a bit, you're bound to see a bird or fifty flying high above you in the sky. From below, a bird's underbelly is exposed and its broad wingspan epitomizes freedom. Changing our perspective can create some unique pieces of art.

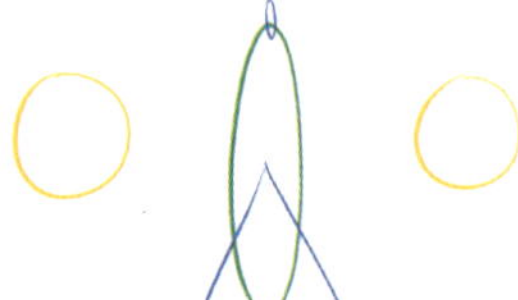

STEP 1 Lay out some guidelines.

- Draw an oval (green) for the body of the bird.

- Leave some space on each side about the same width as the oval and draw two circles (yellow).

- Leave a little more space this time and create a much smaller circle on each side.

- Draw a triangle (blue) from the center of the oval to the bottom of the oval.

- Draw a tiny oval at the top.

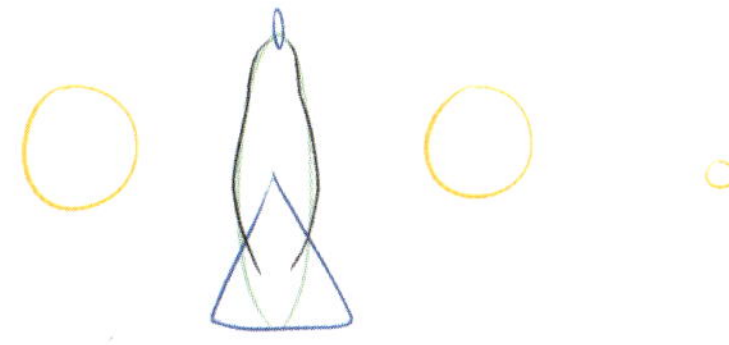

STEP 2 Begin drawing the bird by starting at the top, forming the head. Curve your line outward and then back inward toward the top to form the neck, then curve outward again, stopping in the middle of the triangle. Draw these lines on each side.

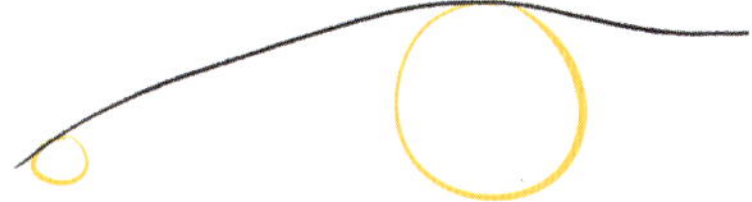

STEP 3 Starting at the indent at the top of the oval (or the neck), draw an S-curve to form the top of each wing. This line should dip downward slightly and curve upward again around the circle guide, then stop at the outermost circle.

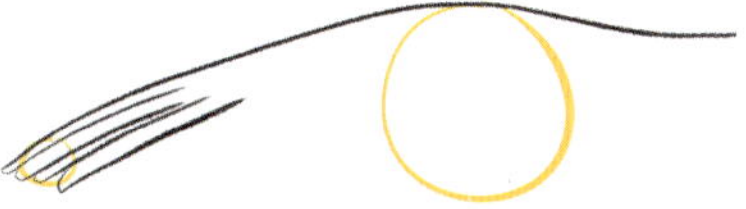

STEP 4 Begin forming feathers in the wings by drawing lines that connect to each other in little C-curves that straighten inside each feather. Depending on which bird you choose, you may want to stagger a couple of feathers in the wing. Doing a quick image search online of your favorite bird will be helpful in determining these characteristics.

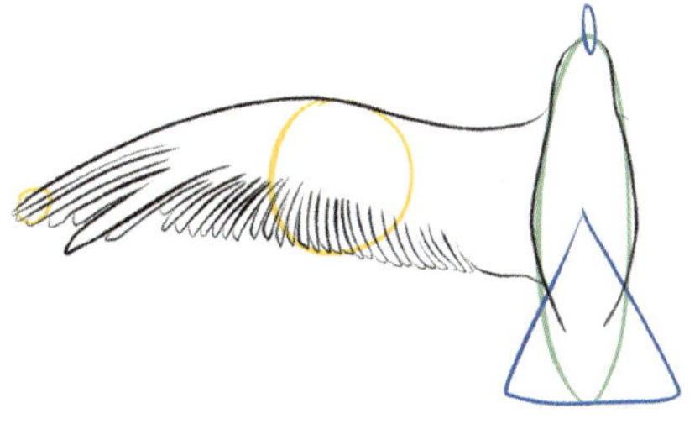

STEP 5 As you get closer to the body of the bird, make each inner feather line shorter so the feathers taper. Connect the wings to the body with a final small horizontal line.

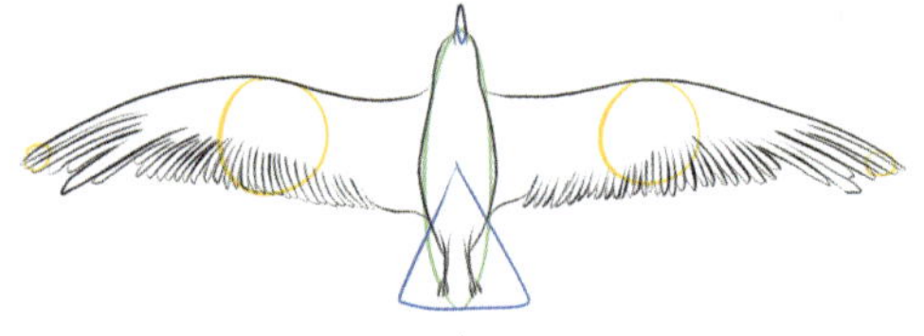

 Follow the small oval guide at the top of the bird's body to add its beak. Then add the bird's legs and feet. Just inside the bottom of the main oval of the bird's body, draw two concave C-curves very close to each other for each leg, then smaller C-curves to make the feet.

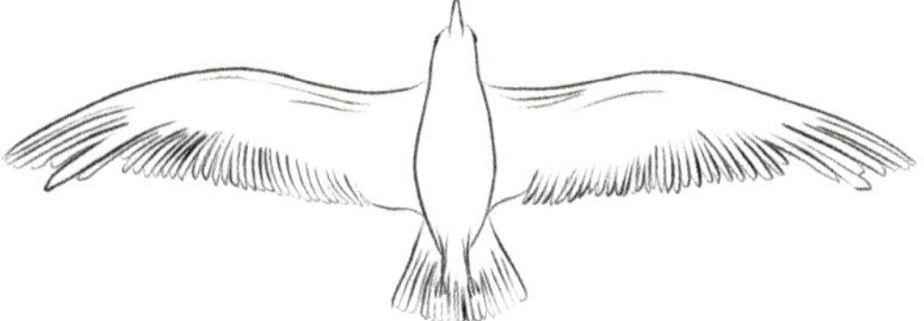

STEP 7 Follow the triangular guide to draw the bird's tail just as you did the wings. That's it!

PUT IT ALL TOGETHER

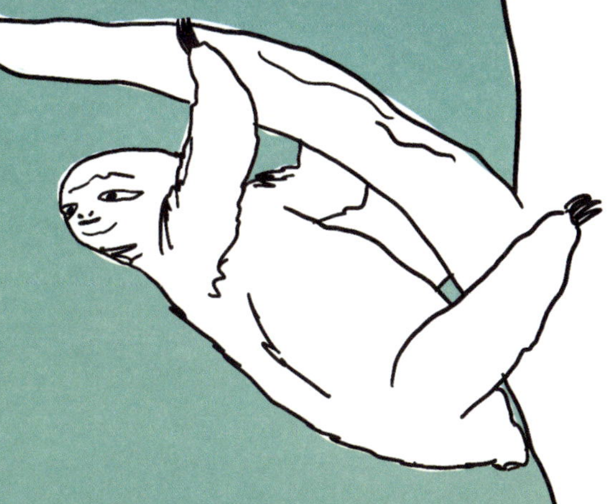

One of the things that we too often neglect in our very personal creative journey is celebrating milestones. We start out with a goal and we work crazy-hard to achieve it and we end up adding new elements to those goals and forget to pay attention to the progress we're making. It's all about those steps it takes to get there. It's far too easy to see examples of the things we aspire to do and create and compare our work with negative reflection. If you want something bad enough, though, you must commit to the process. And when you've made it to your goal—because trust me, if you're committed and you put in the practice, you will get there—when you've made it, you most likely won't realize it. Why? Because at that point your big goal will be different than today's big goal. You'll be shooting higher, reaching further. And that's okay. Here's some good news: You've made it this far. You've committed to the process. Take time to reflect on that. When you first sat down and opened this book, you were starting a journey in hopes of getting to this point, and now you're here. That desire to get better and improve your skillset is an undying passion that you should embrace and celebrate! At one point, your goal was to be where you are RIGHT NOW. Celebrate this moment. Celebrate your journey. You've done an amazing job. Go you!

You've just been on an exploration discovering drawing techniques such as curves, mark making, working with different angles and perspectives, and you've also played with color. You've discovered how to get your desired finish with just a little brush control and paint. You've learned about dozens of natural items, including leaves, flowers, and birds and fish. But there's so much more to explore! That's the best part about nature and about art. It goes on and on. Let's merge some of the things we've covered by moving into composition, landscapes, and more!

FLOWER ARRANGEMENTS

Bouquets make for some of the most beautiful illustrations, but where do you start? How do you arrange flowers and fillers and greenery to make the right composition? The first thing to think about is where you want your focal point. What flowers do you want to stand out the most? What mood do you want to evoke? Do you want something classic? Perhaps a carefree, unstructured bunch of wildflowers? Your primary flower is your eye-catcher. You don't want a secondary flower to drown out a classic bouquet of roses, as the primary flower is what sets the mood. Bouquets are dimensional, so these flowers should be staggered in height and some might sit at an angle or be seen from behind. This is a stylistic choice, just as many other facets of our lessons are. When we draw flowers with their faces pointed our way, it creates more of a doodle-like effect—playful and youthful.

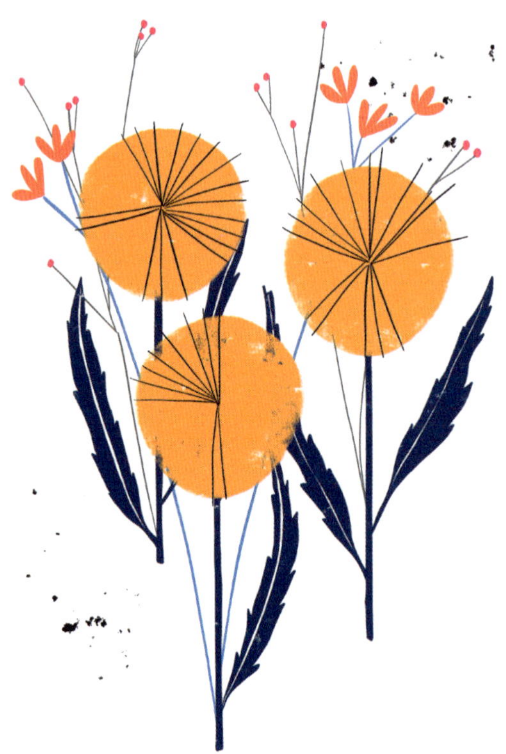

Classic Bouquet

Timeless and sophisticated, classic bouquets have a clean, compact, shapely silhouette. I typically start with three flowers as a focal point. They can be facing outward, upward, or angled. Refer back to The Flower Study on pages 100–123 if you need some flower inspiration.

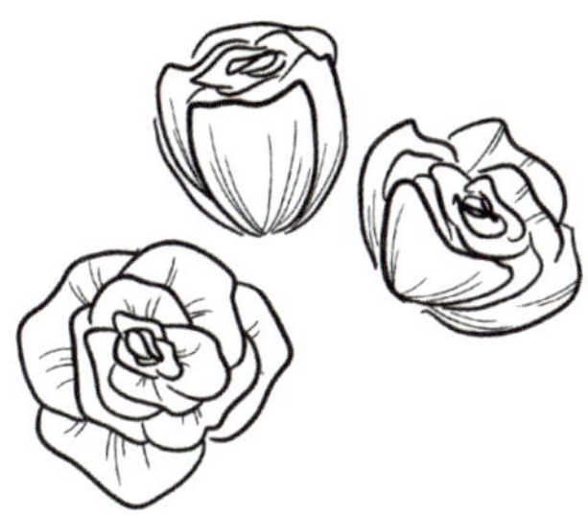

STEP 1 First draw three flowers, and angle them to the left, right, and center. In this example, I've drawn all three angles of a rose.

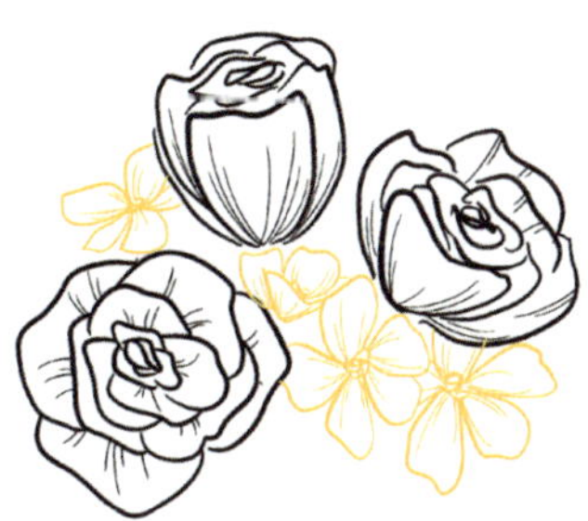

STEP 2 Next, add some secondary flowers. These flowers aren't small enough to be considered filler flowers (like baby's breath), but they're small enough that they won't draw attention away from my main three flowers. Tuck these flowers behind the others if it makes sense. You want to fill in that empty space.

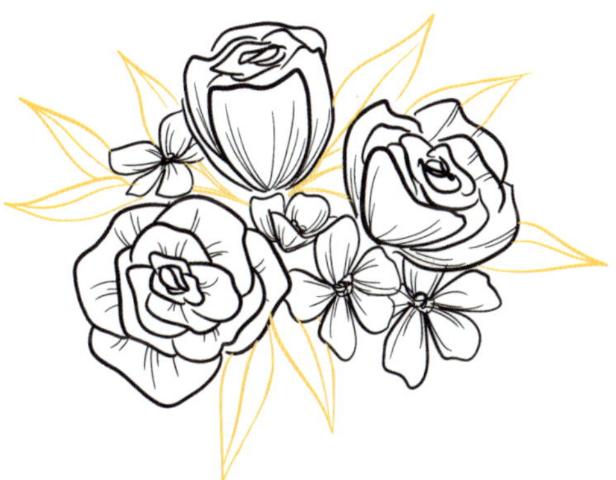

STEP 3 Choose three main points where the leaves will branch out and then add them there in different quantities. For example, the top left has three leaves while the bottom has two and the right has three that are spaced farther apart; make them all different so they won't look forced. You can choose to keep the illustration as is, or you can add stems to each leaf and flower.

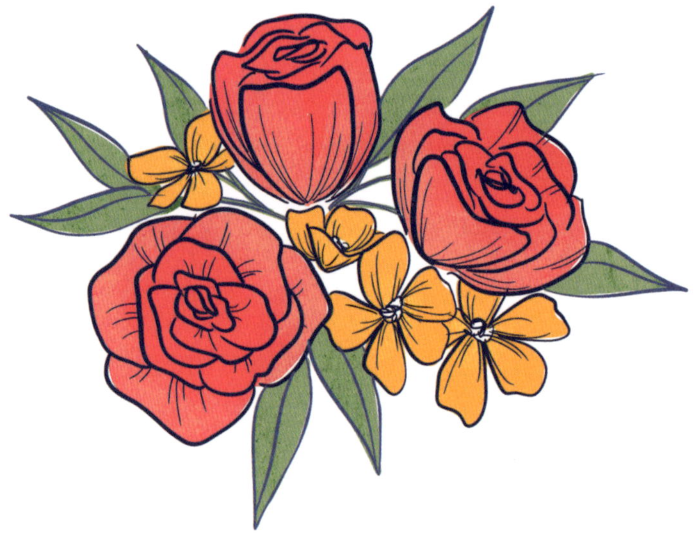

 Try a particular color scheme to evoke a mood. I opted for some warm red and orange tones. You could try pinks or royal blue and violet.

Wildflower Bouquet

Wildflower bouquets are loose and unkempt. Drawing these involves more organic and loose drawing. Let yourself go and forget the rules. It's a beautiful thing, embracing imperfection. Let's walk through an example. Several of these shapes aren't specific flowers but imaginary. Get creative and see what comes out when you think of wildflowers. And don't underestimate weeds. They have a bad rap, but they can also be quite lovely. Small details can often shine even more than a full scene. A simple leaf instead of a bouquet, a weed instead of a field of flowers, and even a single feather instead of a bird will stand out when featured in an art piece.

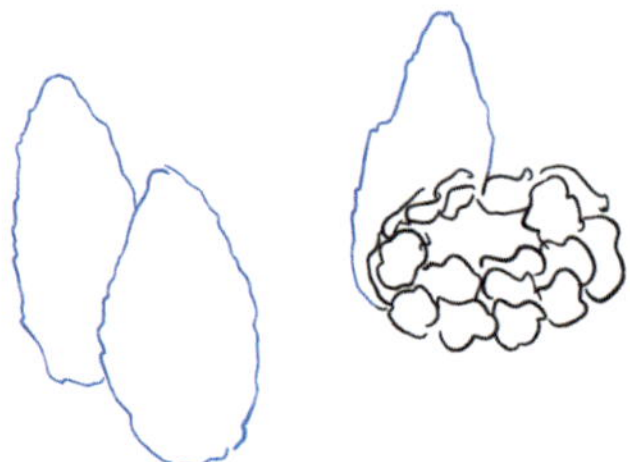

STEP 1 Draw a cluster of small, wavy circles. Keep the upper center of the cluster open. Add some jagged-lined oval shapes with tops that are narrower than the bottoms. Place these randomly.

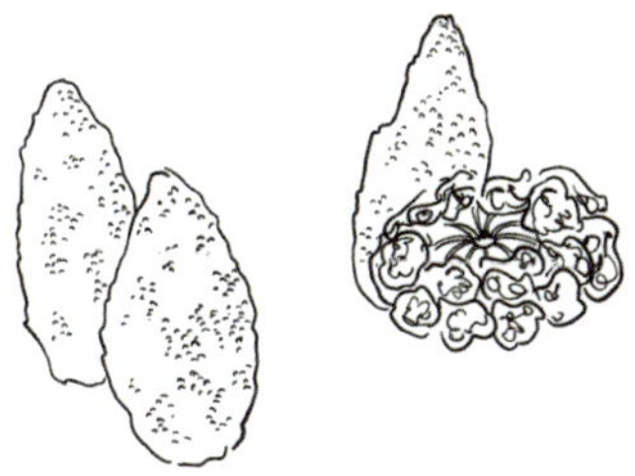

STEP 2 Add small scribbles to the insides of the first shape you drew. Add tiny C-curves to create patches on the oval shapes.

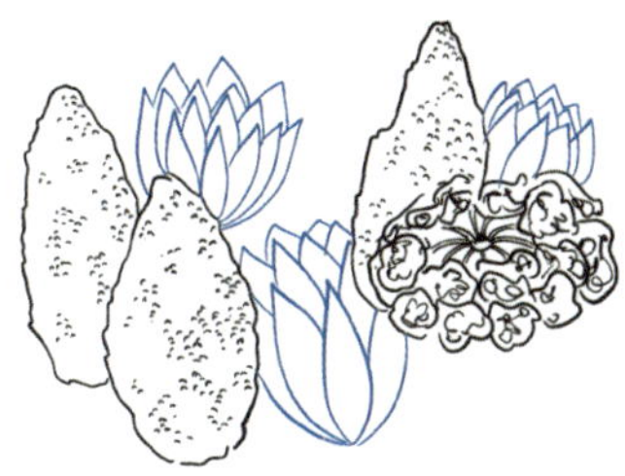

STEP 3 Tuck a few flowers into the background. Create simple petals that have C-curves and meet at a point. Overlap these petals until you have a full flower. Use the middle, sides, tops, whatever fits best in your illustration. When you're finished, add simple line work coming from the petals' bases, adding those details we love so much.

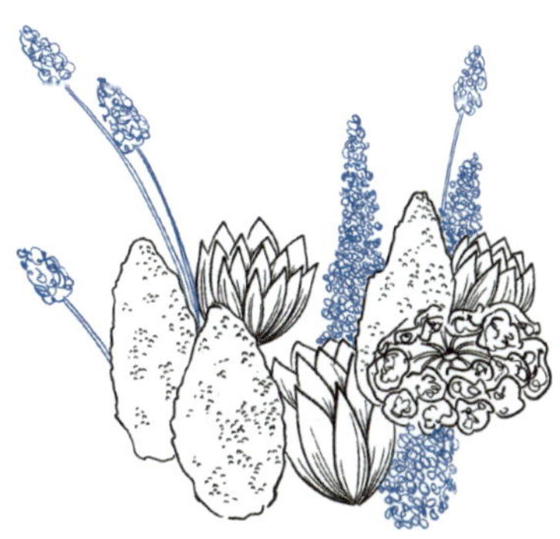

STEP 4 Next, draw tiny circles, almost in a scribbling motion, to create long narrow shapes with pointed tips. Draw a few of these on stems as well. The stems should reach higher and wider than the center of the bouquet. We're starting to stir things up.

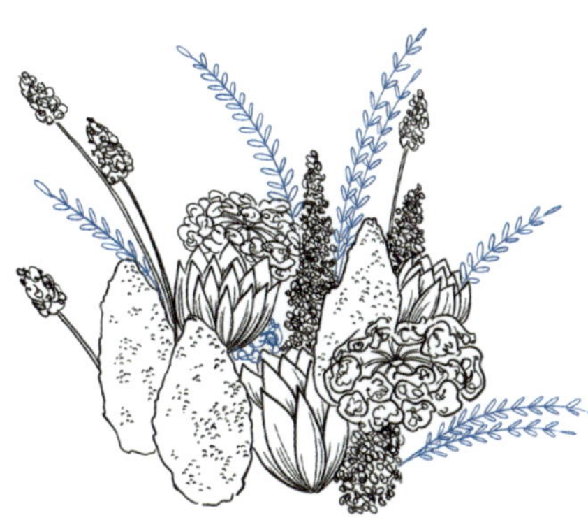

STEP 5 Create additional stems reaching upward and outward, only this time add tiny leaves in loop shapes all the way down. At this point, you may notice some sparse areas or holes near the top or sides of your bouquet. You can fill in these areas with flowers you've already used in the composition.

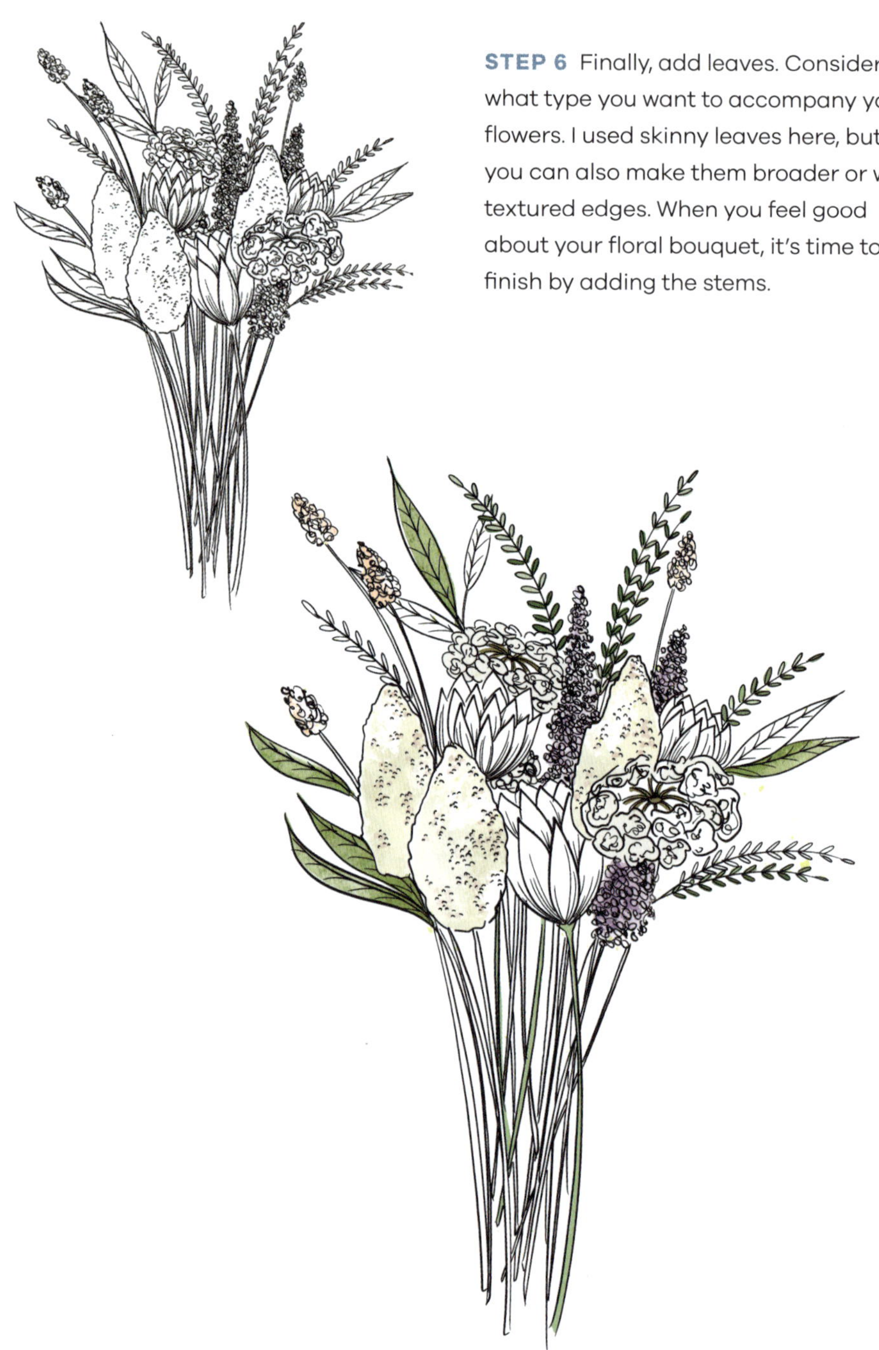

TO ADD COLOR Try a palette of neutral tones, like buff and ochré, and muted greens, like sage and olive. Experiment with leaving some elements uncolored.

Floral Wreaths

You know how adding a banner to something makes it look more complete? The same goes for wreaths. There's something truly lovely about framing a word, announcement, or photo with a pretty floral wreath. They are easier to draw than they appear. I'm going to teach you a trick that will squash the idea that you can't draw a circle without the right tool. I actually came up with this on the fly when I was teaching a holiday wreath workshop to a crowd of fifty people and didn't have anything to draw a circle with! Worse, I didn't have anything for anyone else to draw a circle with. Empower yourself. You're creative. You're resourceful. You got this.

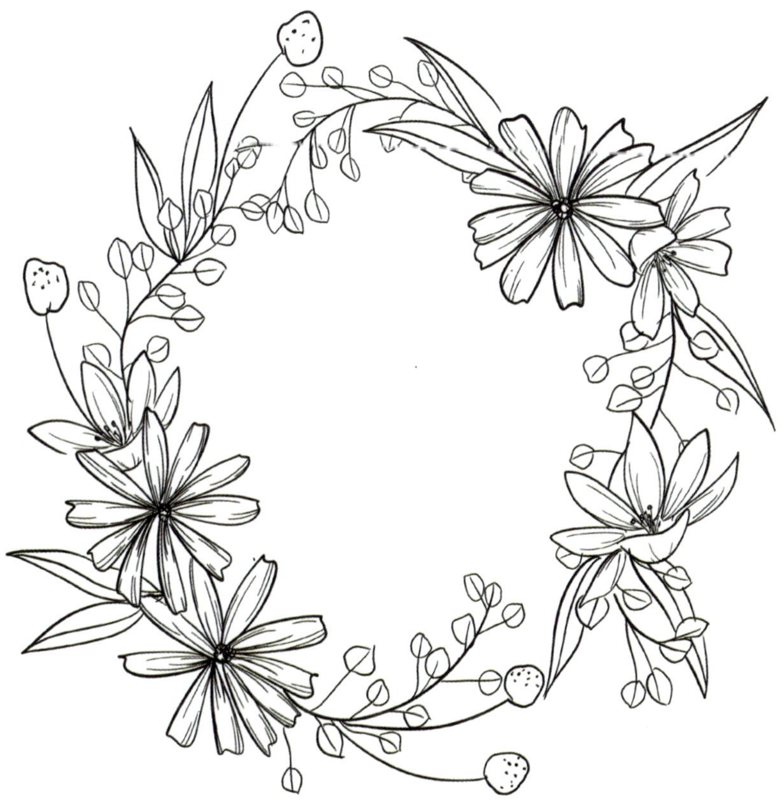

STEP 1 Start off with a dot in the center of where you want your wreath.

STEP 2 Make another small dot where the left side of your wreath will be. I recommend doing this on the side of the paper that is shortest so you don't accidentally overshoot and make a dot too far away and then run out of room on the shorter ends. Remember to create your guidelines far enough inward from the edges of the paper so you have plenty of room to add botanicals. Now think of the circle you're creating like a compass or a cross. The middle dot is the cross and the left dot is the west side or left point.

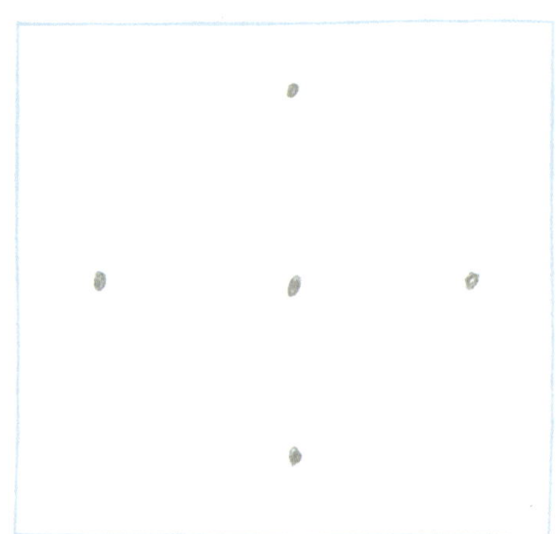

STEP 3 To get all of the dots equidistant from the center, lay your pencil (or pen) flat on the paper with the tip over the dot you drew to the side. Note where the center dot lies in reference to the pencil. Usually, there's writing on the pencil and you can make a mental note of exactly what aligns, or use your thumbnail to make a slight indent. Turn your pencil upward and align the center with the mental measurement you took. Wherever the tip of the pencil lies is where your top dot will go (aka north dot). Repeat this method for the right (east) side and bottom (south) side.

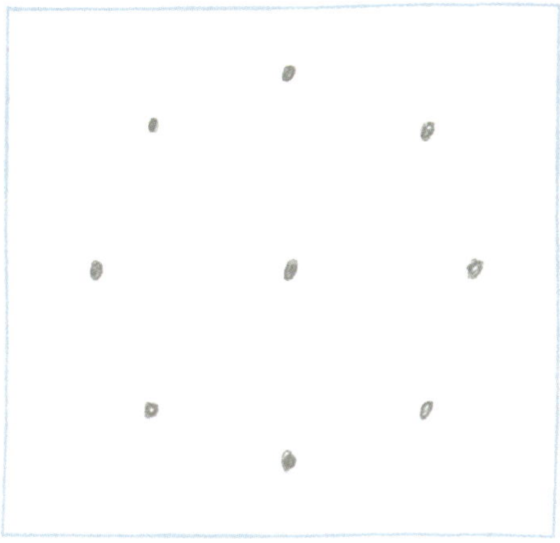

STEP 4 Not too difficult, right? There's one more part to this. We need to be sure we make a circle, and the four points we've made won't guarantee that it will be round enough. Take the cross and turn it so you're now making the points on the diagonal, in between your first four points.

DRAW A BOTANICAL WREATH

Now it's time to connect the dots. This isn't your regular connect-the-dots exercise, though. All of these lines will be curved, since we're making a circle. Now that you have your guide, let's create a botanical wreath.

Remember this order: Start with your main flowers, add secondary flowers, then fill the empty space with filler flowers and different leaves. I'll walk you through it.

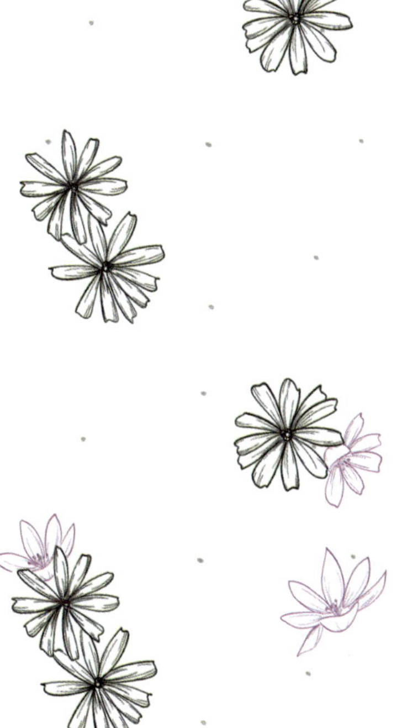

STEP 1 Choose a flower. This can be the most difficult part of the whole wreath. Choices, ya know? Pick three places on your paper to draw your focus flowers. You can even put two flowers next to each other.

STEP 2 Add some secondary flowers. The amount you add is up to you, just make sure they don't take away from the main flowers. They can go on both sides of your main flowers or be sprinkled a few places. I like to keep mine near the other flowers because I find that it's the perfect balance before adding leaves.

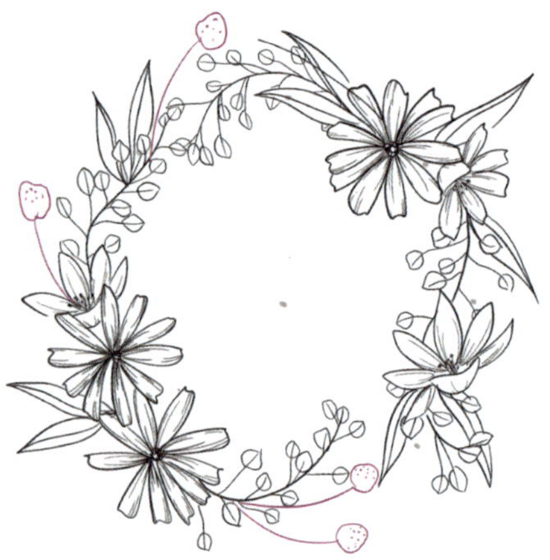

STEP 3 Next add your leaves around the circle template. The types of leaves that you choose can completely change the look and feel of your piece, so think about that before jumping in. Another feature to consider if you opt for leaves on delicate stems is that these can branch off of the flowers and fall inside or outside the circle base, which then opens up your wreath and makes it a bit more playful.

To finish up, add some small filler flowers, like simple Billy buttons. These are my favorite flowers to add to arrangements.

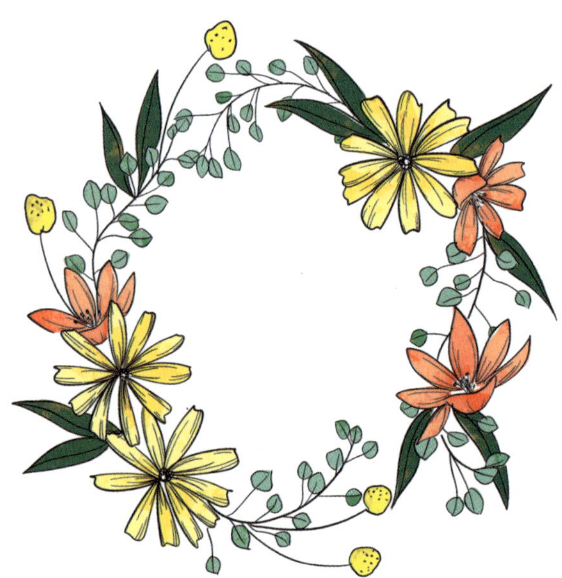

TO ADD COLOR Play with different greens so each style of leaf stands apart. After laying down your color, grab a dry sponge and press it on the paint while it's still slightly moist. This can add some pretty fun textures!

CREATE A MAP

Illustrating maps can be *so* fun. You have the power to add only the elements you wish to include, creating a unique view. We've all seen examples of these maps, and they're like eye candy. Visually stimulating map illustrations can be achieved by choosing either beautiful simplicity or heavy detail, or by focusing on a particular color palette. You can also draw a map using a specific theme. Oftentimes this is found in maps of popular landmarks, historical sites, or a city's "best of" guide. In this case, we'll be focusing on nature. You can travel anywhere and stumble across a must-see outdoor wonder. You might also discover upon a hidden gem.

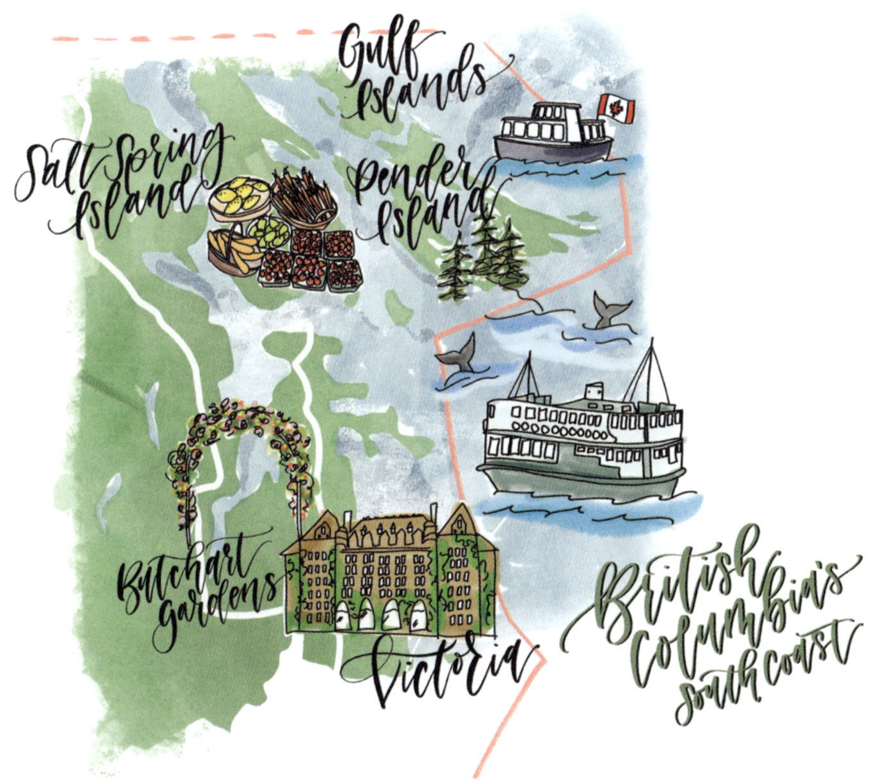

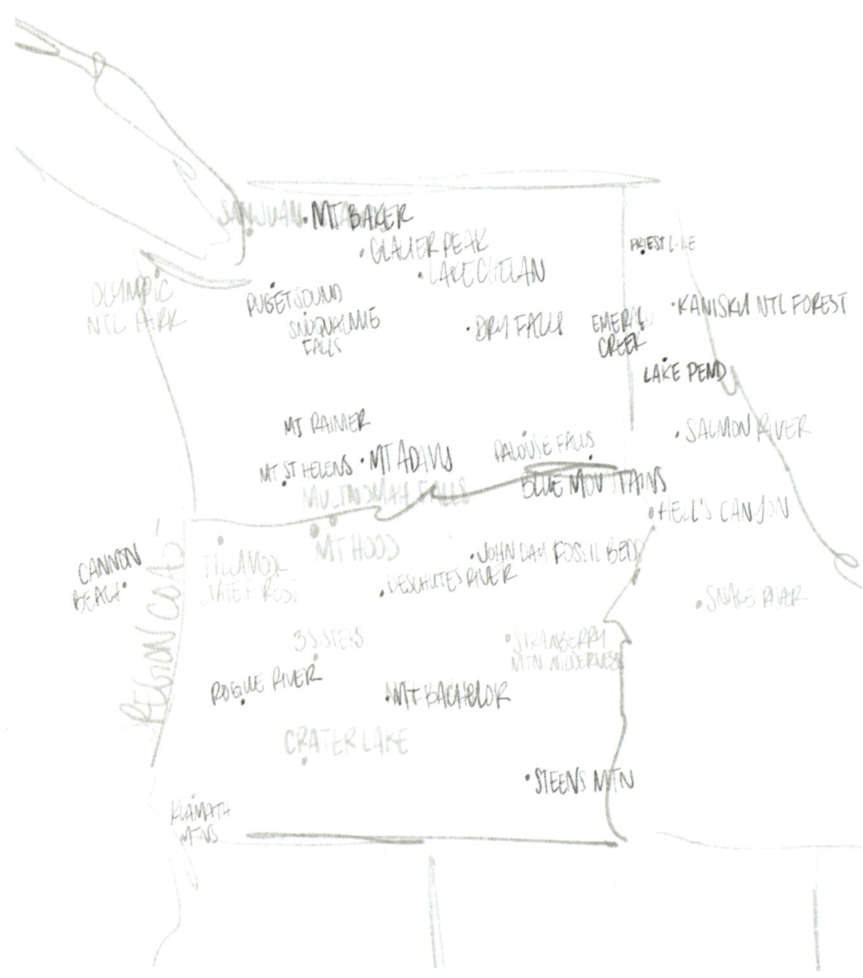

STEP 1 The first step is to ensure that you know the boundaries of the map you're drawing. The map's boundary can fade off toward the edges or be sharp and precise. I'll often use a lightbox and/or tracing paper to trace my maps' borders. Sometimes I highlight main freeways; you can choose whether or not you'd like to include streets.

Next, create bullet points of the places you'll be including. Doing this before drawing will help you visualize how to space out drawings. You don't want them running into each other when you could have easily moved one object slightly to make room for both.

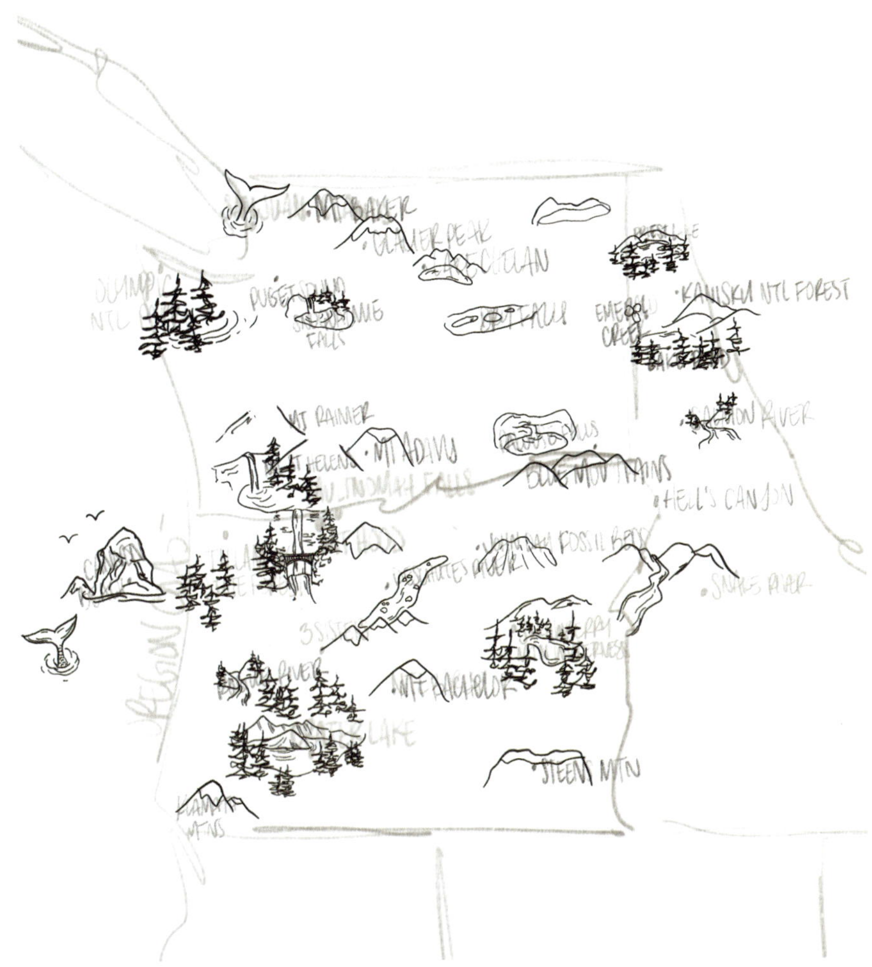

STEP 2 You don't need to worry about placing your drawings in their exact places. You can begin the drawing process on the same paper or you can use a new piece and place your guide underneath. As you begin sketching, you'll see if there's something that needs to scoot over a bit to allow for another item. You might also find that some areas of your map are a bit more sparse. This is a good opportunity to decide if you want to leave some spaces intentionally blank or find things to fill them in. I'll often use this space as an area to insert my map's title. Once your main elements are placed, you can start adding details. You can create texture with mark making or you can add tiny doodles of flowers, trees, or animals.

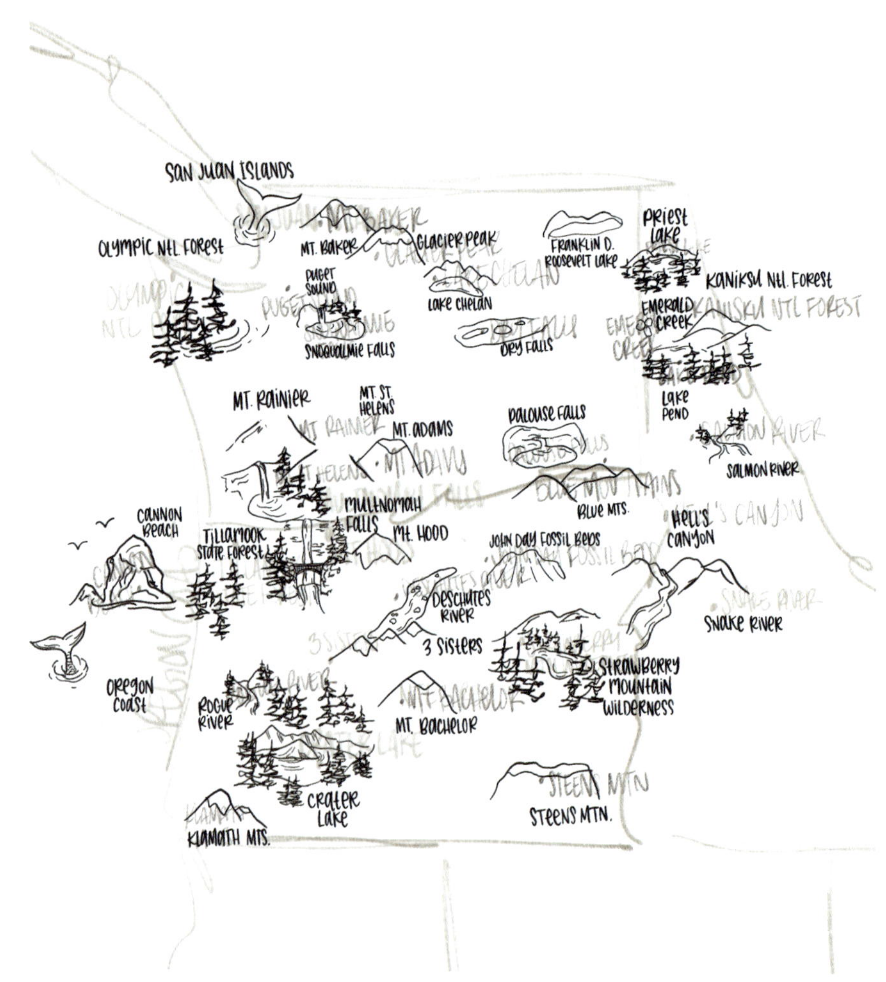

STEP 3 Once your sketches are on your map, you can add any lettering you'd like to include. I always want to feature the names of the places I've drawn on my maps. This part alone can change the whole vibe of your map, so think about the type of lettering you want to use. If you add fancy calligraphy or something ornamental, it won't mesh as well with a quirky drawing style. If you choose a serif font, it won't blend well with a playful color-block style. You get the idea.

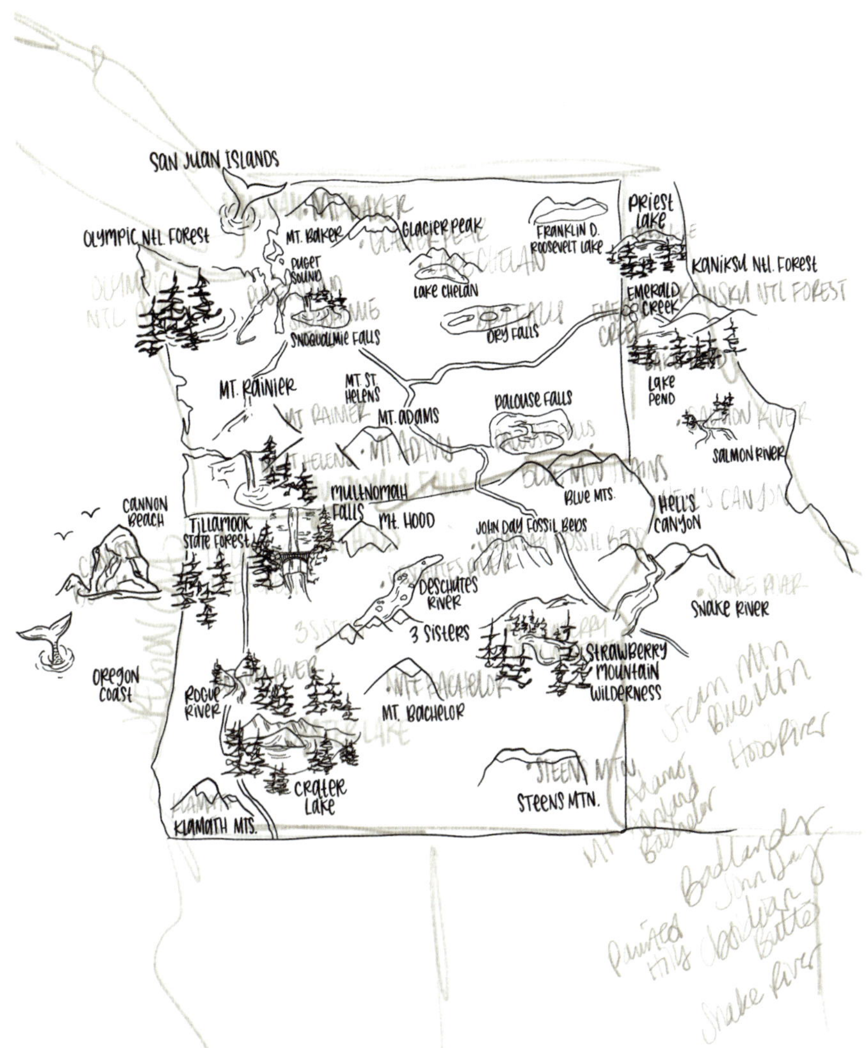

STEP 4 Now you can add the borders of the region you've drawn, if you'd like. I do this after placing the illustrations because I don't want the lines from the borders running through any of the other elements of my map. I avoid this by saving the border until the end.

Pacific Northwest

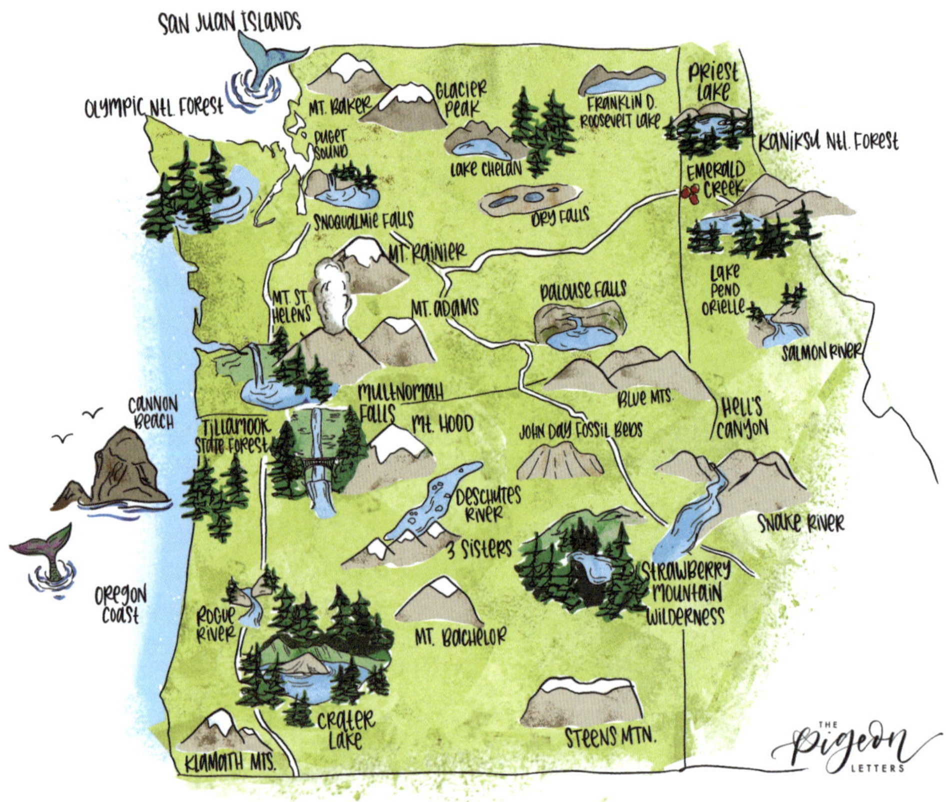

TO ADD COLOR Erase your pencil lines and you'll have a completed map! Black ink maps (or even one-color maps) have their own unique aesthetic, so don't disregard the beauty of simplicity. If you do opt to add color, this is an exploration stage. I encourage you to play with different palettes on a separate sheet of paper to find the palette that will best suit your design. I'm a fan of doing loose sketching and light watercolor washes or gritty textured color, but you might be more attracted to bright pops executed using markers, paints, or digital programs. There's not a wrong approach here. You do you!

OCEAN SCENES

Diving a little deeper into geography, let's take a trip to the beach. See what I did there? Diving a little deeper? Going to the beach? You dive into the water? Oh boy. Anyway, I want to take a look at three different beaches around the world that feature sands of different colors. When we see landscape illustrations of the coast, we usually see a cerulean ocean that meets a khaki bed of sand. Looking closer, you might see additional details such as rocks, trees, and wildlife. But have you stopped to look at the actual color of sand? It might be a warmer tan or a golden beige. I say this because I want you to explore color in your illustrations and paintings.

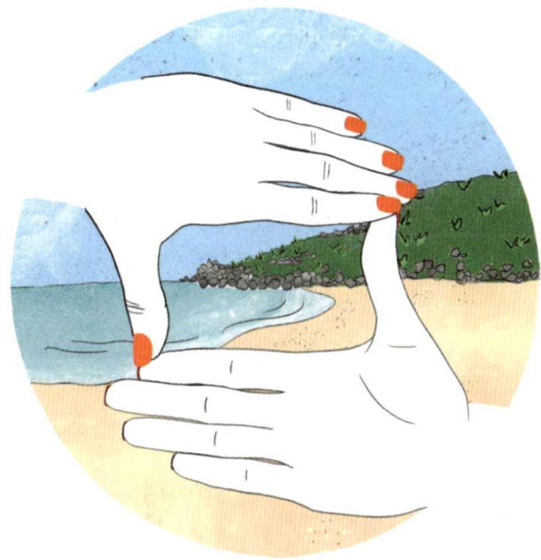

When you look at a beach scene, use a viewfinder to help with composition. You can create a viewfinder with paper or you can simply use your hands to create a frame. Practice bringing your hands closer and pushing them farther away to create compositions that are closeups or panoramas. Try changing the orientation of your hands to see the frame in both landscape and portrait views. Doing this will help you determine the best composition for your piece.

Once you figure out how you want your composition, look at its elements as shapes. Then separate the features in halves, thirds, or quadrants. If you're drawing a beach scene, seeing exactly where the water sits on your page along with where the sand lies will help you know where to put these elements.

Pink Sand

The pink sand at Les Sables Roses comes from foraminifera, a microscopic organism with a reddish pink shell. The sand mixes with coral, shells, and calcium carbonate, creating a rosy paradise. Les Sables Roses is located on one of the largest atolls in the world, in Rangiroa, French Polynesia. Its pink sand borders an abundant lagoon, ideal for diving and snorkeling to your heart's content. This scene is broken up into thirds. The top third is the sky, and the bottom two-thirds are divided by a diagonal line, with the ocean at the top and the sand at the bottom.

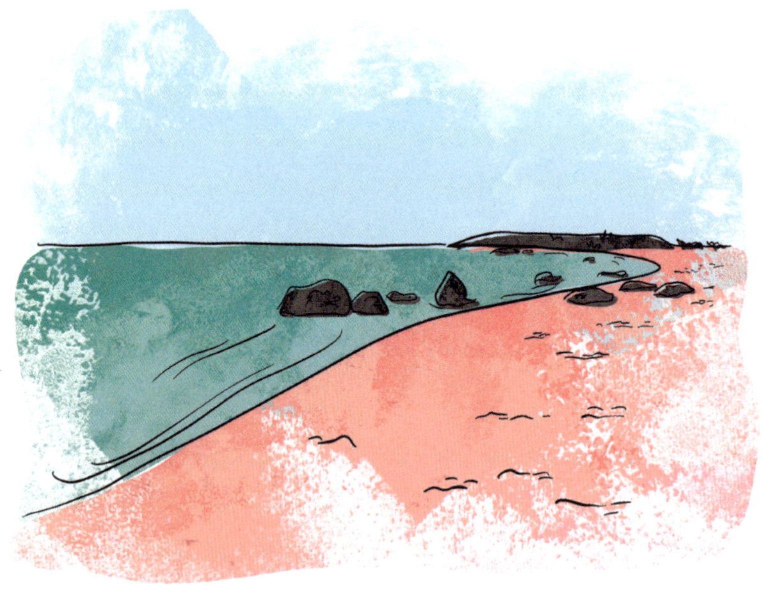

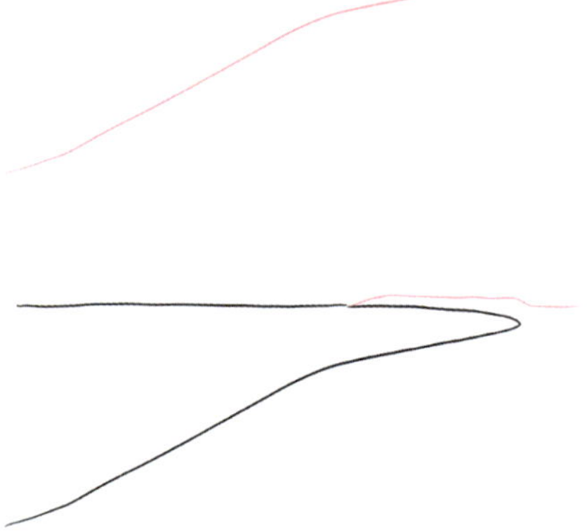

STEP 1 Seeing the shapes broken up this way, choose where you'd like to begin. As always, beginning at the horizon line is usually the easiest.

STEP 2 Continue to create the shapes we see (such as the rocks in the distance) by dragging the horizon line down at an angle to mark the water's edge.

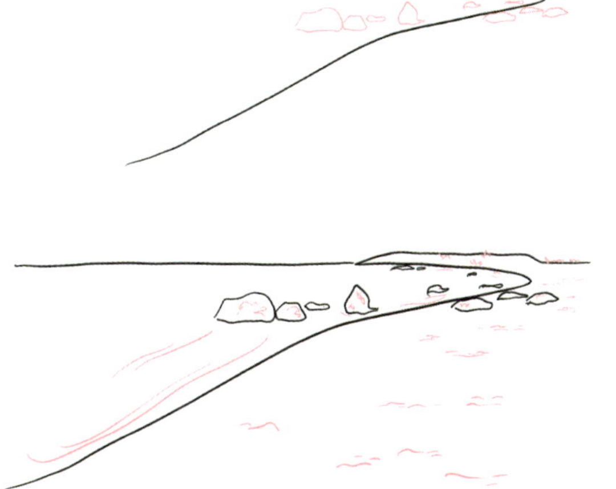

STEP 3 This beach scene has some small rocks, which can be drawn as odd shapes on the top with relatively flat bottoms. The closer to the horizon you get, the smaller they become.

STEP 4 The last part is the detail. Add some lines to the sand and water, remembering that they should get smaller and closer together the farther away they are.

You'll find so many colorful friends here:

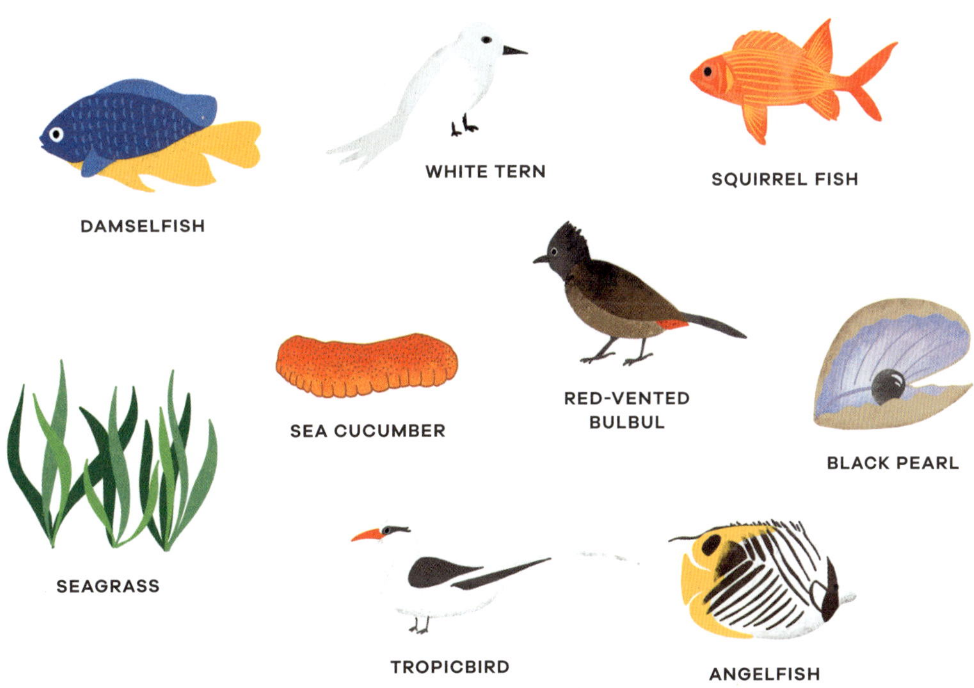

Purple Sand

Off the beaten path, the secluded Pfeiffer Beach in Big Sur, California, has variable purple patches, mainly at the northern end, that are most obvious after heavy rainfalls. The coloring is caused by manganese garnet deposits that wash down from the surrounding hills, supplementing the quartz grains that make up the sand of the beach.

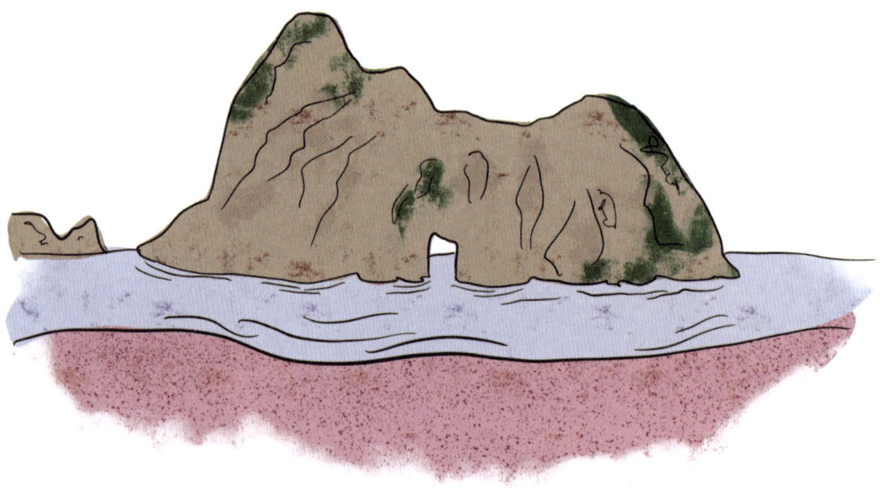

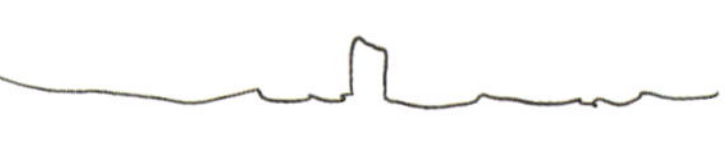

STEP 1 The horizon line in this scene is at the bottom of the rock and along the water. Draw the base of the rock with an imperfect line, leaving a small rectangular hole in the center, which will be the little tunnel within the rock.

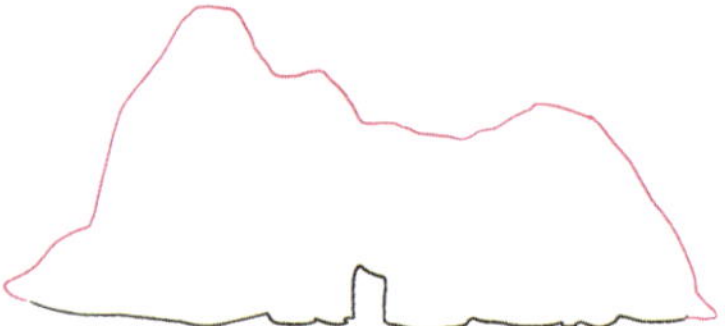

STEP 2 The top of the rock is higher on the left side, dips downward, and then climbs a little higher on the right before returning to the bottom on the right side.

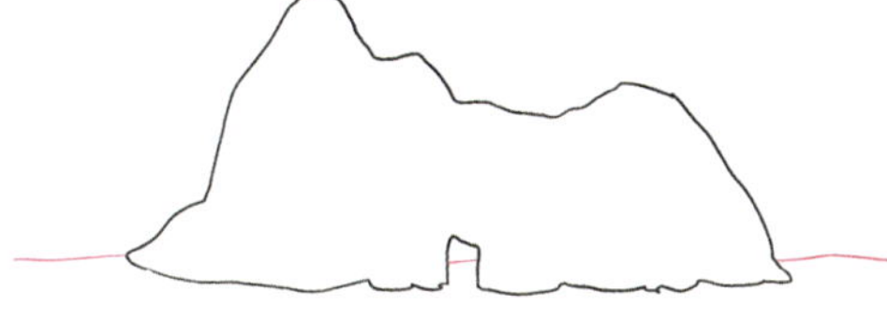

STEP 3 Tuck the horizon line of the water behind the rock by drawing a horizontal line a bit higher than the bottom of the rock. You'll want this line to also travel through the small tunnel in the middle of the rock showing that it's in the water.

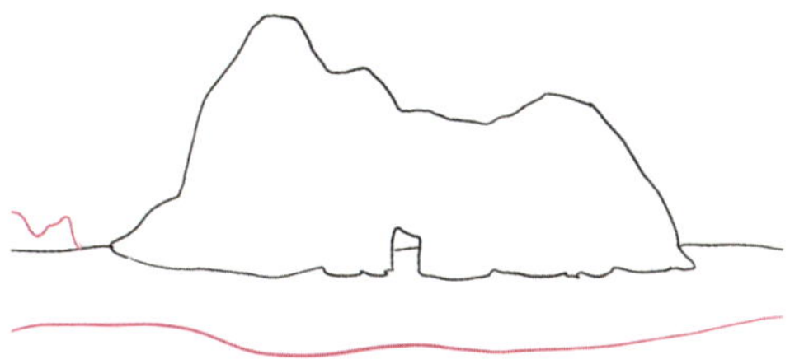

STEP 4 Just below the base of the rock, add another loose line. This acts as the tide line, where the water meets the sand. Also add a couple of smaller rocks to the left of the main rock.

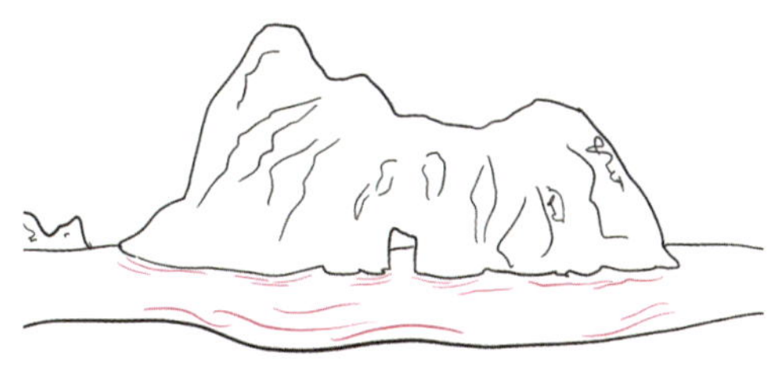

STEP 5 Last, add marks to the rock and water to show depth on the cliff and movement in the ocean.

More nature to find at Pfeiffer Beach:

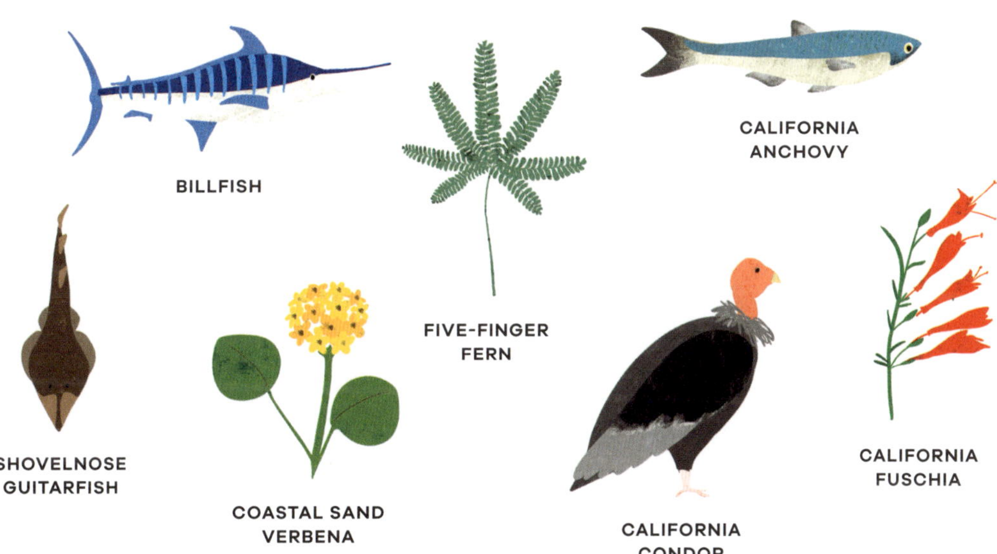

Black Sand

Reynisfjara is a world-famous black sand beach on Iceland's southern coast. According to Icelandic folklore, there were two trolls that tried to pull a ship from the ocean, but as dawn came, they were turned into solid stone, forming large basalt columns that appear as though they are a staircase to the sky. These symmetrical columns were actually shaped from lava, which is also the cause of the black sand.

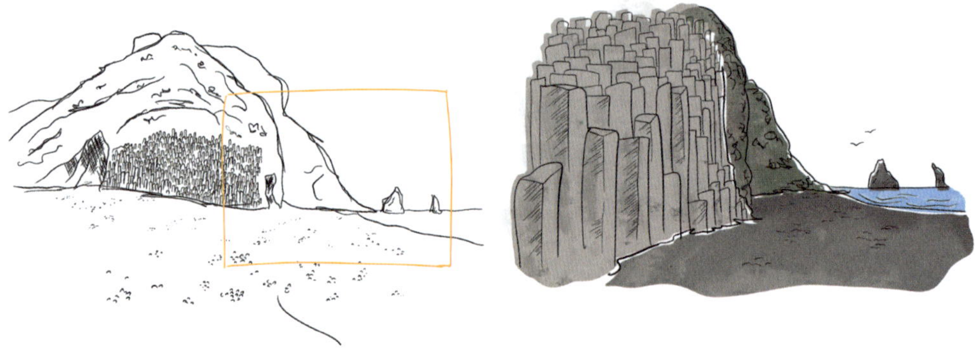

Although this beach is mesmerizing even from a distance, I've used a view-finder to narrow down exactly what I want to draw from this scene. I also decided to shift the angle slightly to focus more on the side of the pillars, as you can see in the illustration above.

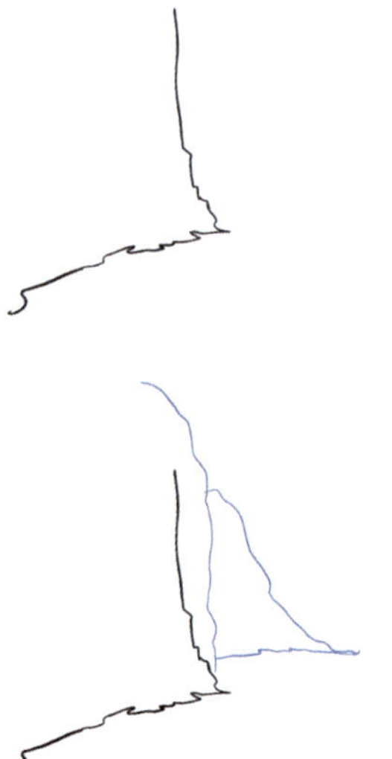

STEP 1 Start off with the base and side of the pillar section by drawing a jagged line at an angle and then sharply upward.

STEP 2 The pillars meet a large rock, so add additional textured lines to show the bumps in its side.

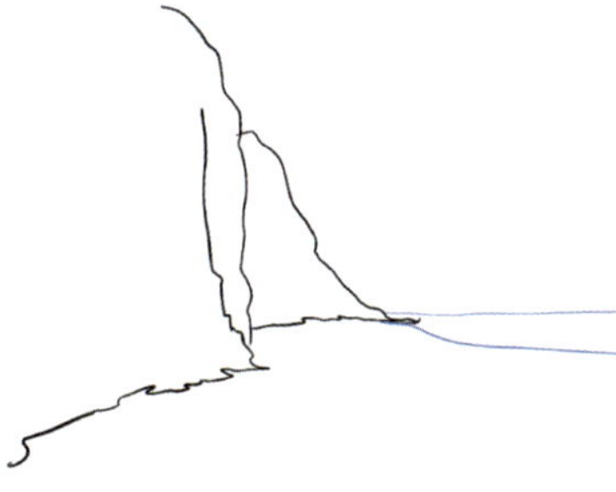

STEP 3 Remember that we're laying out the sections of our scenery in basic shapes and lines. Now draw the ocean horizon line and a slightly angled line for the shoreline.

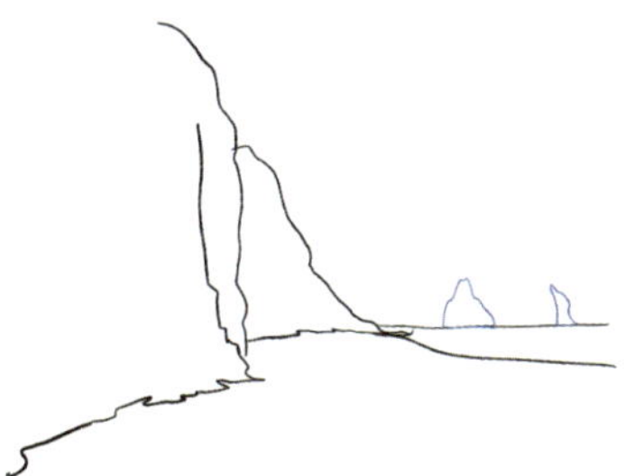

STEP 4 There are a few large rocks in the distance so draw their silhouette at the base of the horizon line. This gives the illusion that they're rising out of the water.

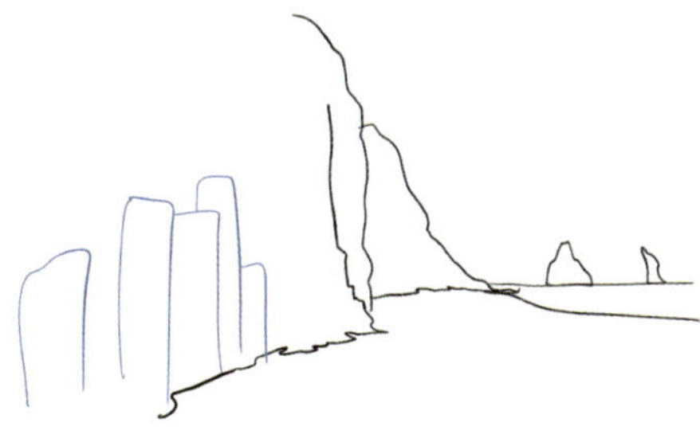

STEP 5 Since we're looking at the pillars at an angle, the left side of our drawing will be the area closest to us. The pillars to the far left will be wider than the ones toward the center.

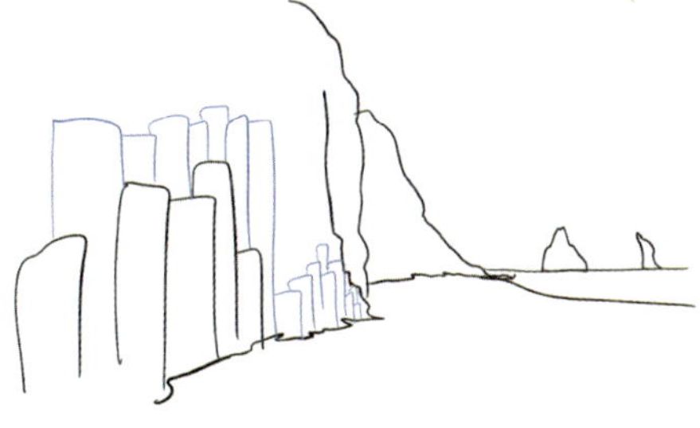

STEP 6 Can you spot where the focal point is? If you've guessed the part of the rock that sits in the middle and meets the sea, you're onto something. This is one-point perspective, which is when you have a focal point on the horizon line and everything converges toward that point. Pretty cool, right?

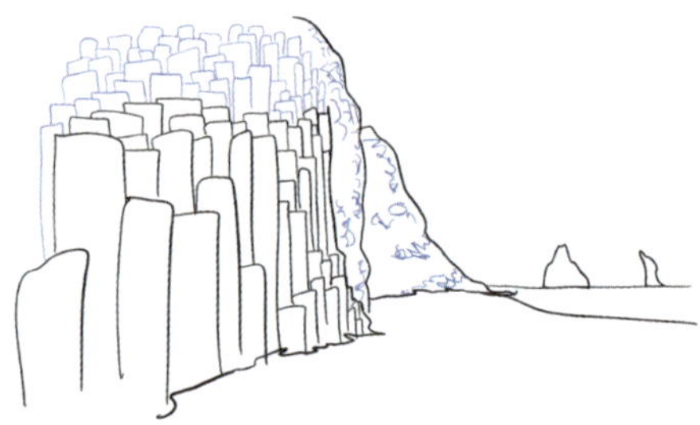

 Continue building pillars above each other until they reach the top. When adding detail to rocks, I use the same technique I do for trees (see pages 43–46). I focus on specific areas by adding random marks to suggest shadows.

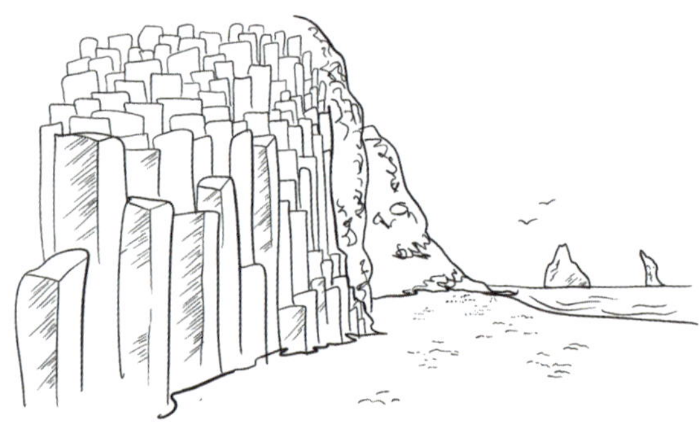

 Everything in the drawing, not just the pillars, conforms to one-point perspective—sand, rocks, and any other details you may want to include. In this case, I've added some small marks for the sand. Don't overdo this part. Don't get crazy covering the entire ground with marks. Less is more! Just remember that the farther away you get, the closer together and shorter the lines become.

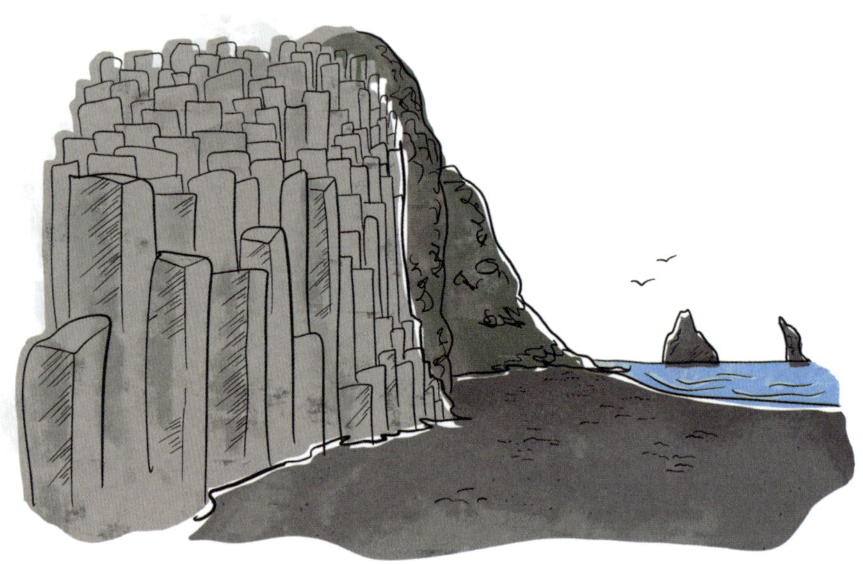

TROPICAL RAIN FOREST

Tropical regions offer bright colors in both flora and fauna. If you walk beneath the lush tree canopies, you'll be met with the bright greens of tens of thousands of different tree and flower species and many medicinal plants. As we trek through our exploration of this exotic terrain, you'll learn how to illustrate different elements that are found in each region. Get ready for some eye-catching color!

The rain forest is home to some desirable plants, including cacao and coffee, and more than half of the earth's known species of animals can be found here, sporting all the colors of the rainbow.

Rain forests are layered with light-starved, sheltered forest floor and under-story trees and shrubs. Leafy canopy trees cover the bulk of the rain forest along with emergent-layer trees that tower over the canopy.

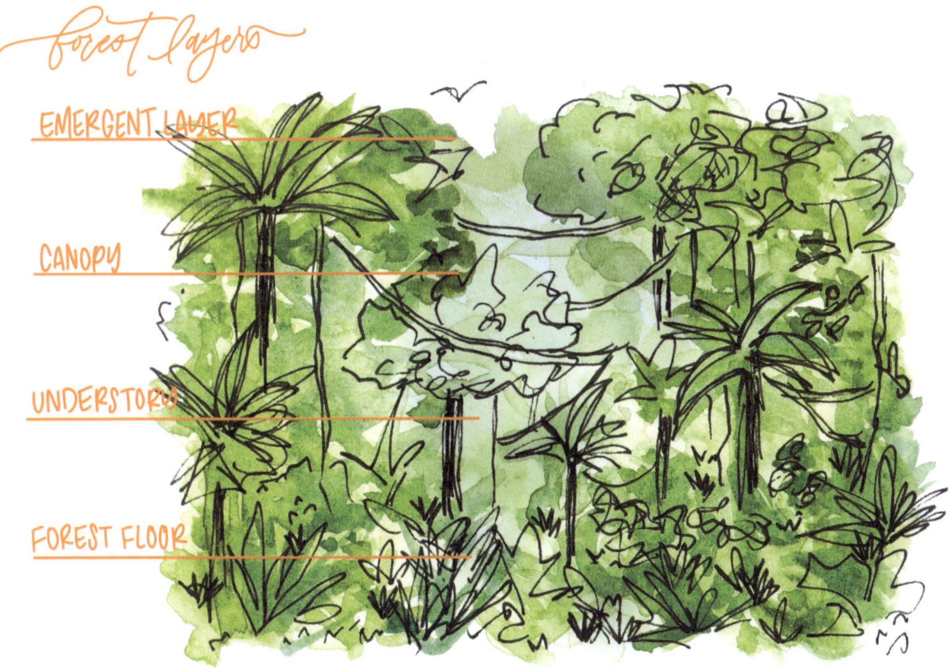

STEP 1 To create your background layer, you want more water than paint on your brush. For a textured look, repeatedly set down and lift up the belly of your brush, quickly dragging strokes around your paper.

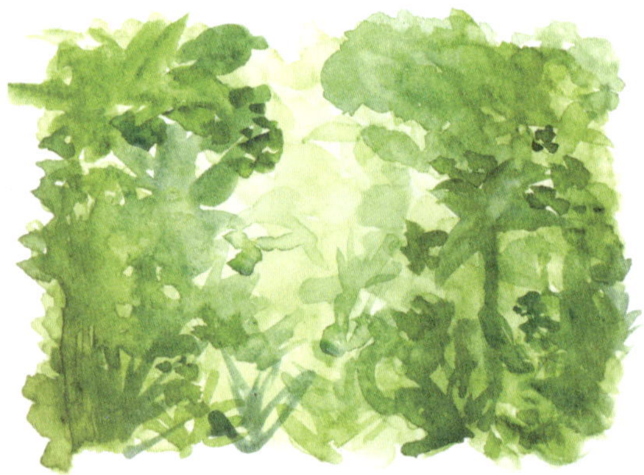

STEP 2 Allow the first layer to dry, then continue with full-pressure strokes, both dragging your brush and simply touching it to the paper to build layers of texture, this time beginning to form plants and trees. You can use the same color, as building upon the watercolor wash will allow it to stand out, or you can introduce a new color. Don't worry about making plants and trees look realistic. Keeping them loose is just fine since we'll be adding ink later.

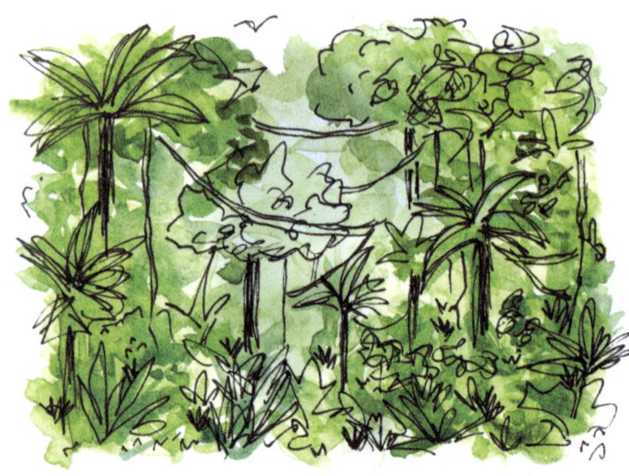

STEP 3 When the last layer dries, begin adding ink. I do this in a sketch style so I can maintain the energy that the jungle gives off. Quick pen strokes forming crooked lines and wobbly movement add character and charm. This is only one example of how you might create a rain forest scene. The idea is to give you one of a plethora of illustration styles to play around with so you can find your favorite method of creating. I want to see you put your pen to paper!

Forest Floor

The forest floor is the lowest layer of the rain forest. Only 2 percent of sunlight gets through the canopy above to reach the ground. Saplings and shrubs grow in patches of sunlight. Fungi, insects, and rodents are found on the forest floor. You'll see dark, moody greens on this layer of the rain forest since it's thickly covered with plants.

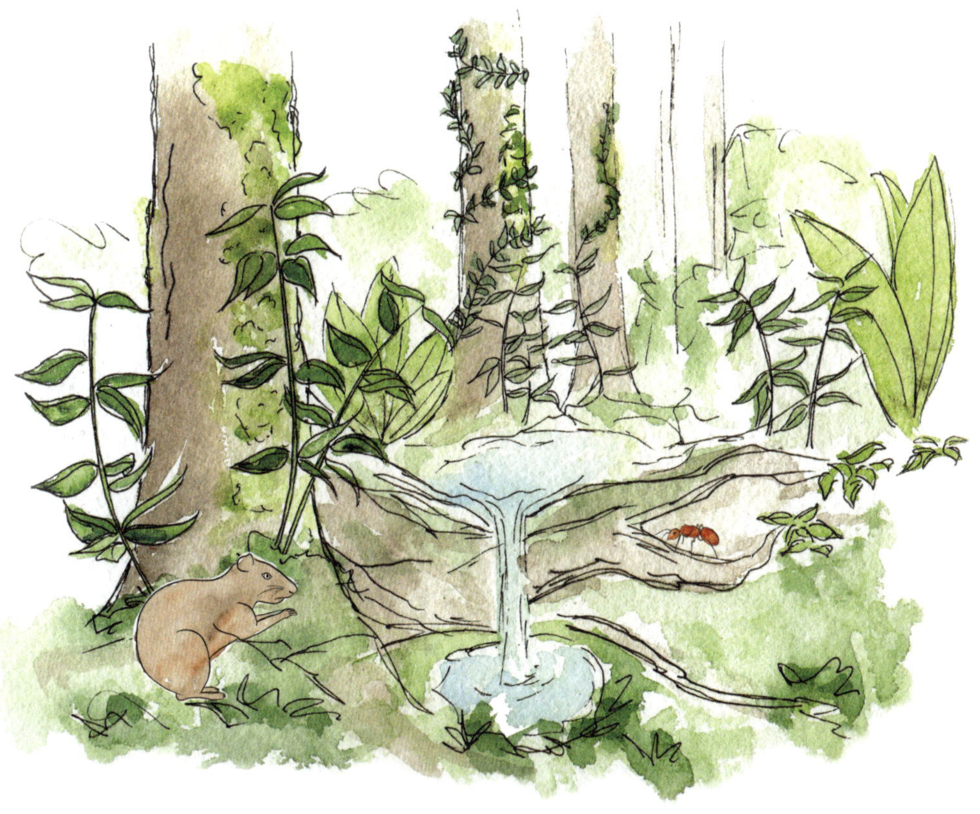

Watching ants for even five minutes makes me tired. They're busy little things with a great work ethic. Little machines, I'd say. If you really watch them, you'll notice that they're quite interesting to look at, and even more interesting to draw!

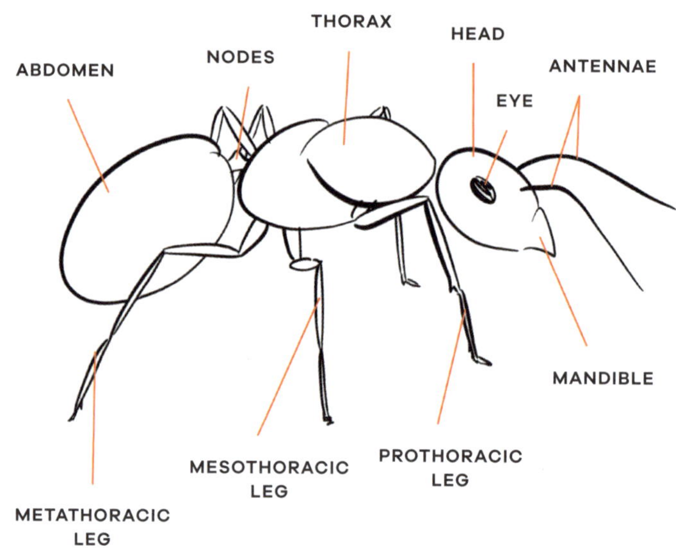

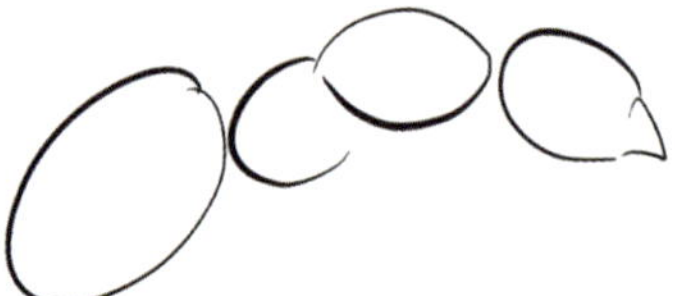

STEP 1 You've probably drawn or seen an illustration of an ant made with three circles for its body. We're going to use these circles but shape them a bit differently: draw the head more oval, with the front pointed for its mouth, and the middle a bit lumpier, made with two oval shapes together. The first is closest to the head, while the other wraps around the backside. The last circle is the biggest. Draw a larger, tilted oval.

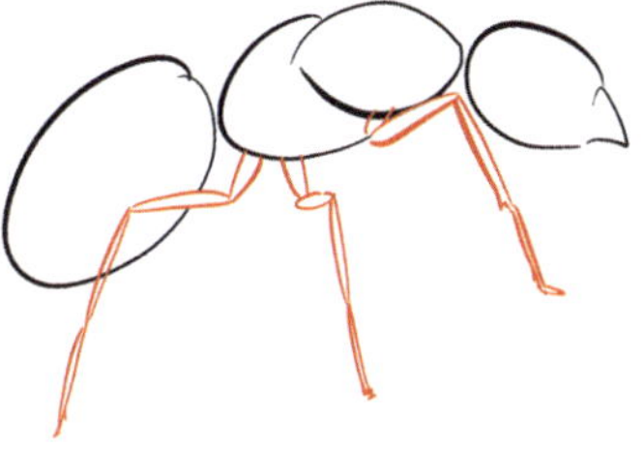

STEP 2 The legs of the ant come off of its center. Rather than quick stick legs, put a little extra time in and draw the legs so they are anatomically correct. To simplify, divide the legs into four sections. The part that connects to the body is the shortest. It acts like a joint with a skinny shape that is more horizontal. Draw the next two sections downward.

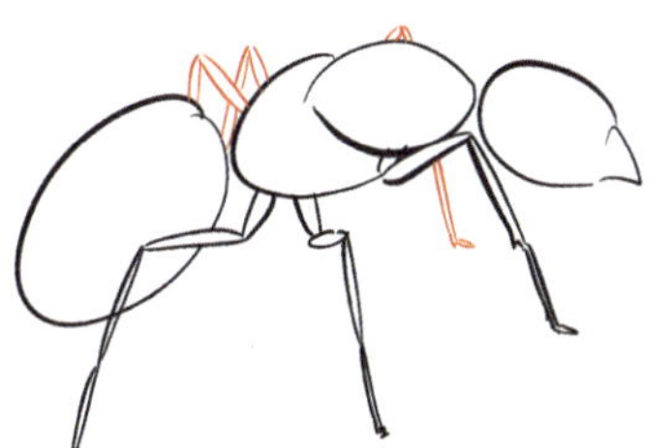

STEP 3 The legs on the other side mirror the front but tuck behind the body. Adding these is fairly simple; just be sure that if you see the bottom and top part, the invisible line (behind the body) is straight so the bottom of the leg looks like it's connected!

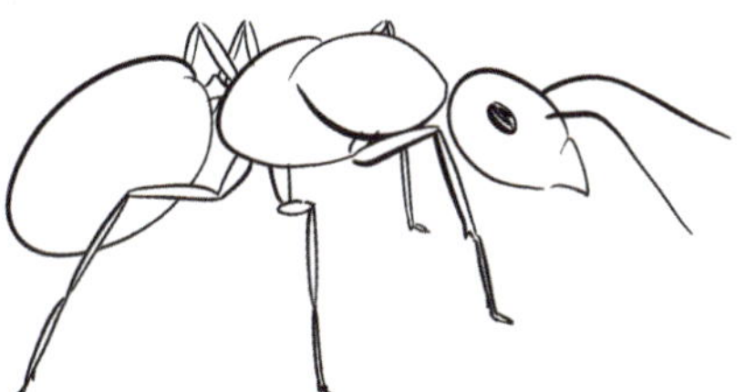

STEP 4 Last, add the eye and antennae, which come out of the front of the head and then bend downward.

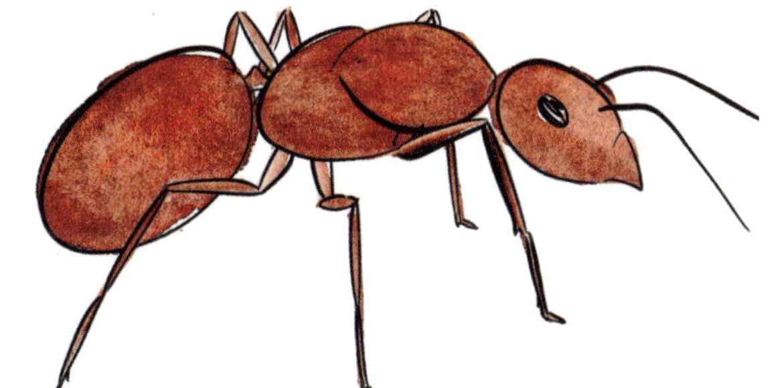

TO ADD COLOR There are so many ant species in the rain forest, you can use various hues of brown to depict them. Fire ants, for example, boast a rich, reddish brown. (I would know from that time I leaned against a tree while visiting an island off Malaysia. I'll never forget those bites, they really feel like fire!)

The agouti is a rodent that looks a bit like a guinea pig and squirrel mixed together. This little fellow is one of the only creatures in the rain forest that can break open the hard shell of the Brazil nut thanks to his sharp teeth.

It's much easier to draw bodies when they're first laid out in guides. You may need to adjust guides and final lines, of course, but having a base to start from will help you.

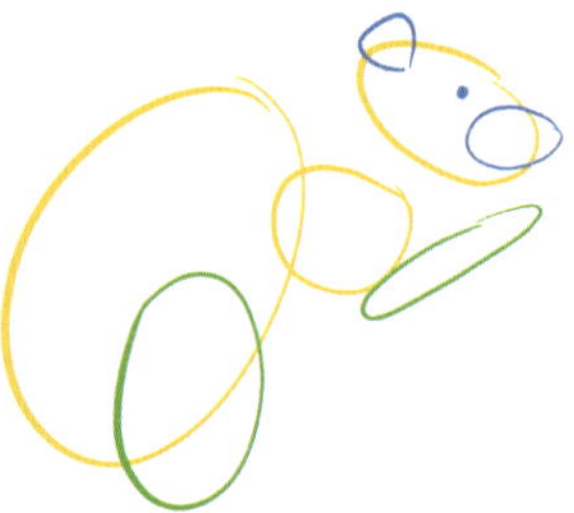

STEP 1 Illustrating rodents might seem a little tricky, but mapping it out with shapes before diving in will help. To begin, draw three circles that will act as a guide for the head, the shoulder, and the back/body (yellow). Then draw circle guides for the leg and arm (green), and circles to assist with the nose, eye, and ear (blue).

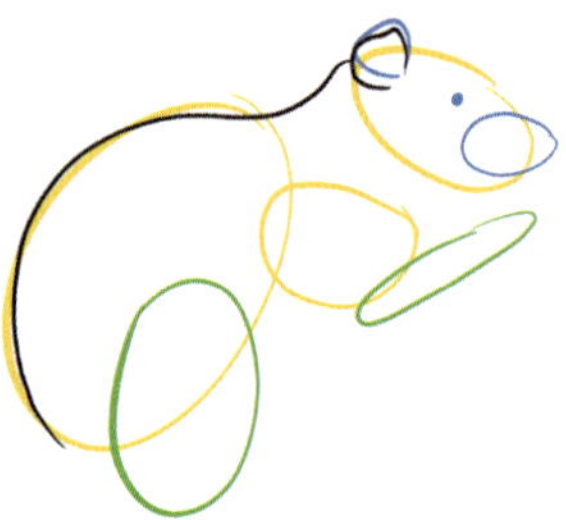

STEP 2 Draw the ear in a round triangular shape with a little dip on the top, then draw a line that sinks inward and arches upward and around the backside. This C-curve forms the top of the neck and back.

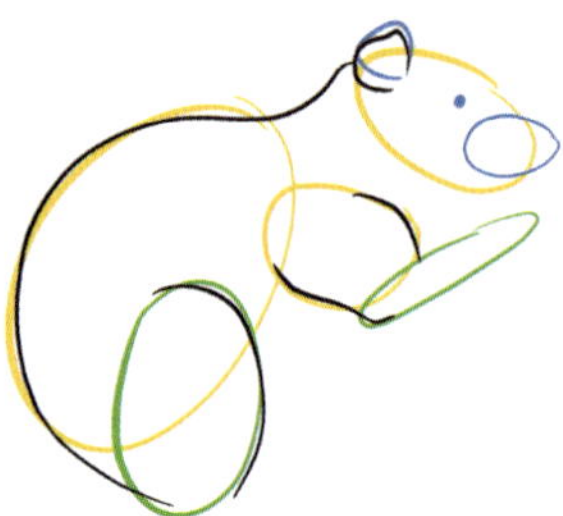

STEP 3 Draw the area for the leg and shoulder and arm. Simply follow your guides for this.

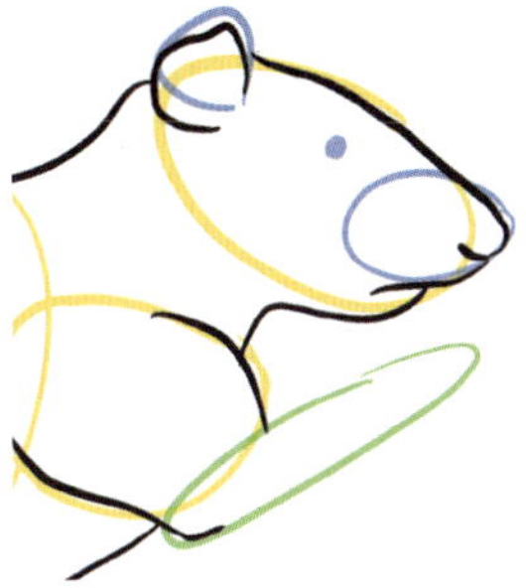

STEP 4 Using the oval guides for the head and face, draw a line down from the ear that stretches a bit past the end of your oval and tucks underneath to form the nose. Then draw a line from the center of the nose inward at the base of the head oval guide to create the top of the mouth. Bring one more line from the middle of the mouth line in and downward to connect to the arm. Look at that adorable face!

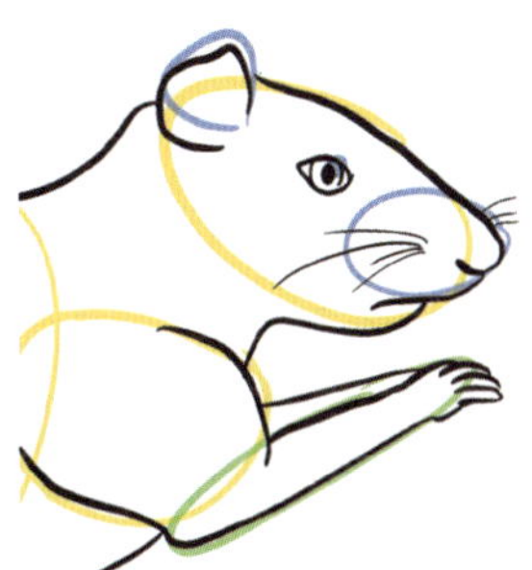

STEP 5 Finish by following the arm guide and adding curved lines for the paws. Er, hands? Or is it the fingers? You get it. Then add another line on the top of the arm to represent the other arm. Do the same thing for the feet. Add an eye and a few darling whiskers and you're set!

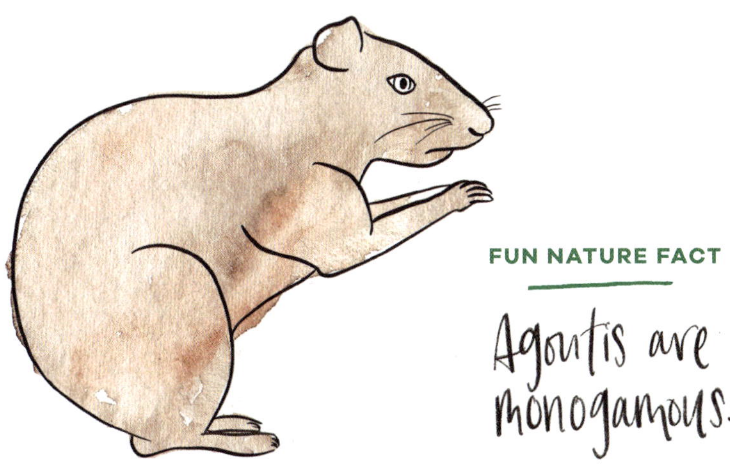

TO ADD COLOR This little agouti just needs a touch of brown.

Understory

The understory is warm and damp and contains many nutritional and medicinal trees and plants. Because little sunlight reaches the understory, plants and trees must have large, broad leaves to soak up as much sunlight as they can. Bananas, mangos, papayas, cocoa, and cinnamon grow here. I don't know about you, but that makes me want to hang out there for a few hours. There's nothing like freshly picked fruit! That said, there are plants that have defense mechanisms to deter critters from eating them; some are difficult to eat, others are tasteless, and some are even poisonous. Lizards, bees, jaguars, snakes, and frogs are just a handful of the creatures living in the understory. Animals such as big cats and large reptiles give this layer of the rain forest a little more color, with their hues of cool browns met with rich browns, deep oranges, and bright greens.

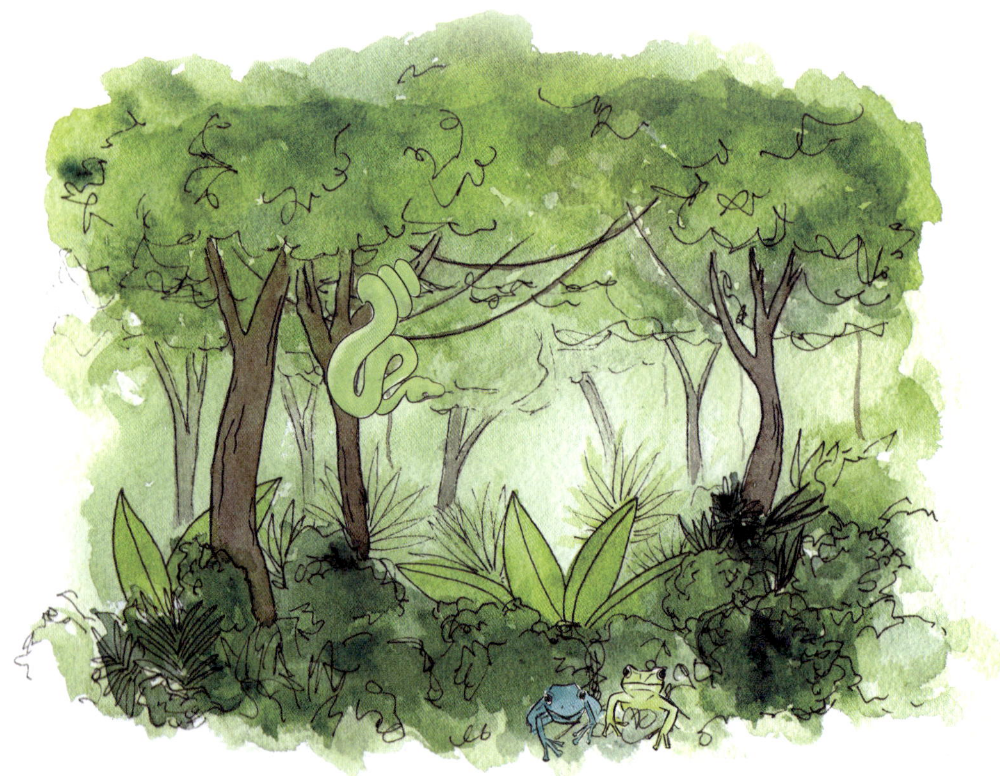

FROG

There are a ton of frogs to be found in the rain forest—tree frogs, poison dart frogs, giant monkey frogs, leaf toads, and more. Although there are some differences among the species of frogs, their overall anatomy is the same. If you can draw a frog, you can tweak the specifics depending on the species you want to draw!

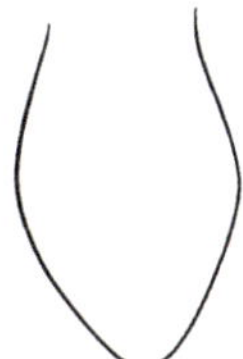

STEP 1 Start out with the shape of the body from the neck area down. The lines for the body curve inward before curving outward and downward and meeting in a small curve at the bottom.

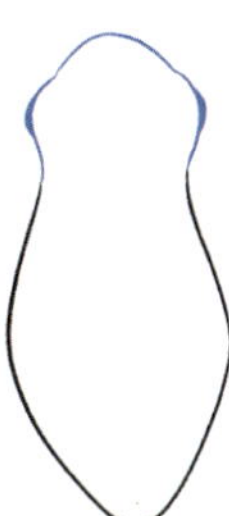

STEP 2 Create a similar but much shallower shape on the top. The lines curve outward and back in for a curved top, which is the mouth area of the frog. Then add two curves on the widest part for its eyes.

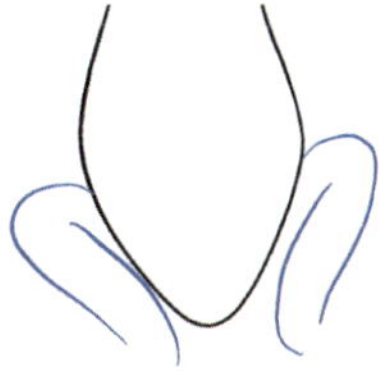

STEP 3 From just below the middle of the main body area, draw a curved line around and down on both sides. Draw another line on the inside of this one curving inward to form the meaty part of the frog legs.

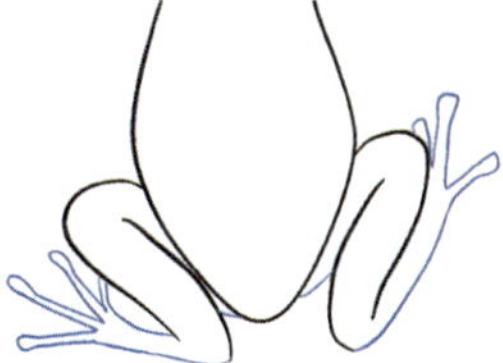

STEP 4 Finish the legs by drawing straight lines outward. Notice that the right side is covered a little by the top part of the leg so only the outside line of the lower part is drawn. Then create the frog's spread-out toes, with the tips a little thicker.

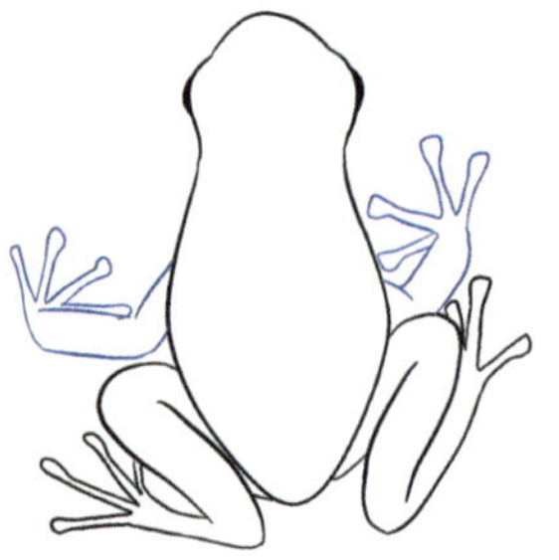

STEP 5 A frog's arms seem a little tricky because they bend differently. Start with a short, angled line downward from the body that bends and reaches outward. The toes turn inward, so with that in mind, draw four skinny lines that meet with little balls at the tips. Use the tips for overlapping on your frog, you can assume the arm is partially underneath it.

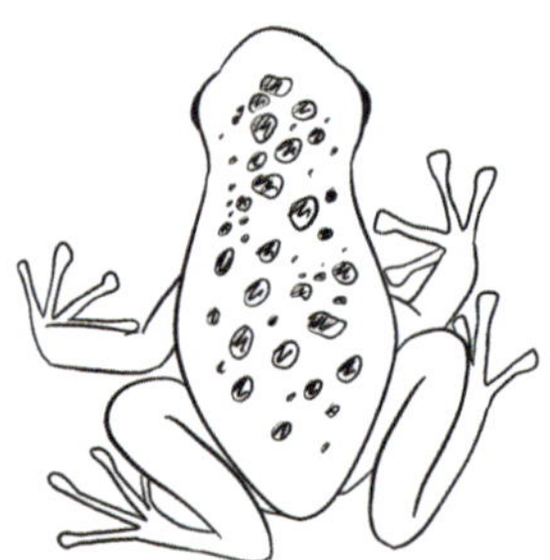

STEP 6 That's it for the form! Now you can add adorable little frog details, like these spots if you want.

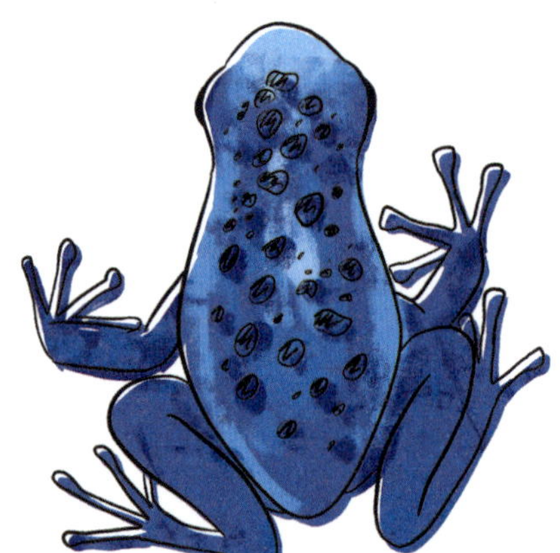

TO ADD COLOR Poison dart frogs come in a variety of bright colors, including blue, red, yellow, and green, and sometimes a combination. Choose a bright hue and lay down a bold watercolor wash, or color in with your favorite pen or marker. Add depth by setting down a darker version of the same color.

Canopy

Canopy trees absorb a lot of sunlight. The trees and plants in this layer are lush and leafy, protecting the understory below from direct light. This is the most productive layer, also known as the habitat layer. Full of fruits and nuts, the canopy feeds most of the animals that live there, including birds, butterflies, tree frogs, parrots, iguanas, monkeys, and everyone's favorite, sloths. This layer is the most colorful of the rain forest. The sun peeks through the emergent layer above to showcase the bold reds, blues, greens, and yellows found in the birds and butterflies.

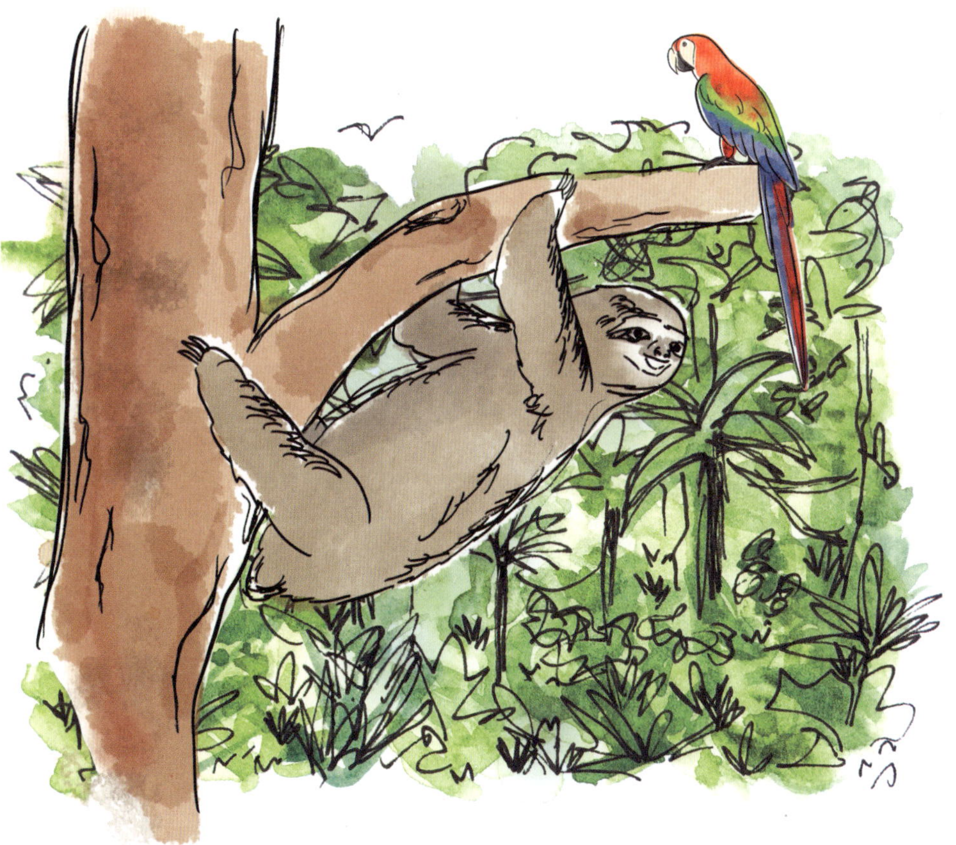

MACAW

Let's put a rainbow on a bird. Seriously, though, how amazing are macaw parrots? If you opt to add color to this bird after you draw it, think about the variety of colors they sport, like blue and gold, green and blue, red with yellow and blue, red with green and blue. . . . This bird is beautiful!

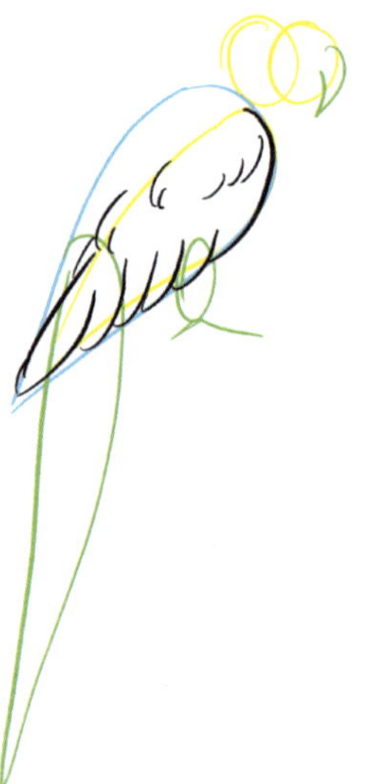

STEP 1 Just as we mapped out the shapes of a bird's body in The Bird Study section (see pages 150–151), we'll apply the same techniques to the macaw, which has a longer tail and a longer head. You can create the guide for the head with either an oval shape or by overlapping two circles, whichever is easiest.

STEP 2 Jumping right in, I sometimes like to tackle the wing before the upper back/neck area. Draw the wing with a downward C-curve on the right side, but rather than a straight line along the bottom, create feather shapes as shown. This gives the illusion that the bird has layered feathers. When you reach the end, draw a line from about the middle of the wing to the end, and fill in areas toward the top with curved lines. Don't go crazy—less is more!

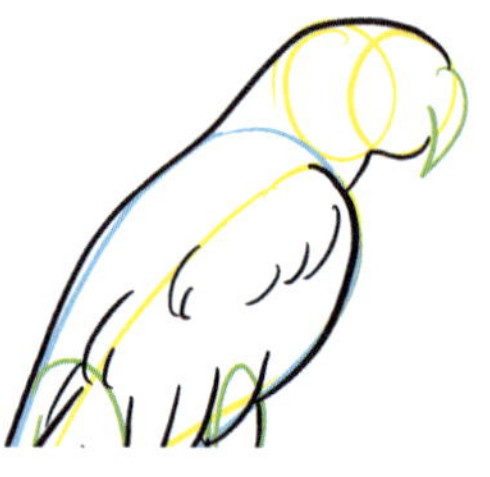

STEP 3 From here, draw the connecting line from the head, rounding downward with a small curve where the shapes meet so the neck is shown. This line connects the backside of the bird to the lower feathers.

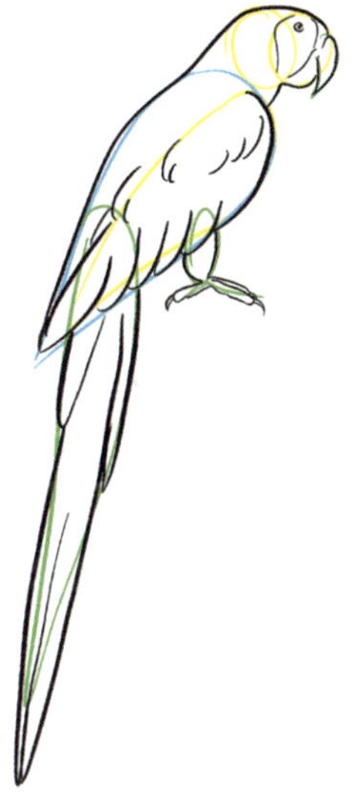

STEP 4 Now we can place the macaw's face, beak, legs, and feet. Remember the bird foot we covered in The Bird Study (see page 151)? Create curved lines for its little feet and then add its foot and claws. The face is highlighted with a couple of light lines around the eye and cheek. The beak curves outward and down into a point.

STEP 5 Finish by drawing the tail. Just as you drew the feathers in the beginning, draw only a couple of long lines slightly curving inward toward the bottom. Keep this area skinny and long. That's it!

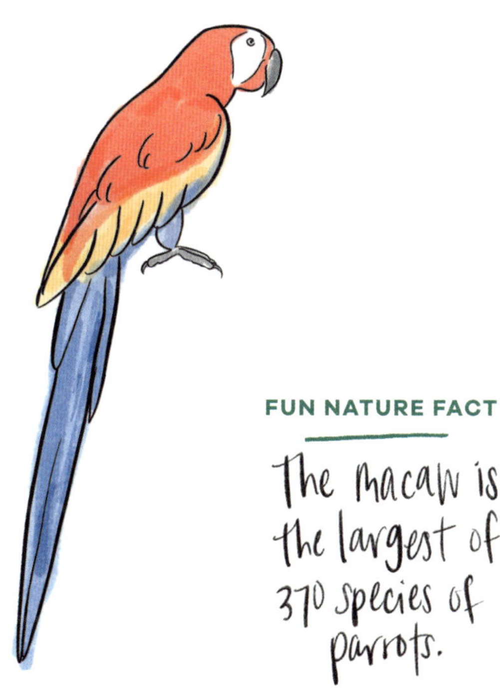

TO ADD COLOR I've gone with the classic red for this macaw. As previously mentioned, if you choose to add color (which you absolutely should on this beautiful, bold creature), there are several combinations to choose from!

SLOTH

You just got a little giddy, didn't you? I get it. This slow, furry animal was pretty trendy a couple of years ago and now stands up on that pedestal with the unicorn and kittens. It helps that it looks like it's always about to laugh, as though it's contemplating whether something was actually funny. Let's draw one so you can create all the sloths and put them up everywhere.

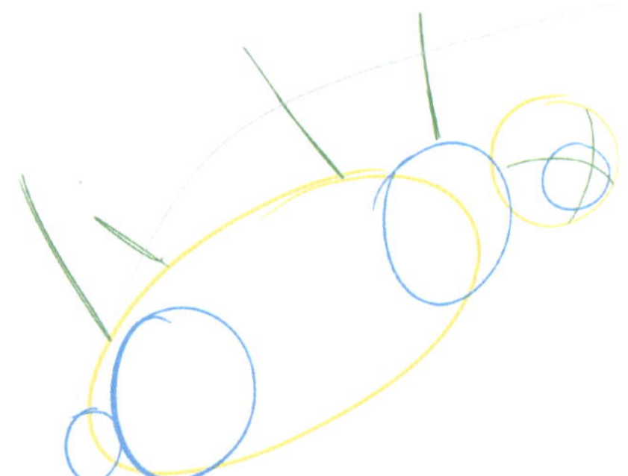

STEP 1 Since sloths are tree-dwelling animals, it only makes sense to draw one hanging from a branch. Draw a light line in pencil coming up and out, acting as a guide for where the tree branch is. From there, draw some shapes to help determine how to lay this guy out. Draw a circle for its head (yellow), then an oval shape for the body (yellow) about the size of three head circles. Then draw four straight lines (green) representing where its legs and arms will be.

STEP 2 Draw a curved vertical line (green) close to the right side of the head circle (yellow) to show the direction that the sloth will face. The second intersecting line (green) is a secondary guide for placing the face. The small circle (blue) inside of the head circle (yellow) will be the area of the sloth's face. Draw it about one-quarter the size of the head circle. Then draw a larger circle (blue) in between the head and body, and another circle (blue) at the bottom. Last, include a small circle (blue) coming from the very bottom, which will be the tail.

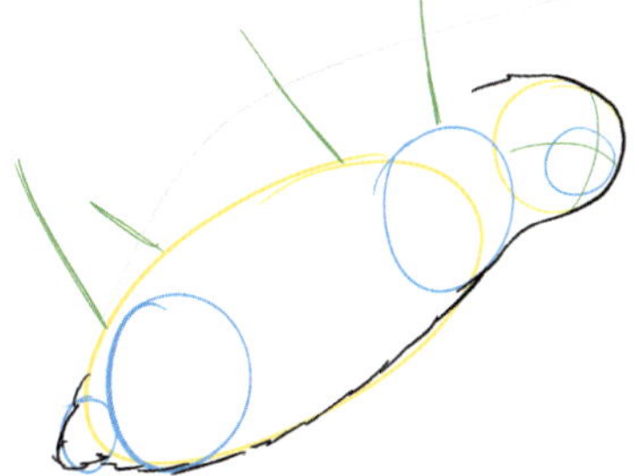

STEP 3 Now it's time to use our guides and draw. Starting with the body is easiest because you can connect all of these weird circles so they make more sense. Circle around the head, dipping in between the circles a little to accentuate the neck. Continue along the bottom of the oval, which creates the sloth's back. Once you get to the bottom, you're going to draw a little nub of a tail. Do you see where my line begins and ends? Leave space so that line doesn't run into the legs. I've also made the line jagged to represent the hair, which might be something for you to try as well.

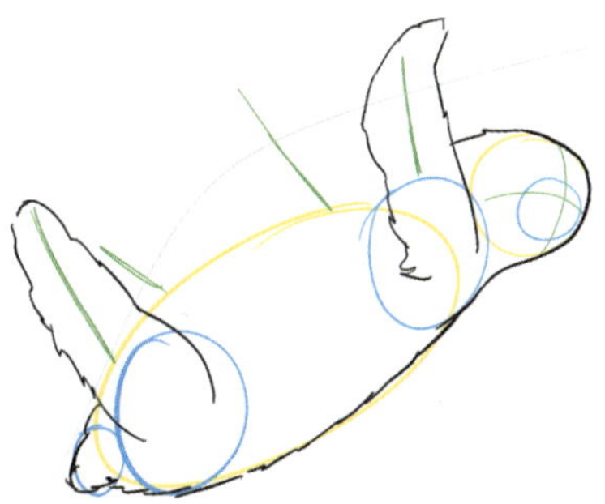

STEP 4 Since we intentionally left room for the sloth's legs, we're going to make those next. Coming from just inside the big joint circles, curve your lines around the outside of the legs the same distance apart on both sides of the leg lines. I've bent the front leg slightly as well. Notice that I've drawn over the line that acts as my tree branch. That's okay for this side, but the leg and arm on the other side will be cut off by this line.

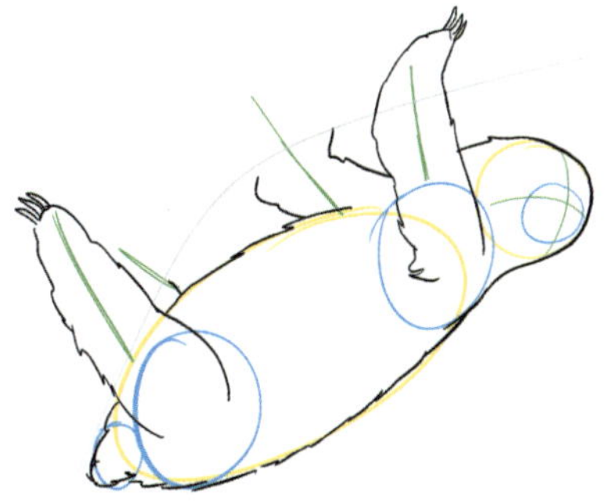

STEP 5 Draw a jagged line to form the sloth's stomach. Add its claws and legs on the other side. Remember to draw only the beginning of these because we want them to appear to be grabbing the tree branch from the other side.

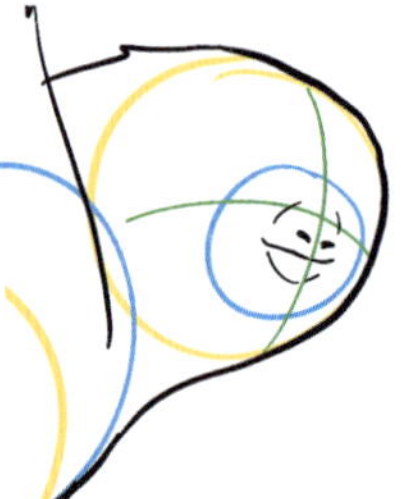

STEP 6 Ready to tackle this cute face? An easy starting point is the nose. It's the central feature of the face, so you can lay this part down on paper and use it as a reference to place the eyes and mouth. Start with the nostrils, one on each side of the vertical line, just below the horizontal line. Then draw a little smirk very close to the nostrils and frame the nose and mouth with smaller curved lines.

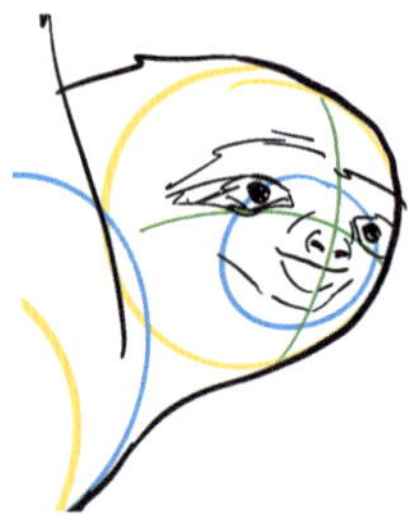

STEP 7 To draw the eyes, place a dot for each eye toward the top left and top right of the smaller circle. Then add a few lines that frame the eyes and are longer toward the outside of its face. You can also add a few lines to shape the face around the chin area.

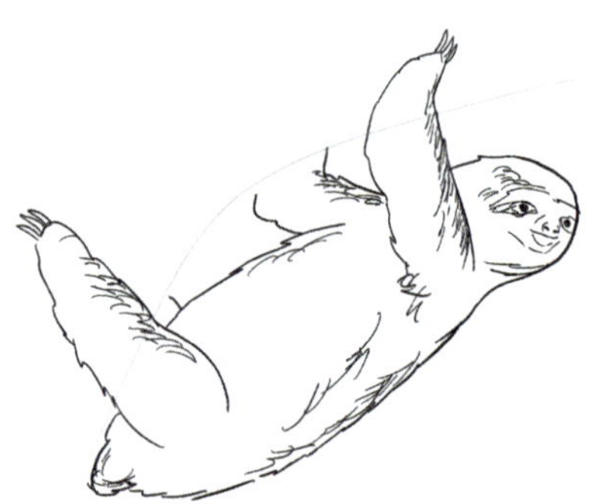

STEP 8 Erase your guide lines and add some marks to give the sloth hair, but remember that less is more. Unless you're going for something crazy-detailed, you don't need to fur this baby up too much.

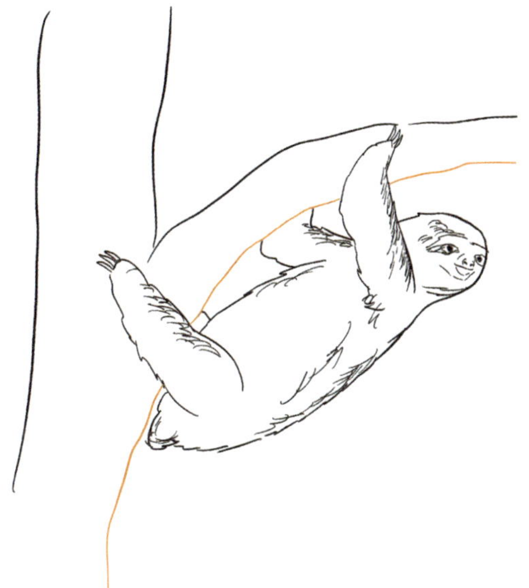

STEP 9 Now it's time to draw your tree. Follow the line you first drew, skipping over the leg and arm on the side closest to you. Draw another line from the inside of the foot and out to mirror the bottom line. See how you just made a sloth hanging from a branch? Now draw two vertical lines that are wider apart for the main part of the tree. You did it! Now make a thousand more. Leave them in random places where people can find them. Sloths will make everyone's day.

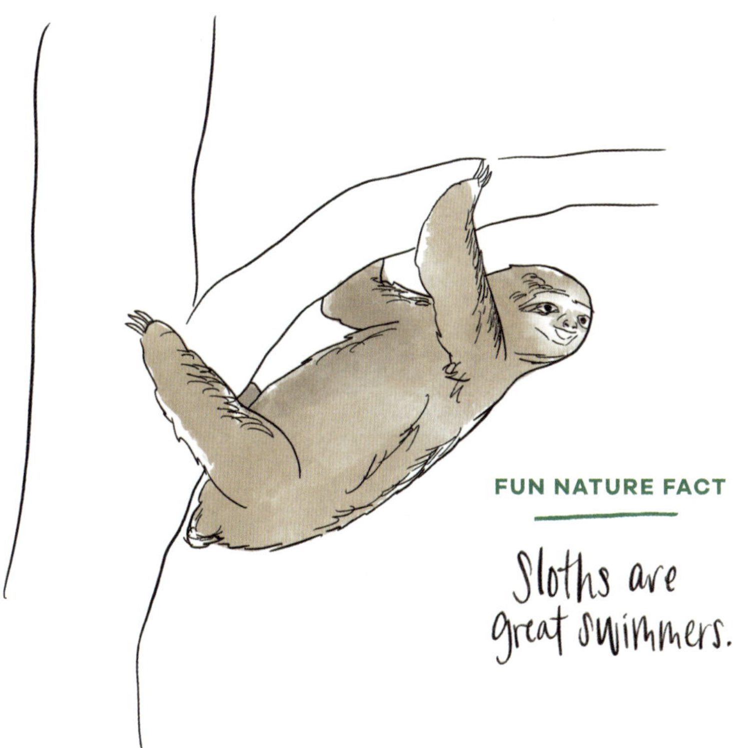

TO ADD COLOR A simple brown wash will do the trick! Speaking of tricks, you can lay a watercolor wash over your entire sloth, then grab a paper towel to dab its face to brighten it up instead of working around it. This will also look more natural!

Emergent Layer

Emergent layer trees are strongly rooted and can grow two hundred feet high. They're hardy trees that live a very long time, and many have built-in defenses in their bark and leaves that make them poisonous to eat or even harmful to touch. This is the top layer of the rain forest, towering above the others, with its greenery exposed to the bright sun. Birds of prey, bats, and monkeys are some of the animals found living throughout this layer.

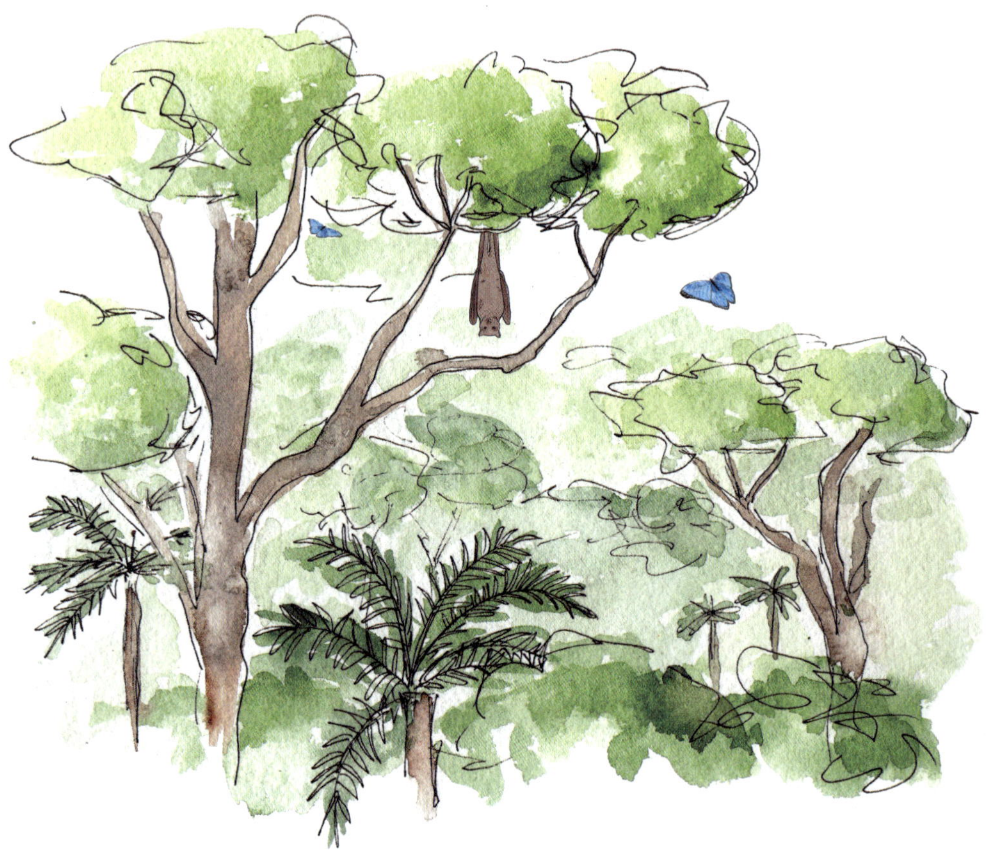

BUTTERFLY

There's nothing like standing in the middle of a swarm of butterflies, also called a kaleidoscope. (Just knowing that word makes these magical creatures even more fantastic.) There are a ton of species of butterflies, but one of the main ones known to inhabit the rain forest's emergent layer is the eye-catching electric-blue morpho butterfly.

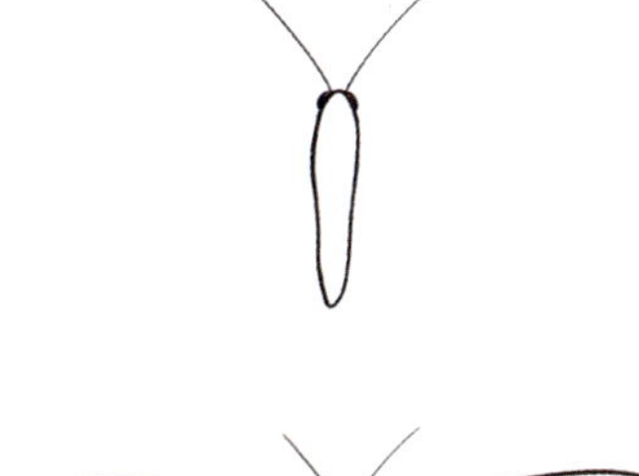

STEP 1 Start by drawing a skinny oval that gets narrower on the bottom half. Add a small dot on either side at the top for the eyes. Even higher, add two thin lines for antennae.

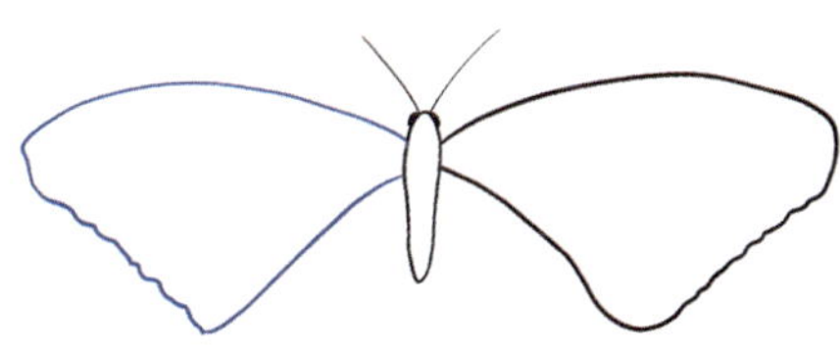

STEP 2 Starting from the top half of the oval, draw a long C-curve about two and a half times the length of the skinny oval you drew. Bring this line inward at an angle with more texture along the outside. Extend the line down just beyond the length of the body and then create a curved line back up, connecting it to the body close to where you started.

Repeat on the other side.

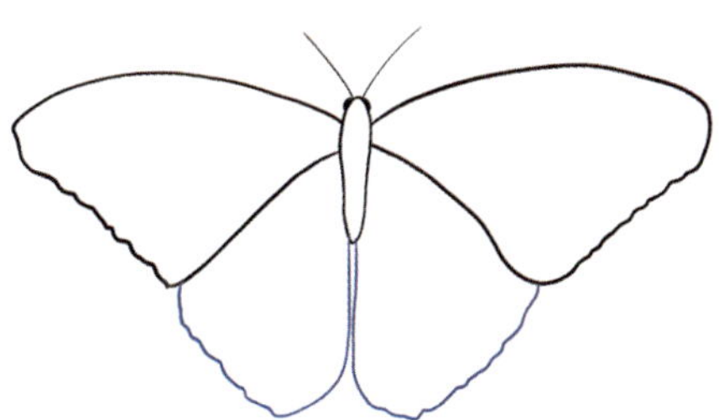

STEP 3 Draw the bottom wing by dragging a line straight downward from the base of the body, extending it about one and a half times the length of the body. Curve it around and, with a textured line, connect the bottom wing to the bottom of the top wing.

Repeat on the other side.

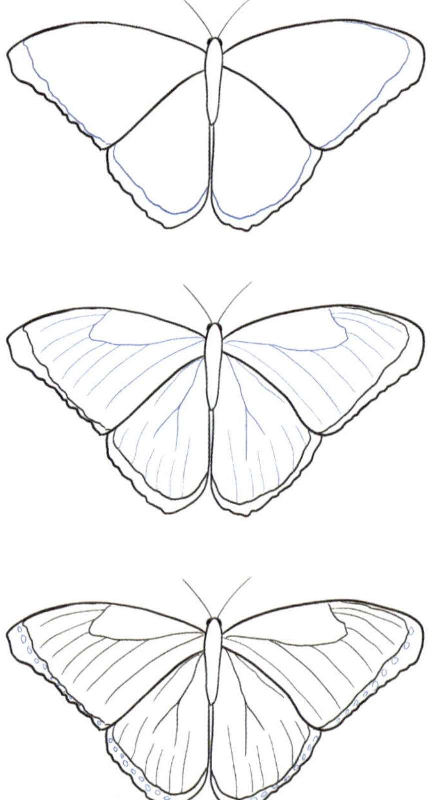

STEP 4 This particular butterfly has unique markings, so draw a line along the perimeter of the wings to show this definition.

If you look closely at a butterfly's wings, you'll see tiny veins in their structure. Draw a line in the middle of the wing coming off of the body, then angle it upward. On the bottom wings, draw lines coming from the middle and downward, then split them off in the middle of the wings into two lines. Create additional lines that are spaced about the same through each wing.

STEP 5 Focusing on features of the morpho butterfly, draw small circles along the edges of the wings, in between the edge and the border near it, as shown here.

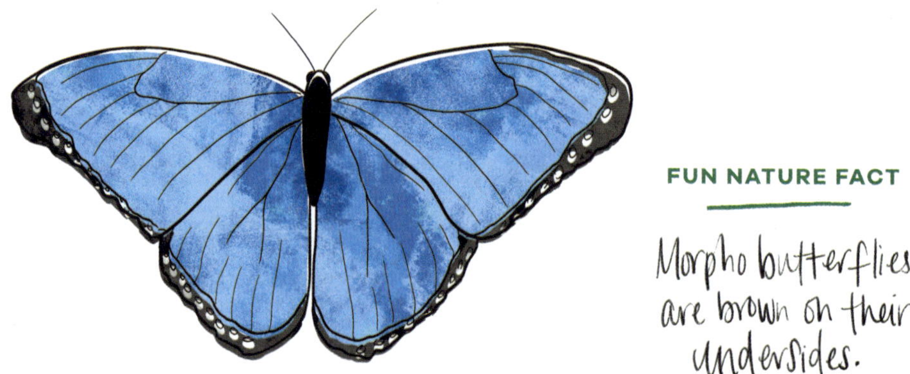

FUN NATURE FACT

Morpho butterflies are brown on their undersides.

TO ADD COLOR Lay down a wash to create a base color and let it dry. Then lay down another wash to intensify the color even more. While your paint is still wet, grab a paper towel, scrunch it up, and lightly dab a few areas to lift some of the color— instant depth and texture!

ARCTIC TUNDRA

The Arctic tundra has a cold, desert-like climate. Vast, treeless grounds are covered in permafrost, and only low shrubs, mosses, and grasses sprout in what is often disturbed soil. There is no deep-root support for vegetation, so the growing season for the hardy plants that can survive in this environment is very short. Despite the harsh conditions, however, quite a bit of wildlife can be found in the Arctic. One that springs to mind is the strikingly gorgeous polar bear.

Polar Bear

It's time to get adorable. How can these powerful creatures be so strong and deadly and yet so cute at the same time? Fun fact: Polar bears have thick white fur to camouflage them in their natural icy habitats, but underneath that bright layer, they have black skin! This is so they can better absorb the warmth of the sun. Pretty cool, right? Although we're drawing a polar bear, you can apply this lesson to other bears as well.

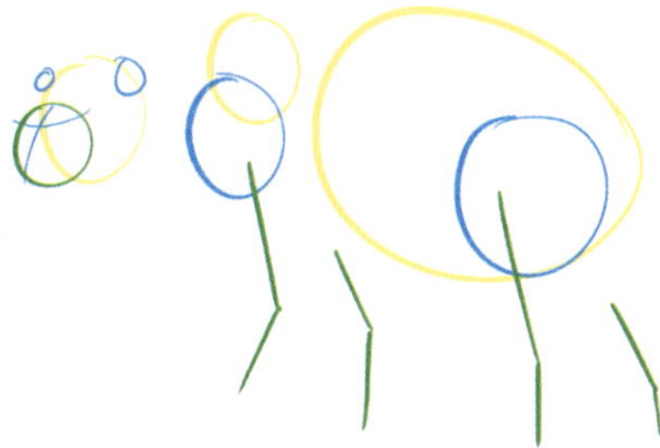

STEP 1 First, let's draw out the guide. Draw circles represent the head, shoulder, and body (yellow). Next, create shapes show the ears and the tops of the arm and leg (blue). Notice that the leftmost small circle for the ear is a bit smaller than the one on the right. This is because we're drawing the polar bear's face at an angle. Because we're drawing the face at an angle, draw a circle about half the size of the head on the lower left corner (green), then add a vertical line close to the left of this circle, and a horizontal line close to the top. Last, add lines for the approximate location of the legs, with bends to help with the shapes (green).

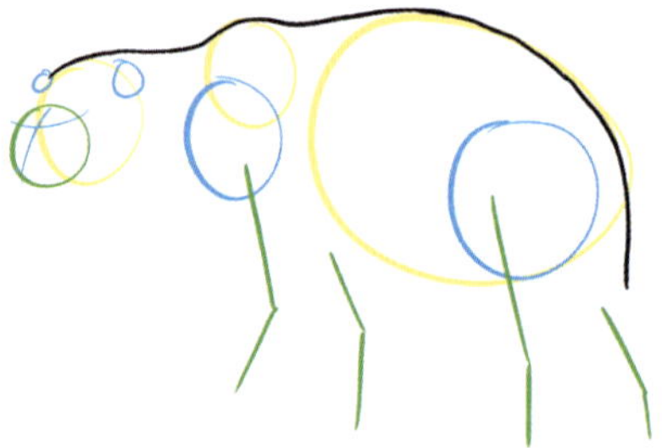

 Once you have shapes mapped out, draw the body using the guide. Start just inside the ear and follow the cylinder shape of the head, dip inward before creating a small arch over the shoulder. This line goes into another dip in between the two yellow circles, then reaches up and around the backside.

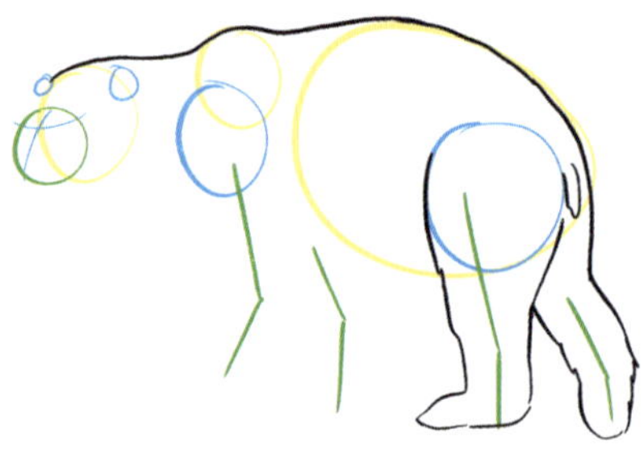

STEP 3 Using the blue back-leg circle as a guide for size, and the lines drawn for the legs as a guide for length, draw the back leg. Create some texture in the lines to represent fur. When you reach the bottom, extend the lines horizontally for the foot. Now, drag the line you drew around the backside outward and down, then back up to connect to the other leg. Add a little tail with a long horseshoe shape close to the outer line.

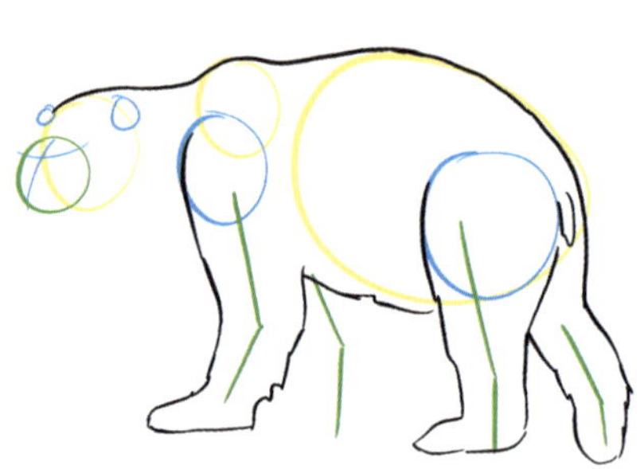

STEP 4 Draw the front leg just as you did the back leg. Then draw the belly of the bear with a textured line connecting the front leg to the back leg.

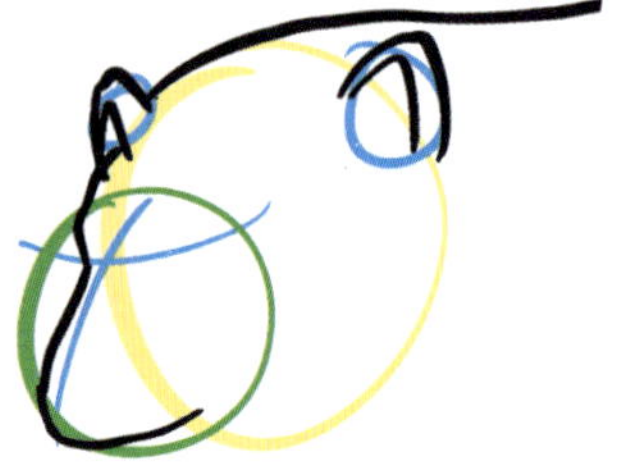

STEP 5 Don't let the three-quarter profile intimidate you. Remember to use your guide. Draw the ears in soft V-shapes, then add similar lines underneath. See where the blue middle line of the face is? Draw a line from the left ear, angle it inward slightly, then continue the line closer to that vertical line. When you reach the bottom of the face's circle guide, curve it around and stop.

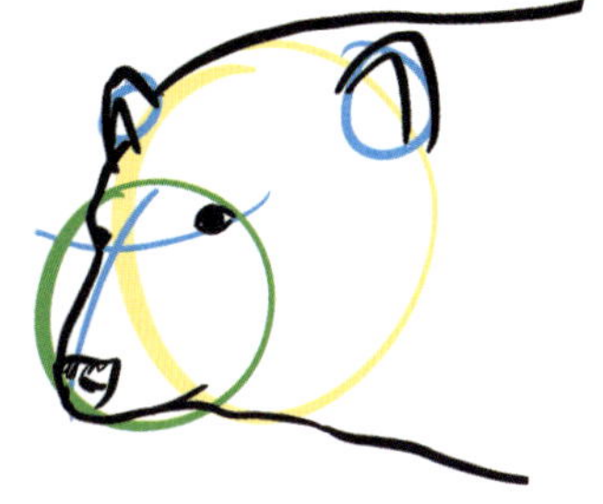

STEP 6 Draw two very small almond-shaped eyes, one in the crease on the left and one where the horizontal blue line meets the edge of the circle. Draw the nose at the bottom of the vertical blue line where it meets the circle by creating a soft V-shape and nostril. Draw a line connecting the chin to the front leg at an angle that matches the line drawn for the stomach.

STEP 7 Now just add some mark-making to show your polar bear's fur!

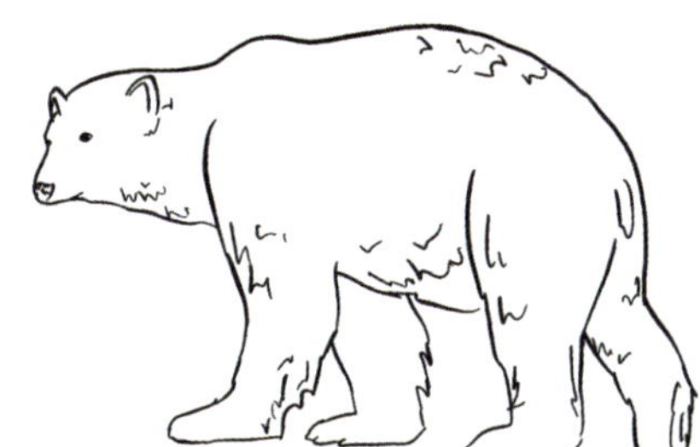

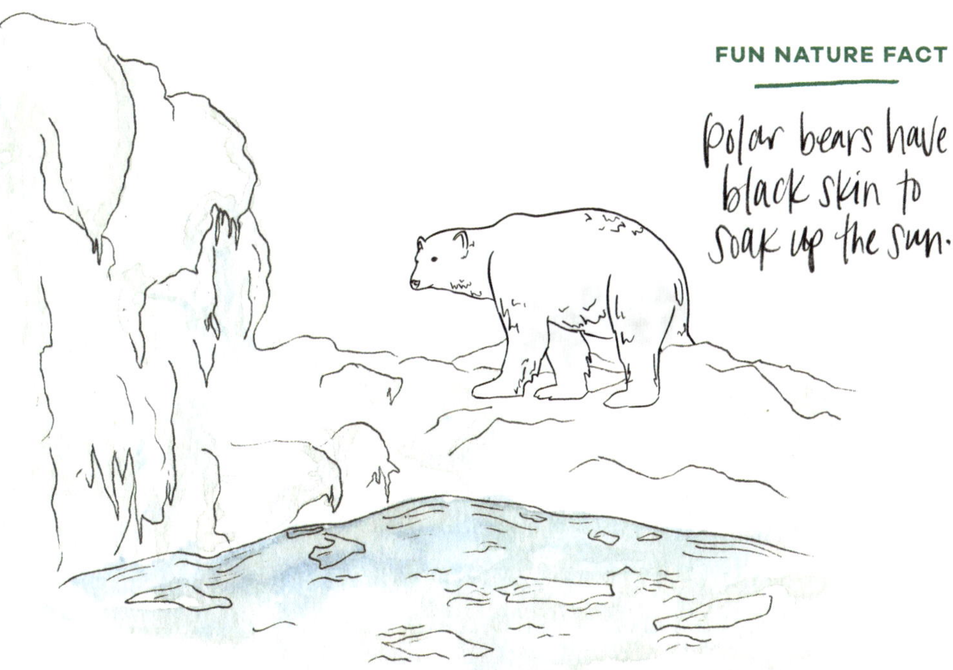

TO ADD COLOR Add color to white by using different shades of neutrals, like gray and beige. Instead of the usual wash, where most of the illustration is covered, you'll enhance only some areas. Adding color to only the underside of the polar bear gives the appearance of a slight shadow.

WETLANDS

Wetlands are saturated with water, and you might know them as swamps or marshes. Some of these areas have permanent standing water, while others gather standing water only seasonally. Wetlands restore and protect water quality and provide habitats for various wildlife.

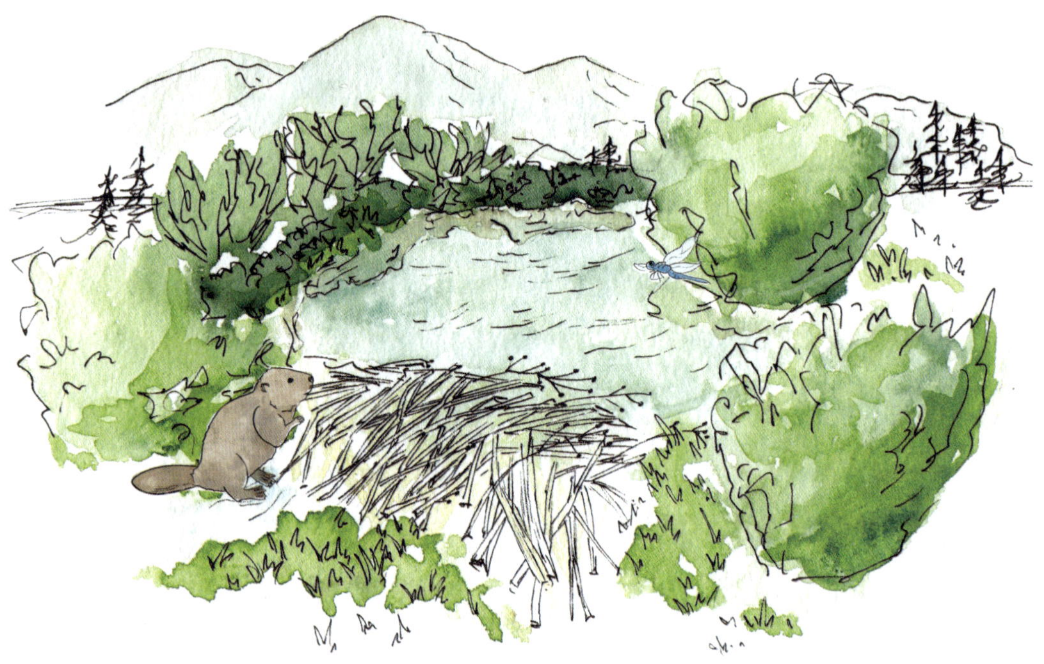

Beaver

When we think of beavers, we immediately think of the dams they build. These dams create ponds of calm, still water in which the beavers build their homes. A few fun facts: Beavers' teeth are orange because they contain a lot of iron; they need those strong teeth to cut logs for their dams. And did you know that beaver teeth never stop growing? Beavers also secrete a substance called castoreum, which smells and tastes like vanilla. You wouldn't think of a wild animal smelling so delicious, right?

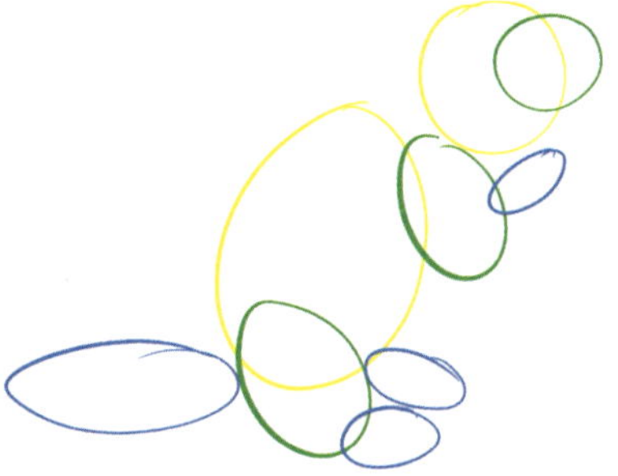

STEP 1 To draw a beaver, first create your guide. The oval body is about two times larger than the head circle (yellow). The arm and leg (green) are oblong shapes that overlap the top and bottom part of the body. The top green circle is for the face, which sits on the side of the head circle. The oval shapes of the feet (blue) point forward from the bottom leg oval (green). The tail sits where the body (yellow) and leg (green) shapes meet, and the hand (blue) attaches to the arm.

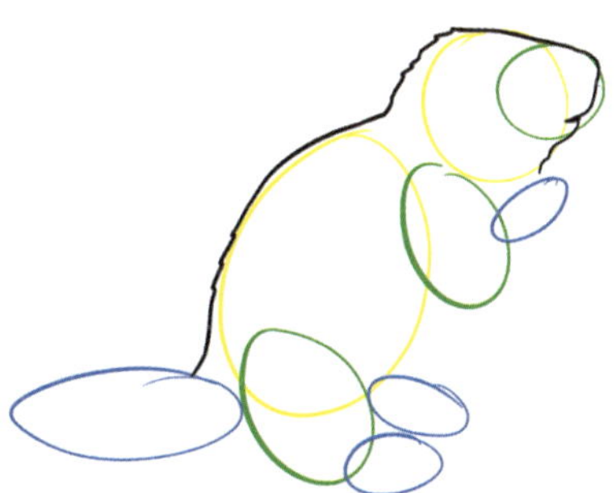

STEP 2 Start with the top of the head and move to the back of the body, with a slight dip between the two for the neck. Draw up and around the body's shape, connecting it with the tail. Then go back up to the top of the head and extend it all the way to the right side of the face circle, creating a slight rounded curve where the nose will be. Continue that line down at an inward angle, then dip it all the way in to start the mouth.

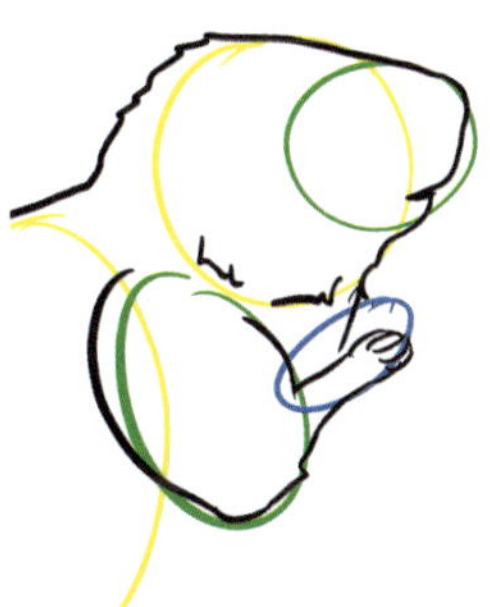

STEP 3 Draw a line following the left side of the upper green oval to create the shoulder and arm, then bend the line to reach toward the bottom edge of the blue oval. Follow the right side of the green oval and create a bend for the skinny wrist and paw. To create the paw, just overlap a few curved lines. Then draw fur markings near the neck. Draw the bottom part of the mouth about halfway out from the top line and use an S-curve to follow the yellow circle.

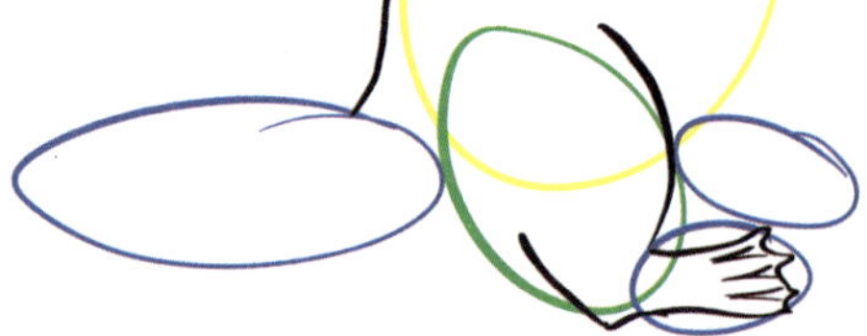

STEP 4 Beavers have webbed back feet. To draw them, follow the bottom green oval, then create lines that curve inward for the sides of the feet. Draw three C-curves to connect these two lines, which creates the webs. On the inside of the foot, draw three long V-shapes to enhance the webbing.

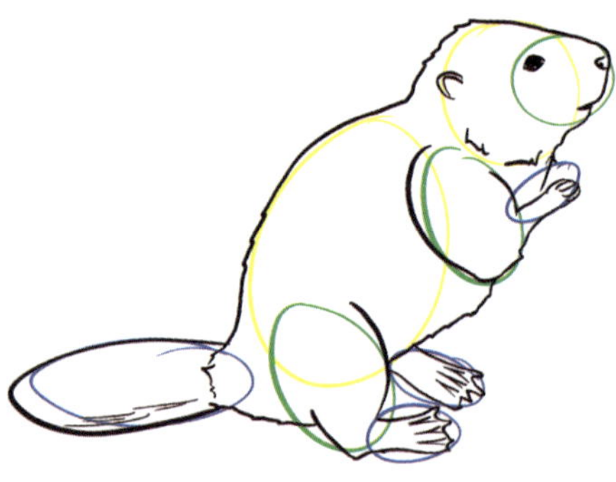

STEP 5 Draw a jagged line to create the beaver's belly from its elbow to the middle of its bottom leg. Then draw its other foot coming from the area where the belly and front leg meet.

To create the face, draw an almond-shaped eye in the upper left area of the green face circle. Add the nose with a sharp curved line and nostril dot, and place an ear on the left side of the yellow circle.

Draw the tail by following the leftmost blue oval, then add a few lines for a little texture.

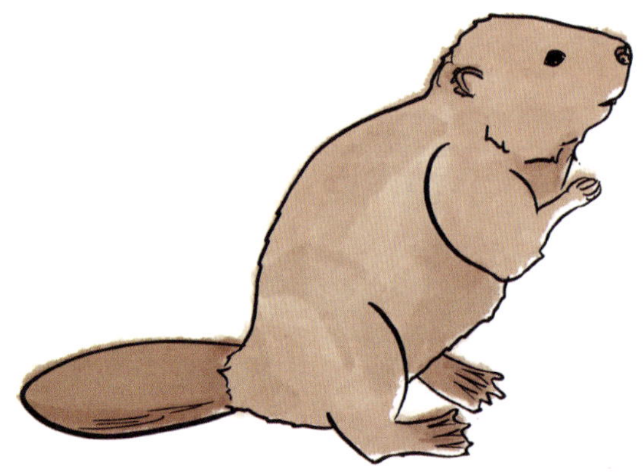

TO ADD COLOR Adding a simple wash in the same color throughout is sufficient. You can then return to the tail and webbed feet with another layer to make a bolder color.

Dragonfly

Dragonflies are both beautiful and impressive. Their wings are like little all-wheel-drive tires, meaning dragonflies' wings can move independently of each other, and dragonflies can fly sideways, backward, and even upside-down. And they can reach speeds upward of 18 mph! They're the ultimate flying machines. If my dream of being able to fly ever came true, I wouldn't mind having a dragonfly's abilities. Let's draw one.

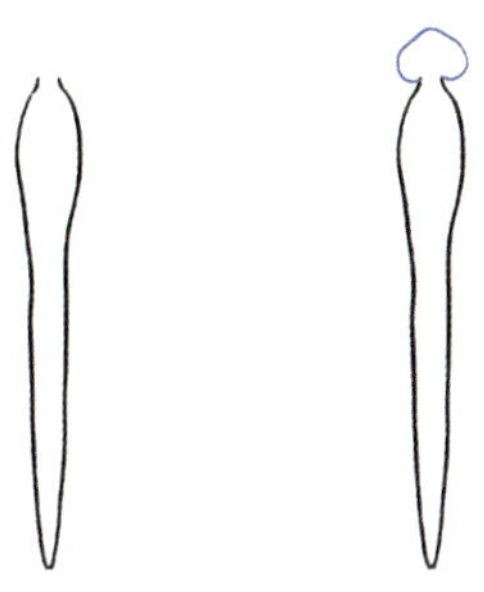

STEP 1 We'll start by drawing a long, narrow oblong shape, as we did for the butterfly only this one will have more of a curve on the top and a longer narrow area toward the middle and bottom.

Draw the head with curved lines that circle outward and back in at the top in an arc.

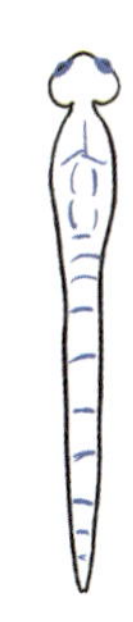

STEP 2 Without getting too far into all of a dragonfly's details, let's draw some simple parts. First are the eyes. Don't be afraid to let these little oblong shapes sit outward from the head. Ever heard the term *bug-eyed*? It exists for a reason! Also draw some small details in the body using quick dashes and small curved lines.

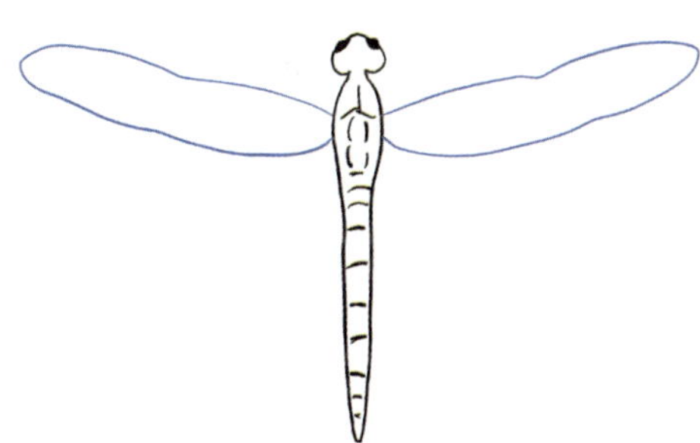

STEP 3 Onto the wings! Starting at the top of the body, near the widest point, draw a line outward about the same length as the body. Dip the wing toward the center for shape. Curve the wing around and back inward, repeating the slight dip inward and then connecting it close to where you began. Repeat on the other side.

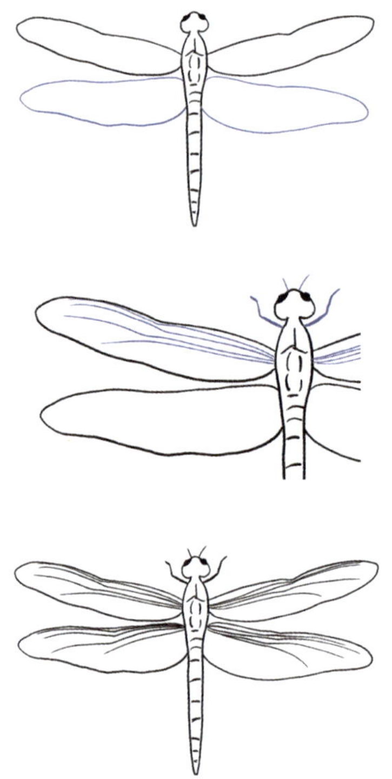

STEP 4 Create a second set of wings just below the first set. Notice that these are a tad shorter but a little wider, and they curve upward a bit more at the bottom.

STEP 5 Add a few thin lines through each wing toward the top, with the lines underneath shorter than the others. Add the two front legs coming off of the top of the body. Notice that they have a slight bend. Don't draw the other legs, as they are beneath the wings. Add short antennae just inside the area where the eyes sit.

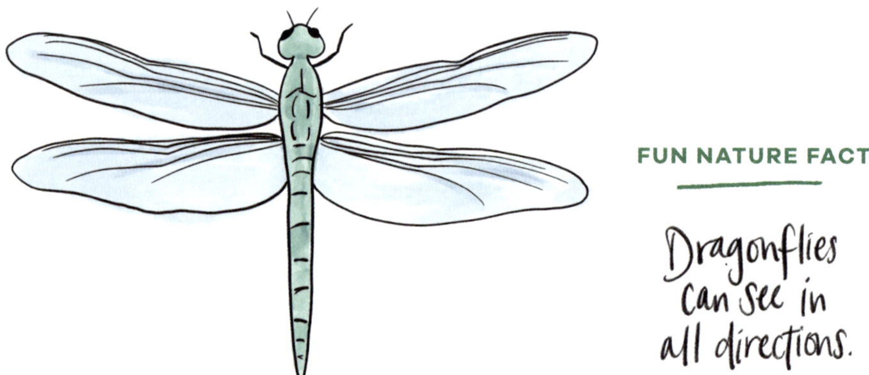

FUN NATURE FACT

Dragonflies can see in all directions.

TO ADD COLOR Dragonflies are generally blue, brown, red, or yellow. They can also sport a combination of these colors.

DESERT

Some deserts have arid climates with intense heat and drastic temperature changes. Many animals that live in the desert come out only at night to avoid the heat. Water is scarce in desert regions, so the plants that live there are drought tolerant, absorbing and storing water.

Creating a desert scene is very simple. Use your one-point perspective to draw a horizon line, some dunes in the background, and a couple larger (because they're closest to the viewer) grassy plants in the foreground. Take your landscape a step further by adding a resplendent sunset using bold watercolor washes.

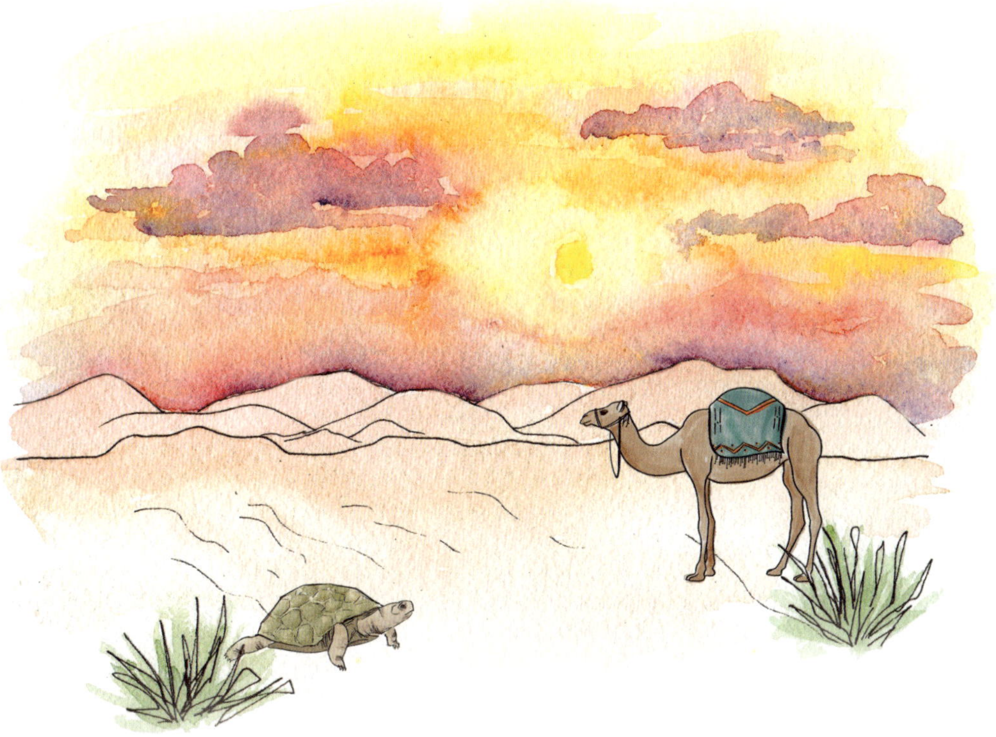

Camel

I love drawing camels. I think they're so interesting, and the flow of their bodies is fun to draw. Do you know the difference between camels with one hump and camels with two? It has to do with the region they're from. One-humped camels are called dromedaries or Arabian camels. Camels with two humps are called Bactrian camels and they're native to central Asia. An easy way to remember their names is by turning them on their side. Drom-edaries have one hump like the letter *D*, and Bactrian camels have two humps, just like *B*!

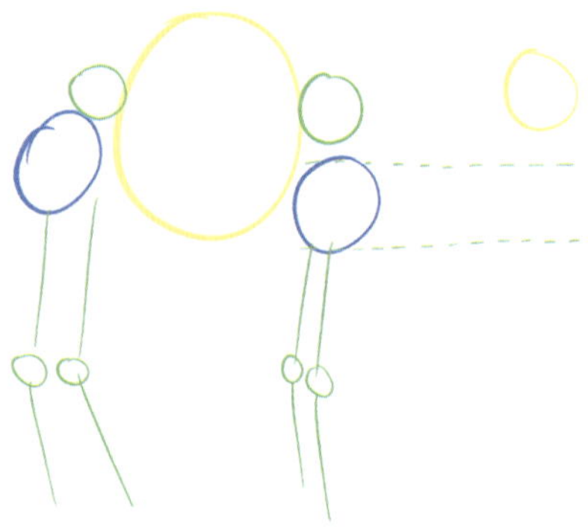

STEP 1 Draw a large circle for the body (yellow). Imagine another large circle on the side of it (as spacing), then draw a small circle toward the top for the head. Draw circles on each side of the body circle (blue); make the circle at the front of the body slightly lower. Add two smaller circles (green) above the ones you just drew and long legs with circles at the knees (green). Draw little dashes coming from the small circle toward the head, we'll use these in Step 4.

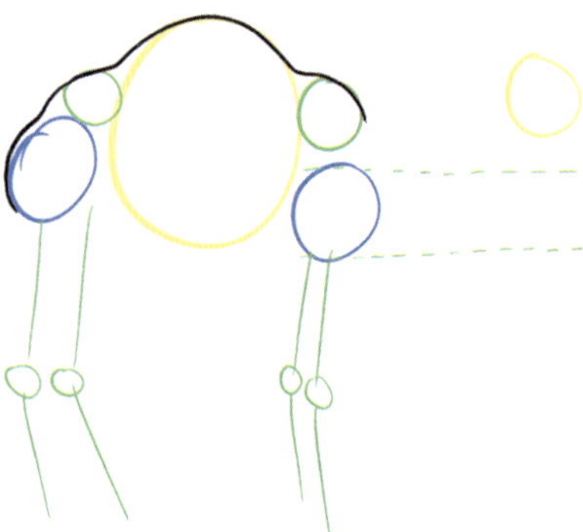

STEP 2 When drawing a camel, we naturally want to start at the part that's the most fun: the hump. Follow the guide and utilize the curves of your circles. Starting from the circle on the top right (green), curve over and dip inward, then curve over the middle circle (yellow) and dip inward before curving over the top left circle (green). Dip inward again, then follow through around the back circle (blue). Stop when you reach the camel's back side.

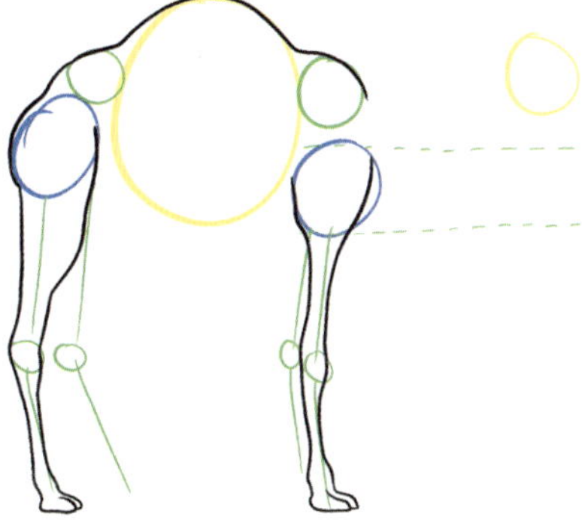

STEP 3 Draw the camel's back leg by using the left blue circle as your guide. Curve around the left side and draw the back of the leg at a slight curve inward until it reaches the circle along the leg guide. Curve outward to follow the circle, then return to a slight curve inward. When you approach the bottom, curve outward for the top area above the toes, then outward farther for the heel, and carry that line around to the other side, tucking it in to create a toe. On the other side of the blue circle, curve a line outward until just above the circle in the leg guide, then come inward to make the bottom part of the leg narrower. Make this line follow to just above the back toe, and connect it to the side of the first toe. Repeat these steps on the right side for the front leg, only this time, don't make the top of the leg as thick.

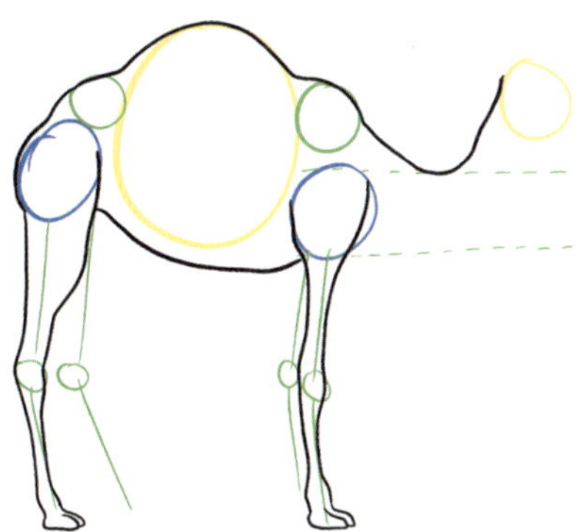

STEP 4 Draw a line connecting the two legs to create the camel's belly. To draw the neck, use the top right shoulder circle (green) and the head circle (yellow) as a guide. This is where our dashed lines come in handy. Dip your line down to touch the top dashed line, then return upward to connect to the yellow circle.

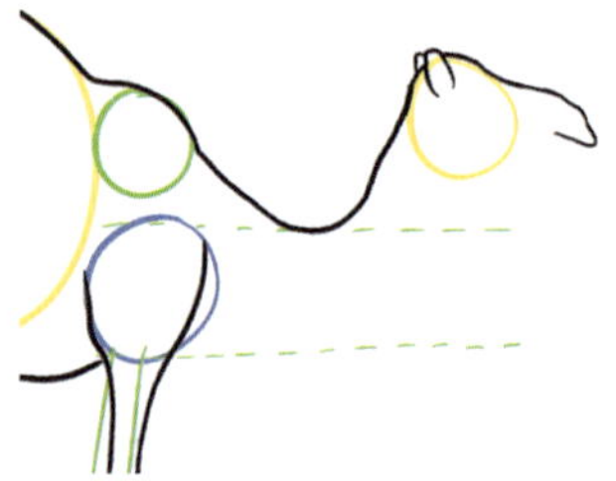

STEP 5 Draw a horseshoe shape on the top right of the head circle to create the camel's ear. Draw the head by following the circle and then, when you reach the top right, extend your line about the same length as the circle and tuck it under to create the nose and top part of the mouth. Tuck another small horseshoe on the left of the first ear to show it peeking up from the other side.

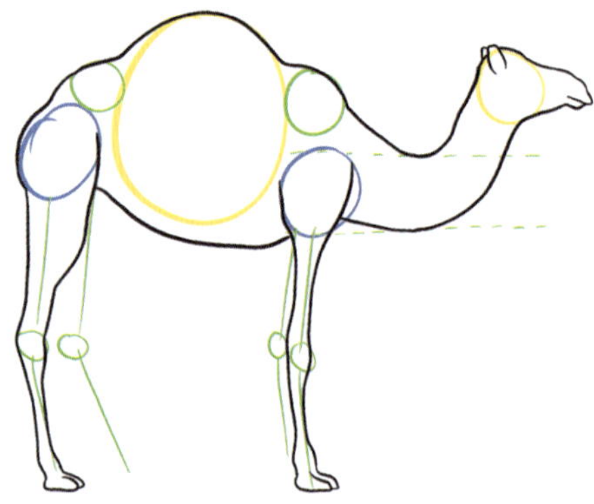

STEP 6 From the nose, come just inside the top of the mouth line and create a lower jawline very close to the top, coming inward and connecting the line to the yellow circle again. From here, dip your line down to the bottom dashed line and connect it to the front leg. Be sure that this line leaves the right amount of space for the neck; you don't want it looking too thin or too wide.

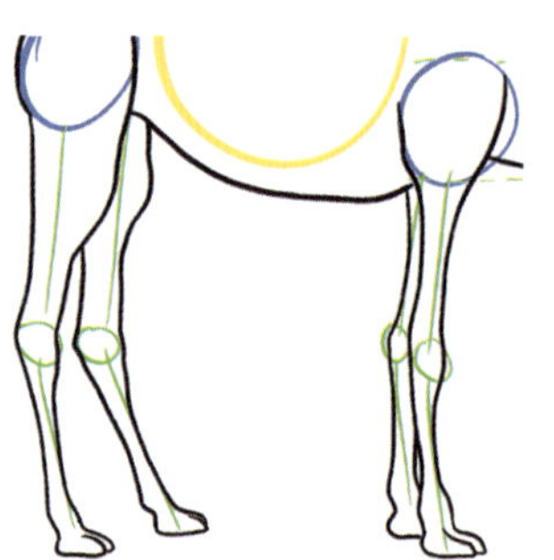

STEP 7 Draw the legs on the other side of the camel by duplicating the legs you already drew. These lines should connect closely to the other legs and to the belly.

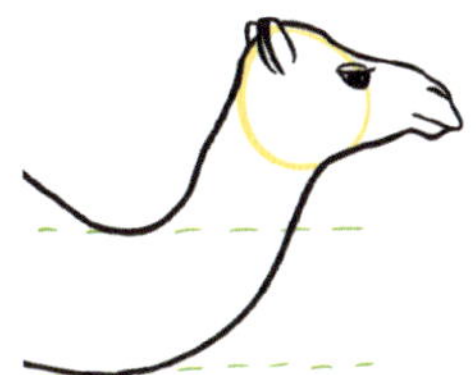

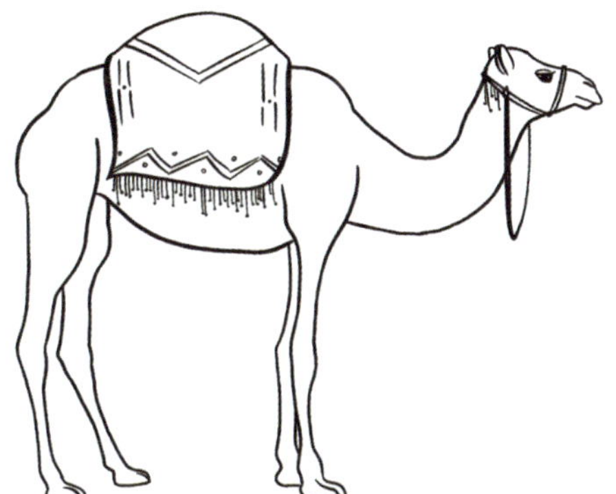

STEP 8 Draw the camel's eye on the top right of the yellow circle guide for its head. Create a thin almond shape for the eyelid, then a curved line underneath. Add the iris. To draw the camel's nose, just make a small slit at an angle close to the top of the head on the right side. That's it!

STEP 9 If you want to get fancy, give your camel a little blanket by pulling two lines straight down from its hump and curving around the edges on the bottom. Add a fun design and a few tassels!

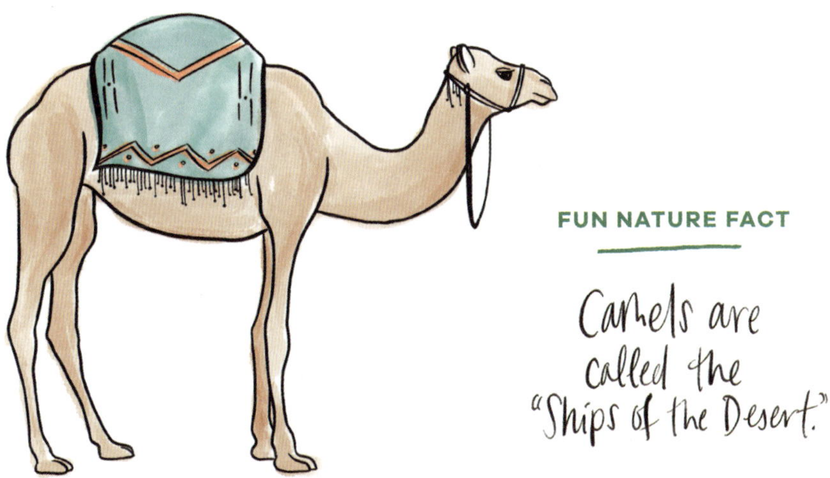

TO ADD COLOR Camels are helpful companions for nomadic desert tribes, as they are useful for transport and for their milk! Let's assume this cutie is your desert ship and you've adorned him with a luxurious blanket in your favorite color.

Tortoise

Did you know the desert tortoise can live for more than eighty years? There's actually no way of knowing the exact age of a tortoise unless you witnessed its birth. This little guy is endangered due to poaching, diseases, predators, and litter. (Here's a friendly reminder to properly dispose of your trash and recycle as much as possible.)

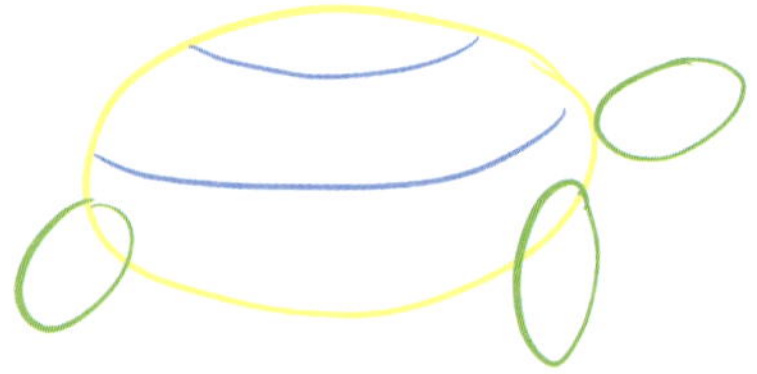

STEP 1 Begin by drawing guidelines. Draw a large oval shape, representing the tortoise's shell (yellow). Overlap two oval circles (green) for legs, then add another oval (green) to the side for the head. Draw two curved lines (blue) inside the shell.

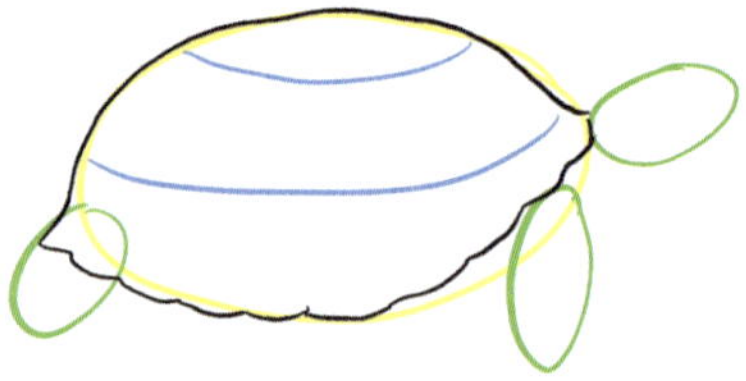

STEP 2 Begin shaping the shell, starting with a C-curve near the head and following the large oval on the top, then dropping down to follow the back leg. Create curved lines along the bottom of the oval and, rather than following the oval all the way through, use the top of the small oval on the right (front leg) as a guide to meet back up where you started.

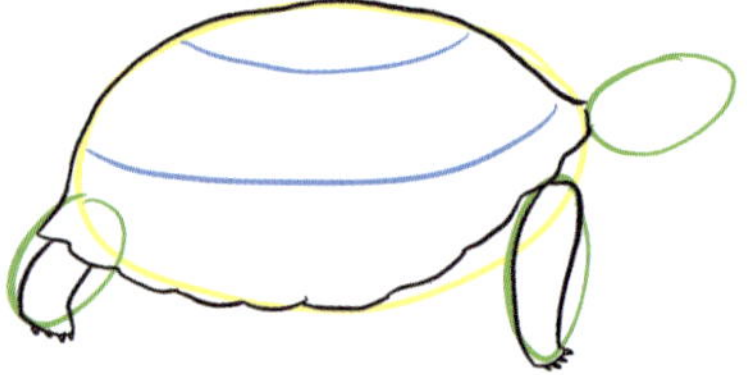

STEP 3 Add the front leg with a curved line at the base of the shell, reaching down into a boxy end. Add little claws along the base. Do the same thing for the back leg, leaving out the top curved line. Instead, have it connect to the shell.

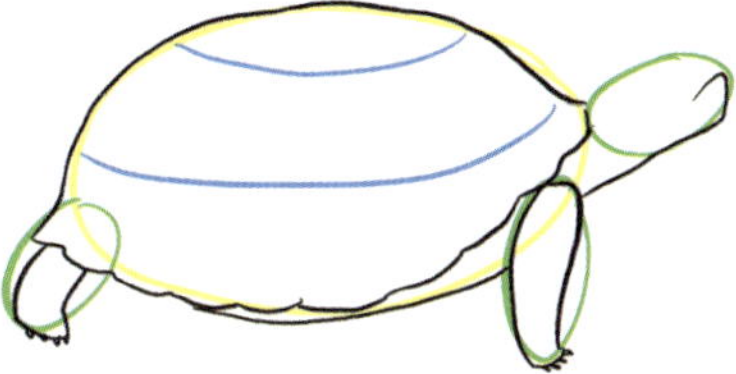

STEP 4 Starting at the bottom of the shell, about a third of the way from the left, begin a smooth line very close to the shell and connect it to the front leg. Starting from the other side of the front leg, draw a line connecting to the oval of the head. Bring that line straight up when you reach the side of the oval, and curve it back inward to start the mouth.

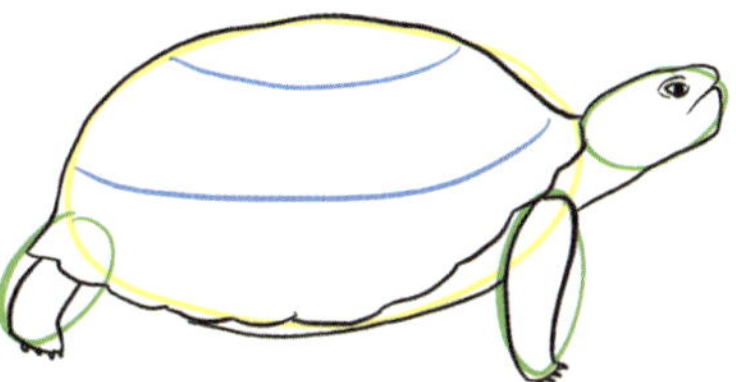

STEP 5 At the point of the shell that transitions from the top to the bottom on the right, draw a curved line that traces the top of the head oval. Curve the line inward at the edge of the oval and into the mouth line. Draw an almond shape for the eye. You can also add little curved lines on the top and side/bottom to accentuate the eye.

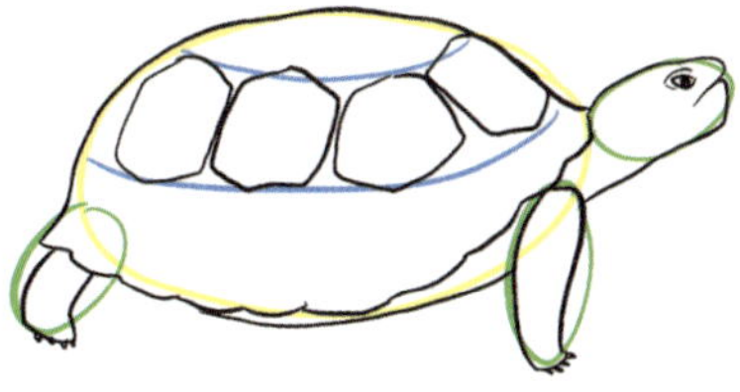

STEP 6 The shapes on a tortoise's shell are both somewhat round and somewhat pointed. Draw this loosely with five to six points. In the middle section that sits in between the blue lines, draw four large, somewhat round, somewhat pointed shapes.

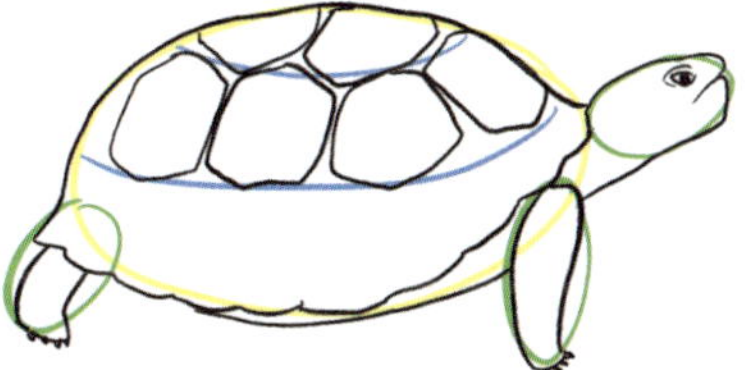

STEP 7 Using the middle row of shapes as a guide, draw two more of these shapes on the top of the shell, dipping the points between the shapes on the middle row, fitting them together like pieces of a puzzle.

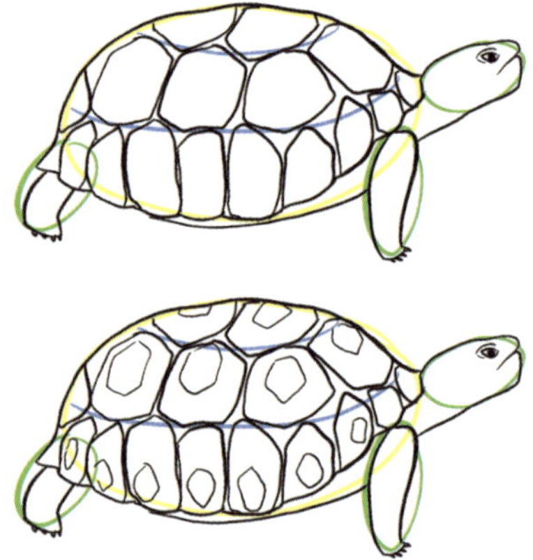

STEP 8 Draw narrower versions of this shape in the bottom section and then connect them to the bottom curved lines of the shell.

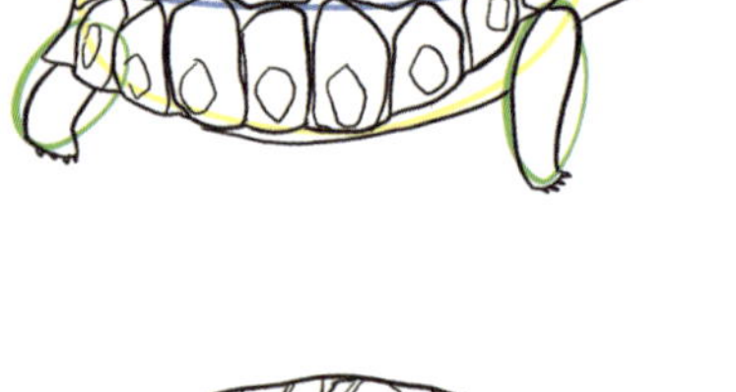

STEP 9 You can leave the shell as is or add additional detail. To accentuate the shape of the shell's segments, draw a smaller version of the shapes inside the first set, using a thinner line.

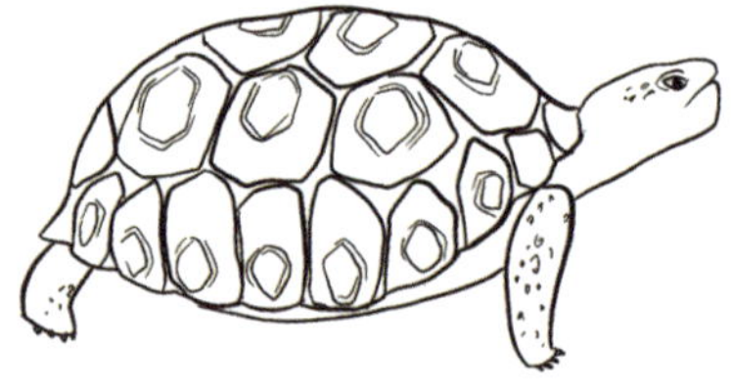

STEP 10 From here, you can add even more lines if you'd like. You may also opt to add some detail on the skin, like small curves to represent scales.

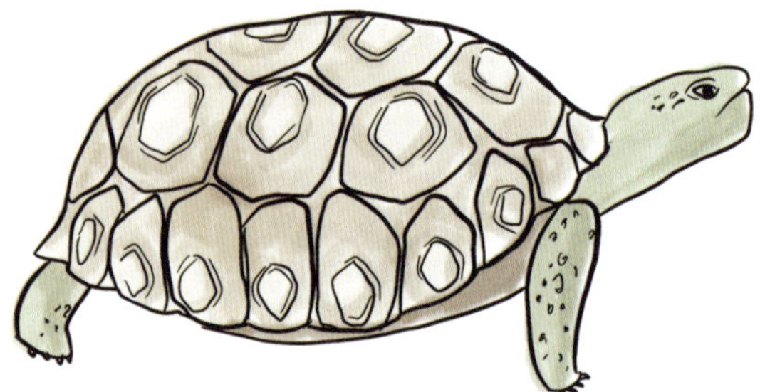

TO ADD COLOR Here's another opportunity to use a flat watercolor wash to create dimension. Paint a wet-on-wet wash, then dab the tip of a paper towel in the center of each hump on the tortoise's shell.

FIND YOURSELF

I probably don't have to get into how much eye candy there is in the world, especially in nature and illustrations. We've discussed trees. We've nailed down our flowers and arrangements like pros. We've explored some animals in different regions of the world. We've got the beach scene broken up. We've covered landscapes. Now, what are you going to create?

Brilliant creativity belongs to individuals and their perfect, wondrous minds. Embrace yours. Allow yourself to grow. Own your journey. Don't ever come down on your practice. Not everything you create is meant to be a finished piece. In fact, you should have a stack of exploration pages, practice pages, and drafts before you get to your end result. That said, during this exploration stage, you may find that your finished piece is the very first piece you created. That's the beauty in exploring and allowing yourself to expand outside of what you think you need to create. Sometimes exciting doors will open and you'll find a part of yourself dabbling on a whole new level. Or you'll look at your collection and feel validated knowing that one of your first pieces speaks the truest form of you. More than anything, sit down with your sketchbook and start. Just start. That book is your safe place, free of judgment. It's where you'll find yourself. #embracetheimperfections

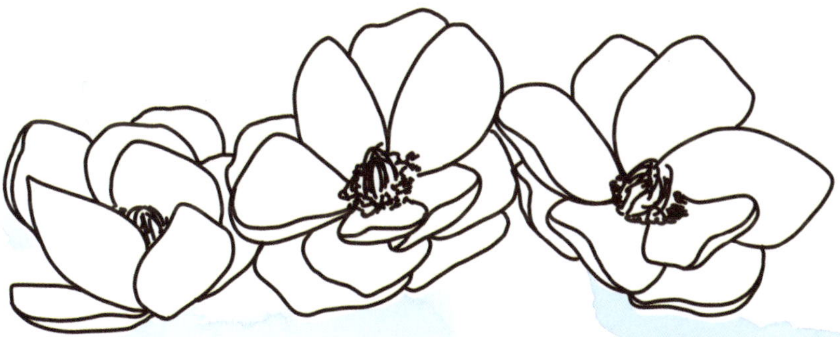

ACKNOWLEDGMENTS

More than anything, I want to thank my wife, Laura. She has been my biggest cheerleader, business advisor, and motivational push. Thank you to my mom, my dad, and my grandparents for submerging me in the arts and never letting me miss an opportunity to express myself creatively. To everyone who has ever reminded me that I must incorporate mindfulness in my life, thank you. I resisted this idea for so long because I couldn't turn my mind off. Finally, I was guided on how to accept and discover, and mindfulness became a part of my journey. I thank God, Mother Nature, science, whatever you believe in, for this stunning Earth that I've been able to sink my toes into—what an amazing place full of constant inspiration. Creating art based on nature has been the best companion to enhancing my mental health. Thank you to my phenomenal editor, Ashley Pierce, my entire team at Ten Speed Press, and my agent Carrie Howland for all of your shared passion on this project and for helping me bring this book to fruition. Last, thank you from the bottom of my heart to my readers for allowing me to be a part of your creative journeys.

Nothing will help you build confidence like owning your journey.

Peggy Dean

INDEX

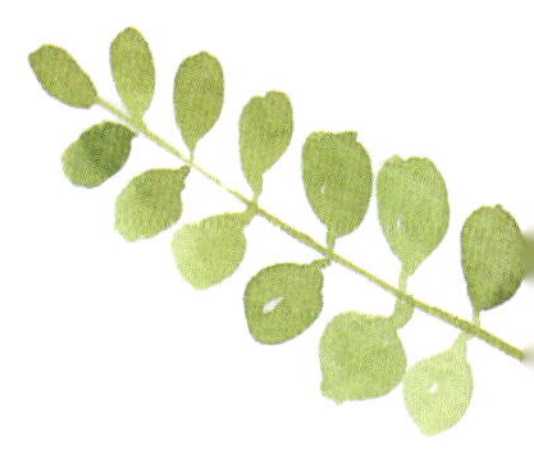

A

agoutis, 184–85
anemones, 87–88
antlers, 96–98
ants, 182–83
archival pens, 12
Arctic tundra, 199–201
Azevedo, Luisa, 95

B

bamboo, 124–27
beach scenes, 171–78
bears, polar, 199–201
beavers, 202–4
Big Sur, California,
    175–76
birds, 148–54, 190–91
black-eyed Susans,
    91–94
blind contour drawing,
    38–40, 41
blue, 28
bluebonnets, 117–19
Boston ferns, 131–32
bouquets, 157–60
brown, 29
brushes, 21–23
brush pens, water-
    based, 14, 79–80
brush strokes, 83–89
bunny-ear stroke, 84
butterflies, 197–98

C

cacti, 137–38
camels, 208–11
canyons, 63–64
cattails, 135–36
C-curves, 33, 84
cherry blossoms,
    100–102
cold press paper, 20–21
colors
    blending, 80–81
    books about, 23
    combining, 26
    complementary, 24
    contrasting, 24
    hue, 25
    layering, 82
    in nature, 27–31
    primary, 23
    saturation, 25
    secondary, 24
    value, 25
    See also individual
        colors
comparisons, avoiding, 7
complementary
    colors, 24
contour drawing, 37–41
contrasting colors, 24
cross hatching, 57–58
curves, 33

D

daisies, 47–54, 68–72
desert scenes, 207–14
distance, showing, 60
dragonflies, 205–6
drawing techniques
    contour drawing,
        37–41
    loose sketching, 42–46
    mark making, 46–59
    shapes and curves,
        33–37
    space and
        perspective, 60–72

E

elements, combining,
    95–98
eucalyptus, 130
experimentation, 4, 90
exploration stage, 215

F

ferns, 131–34
fish, 140–47
flat wash, 77
flower arrangements,
    156–64
flowers
    anemones, 87–88
    black-eyed Susans,
        91–94

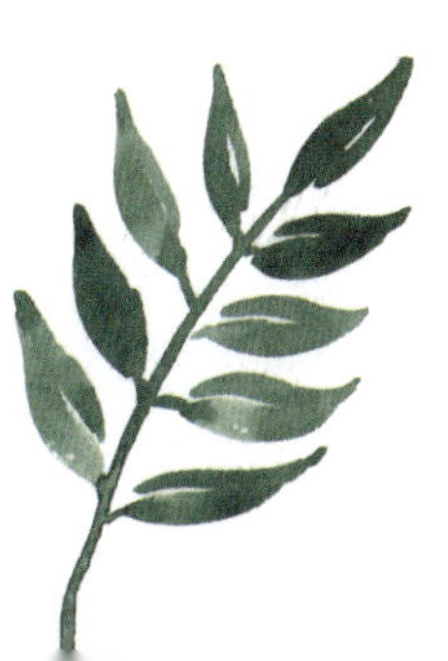

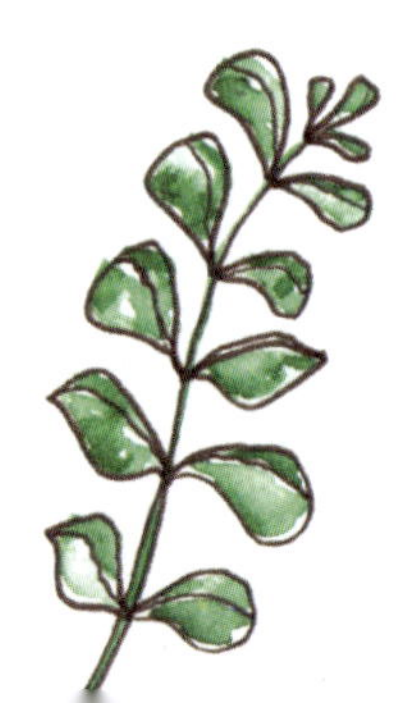

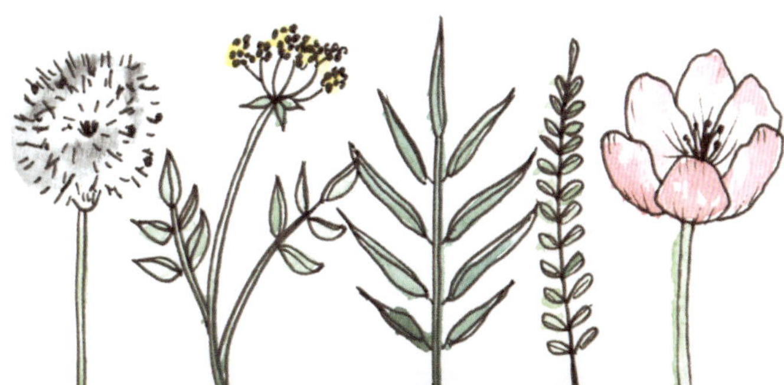

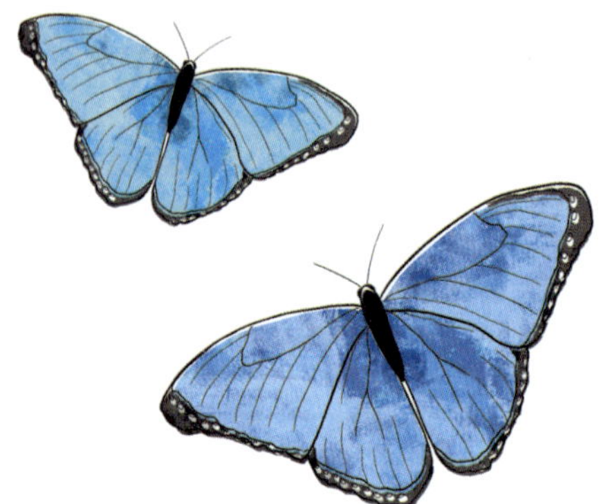

Library of Congress Cataloging-in-Publication Data
Names: Dean, Peggy (Illustrator), author.
Title: Peggy Dean's guide to nature drawing and watercolor:
    learn to sketch, ink, and paint flowers, plants, trees,
    and animals /Peggy Dean.
Description: California : Watson-Guptill, [2019] | Includes
    bibliographical references and index. |
Identifiers: LCCN 2018038938 (print) | LCCN 2018039576 (ebook)
    Subjects: LCSH: Drawing—Technique. | Watercolor painting—
    Technique. | Nature in art. | BISAC: ART / Techniques / Pen & Ink
    Drawing. | ART /Subjects & Themes / Plants & Animals. | SELF-
    HELP / Creativity.
Classification: LCC NC825.N34 (ebook) | LCC NC825.N34 D43 2019
    (print) | DDC 741.2—dc23
 LC record available at https://lccn.loc.gov/2018038938

Trade Paperback ISBN: 978-0-399-58215-8
eBook ISBN: 978-0-399-58216-5

Printed in China

Design by Lisa Schneller Bieser

10 9 8 7 6 5 4 3 2

First Edition